Christianity and Public Culture in Africa

CAMBRIDGE CENTRE OF AFRICAN STUDIES SERIES

Series editors: Derek R. Peterson, Harri Englund, and Christopher Warnes

The University of Cambridge is home to one of the world's leading centers of African studies. It organizes conferences, runs a weekly seminar series, hosts a specialist library, coordinates advanced graduate studies, and facilitates research by Cambridge- and Africa-based academics. The Cambridge Centre of African Studies Series publishes work that emanates from this rich intellectual life. The series fosters dialogue across a broad range of disciplines in African studies and between scholars based in Africa and elsewhere.

Derek R. Peterson, ed.
Abolitionism and Imperialism in Britain, Africa, and the Atlantic

Harri Englund, ed.
Christianity and Public Culture in Africa

Christianity and Public Culture in Africa

Edited by Harri Englund

Ohio University Press • *Athens*

Ohio University Press, Athens, Ohio 45701
www.ohioswallow.com
© 2011 by Ohio University Press
All rights reserved

To obtain permission to quote, reprint, or otherwise reproduce or distribute material from Ohio University Press publications, please contact our rights and permissions department at (740) 593-1154 or (740) 593-4536 (fax).

Printed in the United States of America
Ohio University Press books are printed on acid-free paper ∞ ™

First paperback printing in 2012
ISBN 978-0-8214-2022-5

HARDCOVER 18 17 16 15 14 13 12 11   5 4 3 2 1
PAPERBACK 18 17 16 15 14 13 12   5 4 3 2 1

Library of Congress Cataloging-in-Publication Data
Christianity and public culture in Africa / edited by Harri Englund.
  p. cm. — (Cambridge Centre of African Studies series)
 Includes bibliographical references (p.   ) and index.
 ISBN 978-0-8214-1945-8 (hardcover : alk. paper)
  1. Christianity and politics—Africa, Sub-Saharan. 2. Christianity and culture—Africa, Sub-Saharan. 3. Africa, Sub-Saharan—Church history. I. Englund, Harri. II. Title. III. Series.

BR1430.C475 2011
261.70967—dc22

                    2010047488

Contents

Acknowledgments
ix

INTRODUCTION
Rethinking African Christianities
Beyond the Religion-Politics Conundrum
HARRI ENGLUND
1

PART I: MISSIONARY AND NATIONALIST ENCOUNTERS

ONE
Christian Mission Stations in South-Central Africa
Eddies in the Flow of Global Culture
JAMES A. PRITCHETT
27

TWO
Debating the Secular in Zambia
The Response of the Catholic Church to Scientific Socialism and Christian Nation, 1976–2006
MARJA HINFELAAR
50

THREE
Rejection or Reappropriation?
Christian Allegory and the Critique of Postcolonial Public Culture in the Early Novels of Ngũgĩ wa Thiong'o
NICHOLAS KAMAU-GORO
67

Contents

PART II: PATRIARCHY AND PUBLIC CULTURE

FOUR
The Implications of Reproductive Politics
for Religious Competition in Niger
BARBARA M. COOPER
89

FIVE
Public Debates about Luo Widow Inheritance
Christianity, Tradition, and AIDS in Western Kenya
RUTH PRINCE
109

SIX
"Arise, Oh Ye Daughters of Faith"
Women, Pentecostalism, and Public Culture in Kenya
DAMARIS PARSITAU
131

PART III: A PLURALITY OF PENTECOSTAL PUBLICS

SEVEN
Going and Making Public
Pentecostalism as Public Religion in Ghana
BIRGIT MEYER
149

EIGHT
From Spiritual Warfare to Spiritual Kinship
Islamophobia and Evangelical Radio in Malawi
HARRI ENGLUND
167

NINE
Believing Practically and Trusting Socially in Africa
*The Contrary Case of the Universal Church of the
Kingdom of God in Durban, South Africa*
ILANA VAN WYK
189

Contents

TEN
The Gospel of Public Image in Ghana
MICHAEL PERRY KWEKU OKYEREFO

204

Bibliography

217

Contributors

233

Index

235

Acknowledgments

This volume is a result of the Cambridge/Africa Collaborative Research Programme, which brought four of its contributors to the University of Cambridge for a period of research in 2007–8. The visits were made possible by support from the Leverhulme Trust. The conference at which versions of the chapters were presented was hosted and partly funded by the Centre for Research in the Arts, Social Sciences and Humanities and the Centre of African Studies at Cambridge.

A special debt of gratitude is owed to Derek Peterson, who has provided intellectual and practical support for this project from its inception to the editing of the present volume. The colleagues who participated in the conference as discussants or speakers but whose contributions are not published here are also gratefully acknowledged: Joel Cabrita, Rijk van Dijk, Matthew Engelke, Thomas G. Kirsch, and Anthony Simpson.

INTRODUCTION

Rethinking African Christianities
Beyond the Religion-Politics Conundrum

HARRI ENGLUND

AT THE dawn of the twenty-first century, human tragedy and subsequent surveillance were not the only consequences of epoch-making terrorist attacks in the United States. They also heralded a public outcry over the impact of religion on the hearts and minds of apparently gullible believers. Not only was one religion in particular the target of the public outcry, it also attributed to Islam such powers of inspiration that contextual factors—planetary inequalities, the frustrations of Muslim immigrants in the West, the plight of Palestine, new media and communication technologies—often fell outside the purview.[1] Moreover, such an analysis tended to overlook the persistently motivating and constraining impact a related religion, Christianity, continued to have on political competition in the West, particularly in the United States.

By marveling at the "return" of religion as an all-consuming force, the outcry did little else than reframe the assumptions of secularization whose passing it ostensibly mourned. Following the founding figures of sociology, the thesis of secularization had assumed that modernizing societies would become functionally differentiated, with increasing rationalization spelling the decline of the public significance of religion.[2] What the public concern in the wake of the 9/11 terrorist attacks shared with this thesis was the idea of religion as a subsystem that was separate from others in the structure of society. Its return to the public realm made it imperative to put the lid back on Pandora's box before religious passions would infuse the domains of public life.[3]

Recent anthropological studies of Islamic movements in Egypt and the rest of the Middle East have, quite appropriately, been at the forefront of devising ways out of the impasse with the secularization thesis.[4] Concerned less with theorizing an abstract society than with reflecting on actual, observable practices, these studies have shaken the very foundations of progressive politics among Euro-American academics. The movements, popular among women and young men, have engaged in the redefinition of piety and commitment in which moral and social improvement is as important as technological progress. Their predilections are, therefore, compatible with social activism,[5] and the sounds of mass-mediated sermons that fill the air of public places shape private lives. "Within this context," Charles Hirschkind writes, "public speech results not in policy but in pious dispositions, the embodied sensibilities and modes of expression understood to facilitate the development and practice of Islamic virtues and therefore of . . . ethical comportment."[6]

Progressive sensibilities are challenged by this prioritization of personal conduct over public policy. They are also confronted by the need to rethink the concept of freedom when submission to external authority would seem to be a condition for achieving the subject's potentiality. Far from dismissing adherents engaged in ethical self-formation as belligerent fundamentalists, these anthropologists urge us to "hold open the possibility that we may come to ask of politics a whole series of questions that seemed settled when we first embarked upon the inquiry."[7]

Note how, in this quote, a new understanding of religious formation holds the potential for a fresh appreciation of political practice. The domains of religion and politics are not easily kept separate for analytical purposes once the underlying view of society in the secularization thesis is rejected. Ideas expressed in, and actions taken within, apparently different domains and institutions feed into each other, and what belongs to the public sphere or the private sphere is to be investigated and not assumed. Much as this basic insight informs the chapters in this book, a note of caution must be struck. The appreciation of hybrid and complex forms has long since displaced dichotomous thought in social sciences and humanities, but it has given rise to new problems, notably the question of what the analyst can hope to keep constant when everything is understood to be in flux.[8] For some students of Africa, the ways in which religion and politics can get conflated on the continent become little else than a pretext to assert the primacy of the former over the latter. While admitting that Africans are not busy with religion all the time, Stephen Ellis and Gerrie ter Haar, for example, maintain that "religious thought plays a key role in political life because the spirit world is commonly considered the ultimate source of power."[9] Although these and many other contemporary authors add a suitable dose of cultural relativism to such statements by highlighting religious or spiritual factors in Euro-American public life, others find in their very choice of topics for African studies an assertion of the continent's exceptionalism.[10] Religious thought, particularly as it evokes and wrestles with the occult, would seem to define African experiences in a way that it does not Euro-American experiences.

The approach in this volume is different. Rather than conflating the dichotomy between religion and politics only to reiterate ideas of "Africa's pathological exceptionalism,"[11] the chapters here engage in ethnographic and historical investigation on the complex ways in which Africans have variously appropriated Christian idioms beyond the boundaries of religious expression, asserted a cleavage between religions, kept secular and religious concerns separate, and sought moral and material renewal through Christian practice. In other words, African Christians have constituted, and not merely addressed, domains and categories for moral and political practice and reflection. Even the recent studies of Islamic piety mentioned above may, for all their ingenuity, carry a residual distinction between embodied religious self-formation and liberal modes of self-reflection and critical thought.[12]

It is debatable whether the chapters in this book cast doubt over such a distinction only because of their focus on sub-Saharan Africa rather than the Middle East and on Christians rather than Muslims. Deeper conceptual and methodological issues may account for the difference. Few of the contributors here have isolated religion as the field of their academic specialism; the perspectives they bring to bear on Christianity and public culture arise from anthropology, sociology, history, and literary criticism, as well as religious studies. As for many of the people they write about, the interest in Christianity has evolved as an aspect of engaging with other domains and experiences than religion. The upshot has been to take Christianity seriously as an aspect of life, but the contributors' intellectual and personal backgrounds also allow them to keep its impact in perspective.

Public culture is a notion that facilitates this effort to open up the study of religion in Africa to wider intellectual and pragmatic influences. Less clearly demarcated institutionally than formal politics and more diffuse in its spread than popular culture, public culture prompts questions about how certain events, ideas, and practices assume public significance and thereby cross over the boundaries of their own domains. Among the boundaries these questions address are spatial and temporal configurations, as when the contributors to this volume explore public culture in rural no less than in urban areas, and in colonial and early postcolonial situations no less than in twenty-first-century controversies (part I). The conceptual and pragmatic boundaries that maintain a distinction between the private and the public are likewise considered, as when the relations of intimacy and reproductive and health concerns come to occupy a major public presence (part II). This volume also takes a critical look at assumptions informing academic and popular comments on the apparently explosive public presence of Pentecostal-charismatic Christianity in contemporary Africa (part III). Before introducing these themes in more detail, however, it is important to know more about the ways in which the public impact of Christianity has previously been envisioned in African studies.

Changing Perspectives on African Christianities

The history of the Christian church in Africa is complex, varied, and long. Few scholars would dare to approach that history with the panache that a lifetime of learning enabled the late Adrian Hastings to exude.[13] Not only did he trace the origins of the church in Africa to the earliest centuries of Christianity, he also saw in fourth-century Egyptian Christianity a paradigm for the subsequent history of African Christianity—as opposed to "the history of Christianity upon the continent of Africa."[14] No longer a religion of the urban imperial elite using the scriptures in Greek, Christianity came to hold increasing popular appeal by the end of the third century when most, if not all, of the Bible had been translated into the different varieties of Coptic in Egypt. What was paradigmatic for the quickening of the history of African Christianity over one thousand years later was the attempt to take African languages seriously, often resulting in the first pieces of written literature in as yet unstandardized languages. The close involvement with languages was one aspect of Christianity's impact on life and thought beyond the religious sphere. Conversely, few aspects of life—particularly the struggle for material survival and prosperity—would fail to influence the emergence of Christian identity among Africans.

Introduction

A great historian is marked by his or her skill at discerning what can and cannot serve as a paradigm for patterns in different times and places. Hastings's history of the church in Africa is a narrative of breathtaking complexity, with different denominations, missionary orders, and African initiatives having strikingly different relations to public affairs of profound significance such as slavery, settler agriculture, and colonial rule. It is this humility before historical and political complexity that must inform studies with more modest aspirations, including the present volume.

While seeking to specify and qualify the public role of Christianity in a number of cases, this volume builds on the strengths of decades of historical and anthropological scholarship on African Christianities. Long gone, for example, is a formulaic juxtaposition between mission churches, African-instituted churches, and African traditional religion. These distinctions may well live on in popular and theological thought, and are therefore important subjects of study, but the intellectual case for questioning them was well put by Terence Ranger in 1986.[15] Finding their analysis in isolation from each other to be artificial and distorting, he pointed out, among other things, that churches launched by Africans were not necessarily more in the throes of social change than so-called traditional religion was and that mission, or mainline, churches were no less authentic than African-instituted churches as windows into African religious experiences. Ranger delivered his verdict on the back of several innovative studies of Christian independence in Africa.[16] The wider significance of these studies lay in their emancipation from the confines of structural-functionalism, whose atemporal models had so far precluded a close investigation of social change in Africa. Once it was recognized that no aspect of African social life was sealed off from the forces of change, the extension of their insights into the study of other aspects of religion was inevitable.

The late 1980s saw the rise of increasingly sophisticated approaches to the study of historical transformations through the shift of scholars' focus from Christian independence to African encounters with mission Christianity. A culturalist turn in anthropology and history facilitated this shift, much as many anthropologists and historians continued to relate their findings to the material processes of colonial exploitation.[17] Ostensibly devoted to showing the intricacies of African agency in the face of the missionary onslaught, a major innovation in many of these studies was the insistence on white missionaries as agents no less molded by culture than their black interlocutors.[18]

In order to recover the nuances of cultural ruptures in missionary encounters, anthropologists and historians had to devise new standards of method and demonstration that would make the silences of more formal archives speak. In the work of Jean and John Comaroff, in particular, a rich array of scholars' own reflections on material objects, architecture, agricultural methods, medical substances, and so on, appeared to compensate for the lack of historical records on African voices.[19] Yet this innovation also elicited doubts over the extent to which Africans lacked narratives as a form of historical consciousness.[20] More critically still, a related response was to question the implicit assumption that indigenous debate on religious transformation commenced with the arrival of Christian missionaries.[21] An emerging body of scholarship has indicated the extent to which conversations carried in African languages have predated and exceeded the impact of missionary interventions, with indigenous traditions of reflection making a Eurocentric history an ever more problematic venture.[22]

Although such recognition of African agency may bring us back to the conundrum of authenticity that the earlier work on African-instituted churches grappled with, it does raise the important question of how to acknowledge historical and cultural difference in analysis. Before the current interest in public culture, anthropologists and historians often explored this difference in terms of religious resistance to political subjugation. A range of Christian-inspired prophets and preachers stimulated more or less violent confrontations with colonial rule in different parts of Africa.[23] Karen Fields set a high standard for scholarship by demonstrating how religion remained integral to the apparently secular project of British colonialism.[24] The activities of the Watchtower movement in Malawi and Zambia in the beginning of the twentieth century troubled the colonial administration, because its practices of baptism, healing, and prophecy could be seen to carry elements of political protest.

In a similar vein, Jean Comaroff's study of Zionism in southern Africa highlighted the importance of the religious imagery and nonverbal behavior to black South Africans' resistance against the apartheid state.[25] Healing was a particularly potent practice under the circumstances of exploitation and subjugation. It marked a reintegration of matter and spirit, drawing together the social, spiritual, and embodied experiences that labor migration, among other economic imperatives, had torn apart. Symbolic and physical operations performed on the body through ritual were key to achieving this renewal of the person.

Introduction

The studies by Fields and Jean Comaroff appeared at a time when social theorists were becoming increasingly disillusioned with the Marxist models of false consciousness as explanations for the lack of revolt among colonized peoples.[26] The idea of subtle resistance within culturally specific modes of hegemony seemed an attractive alternative, and these perspectives on African agency provided particularly innovative examples of what the new paradigm could offer. Scholarship has moved on, however, and a general criticism directed against the literature on resistance has asked whether scholars, with their own left-liberal sensibilities, actually looked for whatever glimmers of unconventional politics that poor and marginalized people's lives could contain.[27] In other words, resistance as a category of thought may have been imposed on ethnographic and historical observations. The current conceptualizations of agency, as in the literature on Islamic piety mentioned earlier, emphasize the discourses and structures of subordination as the conditions of its enactment.[28]

A criticism more specifically aimed at Comaroff's argument about Zionism took issue with her view on these churches as sites of incipient political protest. Generalizing about so-called healing churches in southern Africa, Matthew Schoffeleers describes them as conduits of acquiescence instead of protest.[29] Yet wider theoretical and methodological issues continue to intrigue scholars, with some insisting on an expanded and unconventional notion of the political that takes into account church members' own idioms and experiences.[30]

By expanding the scope of what they consider to be political, scholars may or may not redress the limitations of resistance studies. Bearing in mind that Zionists had subscribed to a wide spectrum of political positions in South Africa, Richard Werbner asks, "What weight must we give to the explicit intent of the people themselves as against our inferences about the implicit and the unspoken?"[31] This empirical question requires a conceptual one as its complement: how do scholars conceptualize religion as an alternative source of political commentary and contestation? The idea of resistance as pursued by the Comaroffs, not only in their study of Christianity but also in their argument about witchcraft beliefs as a response to modernity's malcontents, certainly involves a perspective on politics as something else than what takes place within the confines of formal political institutions.[32] It does so, however, by making religious or occult practices seem like substitutes for a sociological and historical analysis.

7

At issue is whether religion is best thought to perform "a second-order process of adjustment."[33] "What allows the Comaroffs," Ruth Marshall has recently demanded, "to assume that these practices are principally modes of interpretation and understanding?"[34] The reduction of religion to a cognitive disposition inevitably diminishes both its practical import and its imaginative resources. It is, after all, not so much politics as religion that requires rethinking, particularly the ways in which it has, as a category of thought in academia, involved assumptions about the relationship between acting and believing.[35] It is a central contention of this volume that this rethinking is achieved more decisively when the concept of religion is paired with the concept of publics rather than politics.

From Politics to Publics

The conceptual and methodological difficulties discerned in the changing perspectives on African Christianities recall the cautionary comment on the recent literature on Islamic piety movements. Problems with a cognitive approach, with the notion of religion as a second-order process of adjustment, are not solved by attributing priority to embodied, non-verbal behavior.[36] The great promise of studying Christianity—and indeed any religion—as an integral aspect of public culture is the way in which embodied, deeply felt experiences can be represented as coexisting with instances of deliberative and critical reason. It is here that a conceptual shift from politics to publics seems particularly productive, because sterile definitional disputes over the scope of the political and the religious can give way to an investigation of what actually assumes public significance in the historically specific circumstances of religious and political contestation. A central interest in such investigation is to uncover the multiple ways in which people seek to make their claims public; how those claims shape, and are shaped by, other public pronouncements; and what insight claims expressed in religious idioms can give into the constitution of moral and political publics.

Note how the notion of public as something that is widely (but not necessarily universally) open and accessible requires a notion of the public as its audience. The chapters in this volume explore claim making in a range of historical and contemporary contexts, but common to them all is the idea that the public is an audience whose members are not known to those who address it in order to make claims. According to Karin Barber, a public can be imagined to be limited or vast, "reaching out beyond the known community to wider populations, whether politically or religiously defined."[37] Crucial to this insight is the idea that a public addressed is also a public constituted—the chapters in this volume bear testimony to the ways in which Christian idioms and practices have informed the emergence of new orders of relationships. Whether public culture is the site for contestation by multiple publics is an empirical question, but the public role of religion can indicate how different publics are, in Michael Warner's words, "structured by alternative dispositions or protocols, making different assumptions about what can be said or what goes without saying."[38]

The insertion of religion into studies of contemporary public life is a relatively recent development in scholarship, and it is important to recognize the specific idea of religious experience and argumentation that often informs this development. Several recent contributions to the anthropology of religion have, particularly in relation to Christianity, registered considerable unease with the concept of belief.[39] Malcolm Ruel's argument about "the monumental peculiarity of Christian 'belief,'"[40] both building on and extending the work of Wilfred Cantwell Smith,[41] has served as a major impetus to this critique. According to Smith and Ruel, the concept of belief is largely a post-Reformation innovation that replaced earlier Christian idioms of trust and commitment with a propositional attitude.[42] Ruel's contribution was to point out the consequences for anthropological analysis, including the assumption that belief is what forms the ground of behavior and explains, therefore, various aspects of cultural and social life. Moreover, to be a believer identifies a person as a member of a group that is clearly distinct from groups of other types of believers. As an interior state, belief also puts the believer in an individual, contemplative relation to his or her God.

For recent anthropology, these critical insights have raised doubts about the concept of belief in the study of Christianity and not only in the comparative study of religion as Ruel intended. When Christian orientations, along with a host of other religious dispositions, are understood as being sustained by acts rather than states of mind, it becomes much less plausible to regard Christians as believers in the senses outlined above. Instead, researchers' attention gets directed, among other things, to the multiple ways in which Christians live their faith practically, how their convictions resonate or conflict with other viewpoints available to them, and how, once they are no longer seen as believers hermetically sealed off from other kinds of believers, they situate themselves in public life.

Whereas recent work on the public presence of religion has often highlighted the role of mass media,[43] this volume pursues its revisionist impulse through a wider range of examples. Mass media certainly loom large in some of the chapters here (especially those by Cooper, Englund, Meyer, and Prince), but the revision of rationalist-secular theories needs to be nourished by other empirical instances than mass-mediated religious interventions. As Birgit Meyer and Annelies Moors have rightly observed, instead of attributing too much significance to the technologies of mass mediation, religion can itself be taken as a practice of mediation.[44] From the use of the scriptures to the mediating efforts of diviners and spirit mediums, various forms of religion have always enabled people to envision and engage matters beyond the confines of their particular lifeworlds.

A related insight into the mediating effects of religion has made much of this recent literature to take issue with assumptions in Jürgen Habermas's theory of the public sphere.[45] The theory is one of the most sophisticated examples of how the assumed public decline of religion comes to be linked to the definition of the public sphere as a domain of rational deliberation. As "the abstract counterpoint of public authority,"[46] the public came into being, according to Habermas, in nineteenth-century Europe with the emergence of the bourgeoisie, whose constitution derived as much from new property relations as from new kinds of public discourse mediated by, among others, the print media, tavern conversations, and art criticism. Although Habermas's historical narrative was presented as a critique, lamenting the erosion of the public sphere in the face of commodification, others have questioned not only the neglect of religion in his idealized notion but also his lack of attention to gender and class in channeling access to the public sphere.[47] As a consequence, the academic debate on the public sphere has expanded the notion's remit virtually beyond recognition, with the sources and sites of deliberation identified not only in religion but in a wide range of other domains.[48] Critical has been the move from a normative standpoint to a descriptive one.

Much as this volume arises from the theoretical ferment generated by Habermas and his critics, it is not primarily concerned with refining the already extensive and complex debate on the public sphere. The conceptual and methodological reflections offered in this introduction should be viewed as an effort to contextualize the empirical cases that form the bulk of this volume. Public culture is hardly a less theoretical concept than public sphere, but precisely because it has not been subject to as extensive theoretical debate as the public sphere, it may facilitate historical and ethnographic analysis without a constant need to refer to abstract and often Eurocentric theorizing. The conceptual shift from politics to publics, as outlined here, involves a number of analytical challenges. For scholars to fully appreciate historical and contemporary variations in the public role of African Christianities, they need to move beyond a number of obstacles: spurious typologies of religion on the continent, models of resistance against political authority, approaches that are deaf to Africans' indigenous conversations about religious and political change, juxtapositions between embodied and discursive modalities, and the legacies of the concept of belief derived from a particular context of Christian theology. These challenges surely represent sufficient theoretical stimulus, but above all they call for fresh empirical work.

Missionary and Nationalist Encounters

It is appropriate, in light of the above-mentioned trends in current scholarship to discuss the mass media and the public sphere, that chapter 1 of this volume takes us where few studies in this vein venture: rural Africa at the onset of the missionary encounter. By describing two mission stations in Zambia's Mwinilunga District, James Pritchett offers not so much a denominational comparison between Protestant and Catholic missions as an account of how their innovations engaged local Africans' aesthetic and epistemological sensibilities. Contesting both the notions that African conversations about social and ideological change began with the missionary encounter and that early converts were marginal members of their community, Pritchett shows that missionary initiatives fed into complex African experiments with agriculture and medicine no less than with fashion, drama, and music. The two mission stations' respective specializations in medicine and agriculture give particularly clear examples of Christian conversion entwining with apparently mundane concerns. Pritchett's narrative recalls historical observations across the continent of medical missionaries as miracle workers despite themselves.[49] Agricultural innovation was no less embedded in particular Christian orientations toward the division of labor, crop selection, and ideas of what constituted an orderly field—all changes that became subject to African experimentation and reconfiguration. Pritchett's chapter releases, therefore, the study of popular and public culture from its association with urban life and introduces a fresh perspective on rural Africa as a site of innovation and experimentation.

Marja Hinfelaar, in chapter 2, complements Pritchett's immersion in a rural district with an analysis of the Catholic Church's input to imagining Zambia as a nation. Her key objective is to historicize the well-publicized pronouncement by Zambia's second president that the country was a Christian nation. By so doing, she challenges evolutionary assumptions that informed much popular and academic discourse shortly before and after independence, claiming that Zambia was on its way toward a secular public culture. In effect, Hinfelaar's chapter serves to historicize not only the pronouncement about Christian nation but also the Catholic Church's influential role in debating and shaping public life across Africa, not least during the wave of democratization in the early 1990s. The Second Vatican Council, in the early 1960s, coincided with the onset of independence in many African countries, and one of the council's consequences was the church's closer involvement in the worldly affairs of justice and peace. This involvement put the church on a collision course with the state in Zambia, because ruling politicians wished to adopt scientific socialism as the new nation's guiding doctrine. Hinfelaar shows how the Catholic clergy's objection arose less from their rejection of socialism as such—some of them were, at the time, veritable experts on Marxism—than from their defense of religiosity and diversity against the looming vanguard politics. However, when the new born-again president declared Zambia a Christian nation, the Catholic Church felt that the pendulum had swung too far in the other direction. Hinfelaar details the shifts in the church's position as it debated the difference between a secular state and a country that has no state-endorsed religion.

In chapter 3, Nicholas Kamau-Goro reveals another facet of Christianity's impact on imagining the nation in Africa. Instead of focusing on any particular church, Kamau-Goro explores another influential figure in Africa's public culture: the creative writer. Pioneering African writers were both nationalists and products of mission education.[50] This double attachment has often resulted in ambiguity, if not hostility, toward their Christian heritage, much as Christian missions sowed the seeds of nationalism by promoting the idea of ethnolinguistic units as polities and by standardizing African languages. Yet their criticism and selective appropriation of indigenous cultures also provoked a nationalist reaction against Christianity. Kamau-Goro shows the ambiguities

Introduction

and paradoxes of Christian allegory and African nationalism in the work of Ngũgĩ wa Thiong'o. He charts Ngũgĩ's transformation from a devout Christian to a critic of Christianity who, nevertheless, remains in his early novels loyal to Christian allegory for his choice of idioms to, in Kamau-Goro's words, "articulate [Africans'] dreams for salvation from colonial oppression." Kamau-Goro's analysis indicates, therefore, some of the ways in which Christianity has shaped public culture in Africa even as it has been ostensibly rejected.

Patriarchy and Public Culture

Public culture is as much a context for defining the boundaries of the private and the intimate as it is the setting in which large-scale public affairs such as nationalism are envisioned. The chapters in part II show how Christianity and public culture influence gender relations, sexual morals, and female empowerment. Barbara Cooper, in chapter 4, focuses on the reproductive politics of a Christian minority in the context of Muslim-majority Niger. Her case is a particularly clear demonstration of how highly intimate and embodied issues such as fertility and reproduction can assume public import. Tracing the history of contestation over the relative sizes of the Christian and Muslim populations in Niger, Cooper dissects the official patriarchal notion that the church was produced and reproduced by the acts of men. Important figures as they may have been, male pastors and missionaries could not have expanded the Christian constituency without the church attracting women and laying claim to children. Cooper builds on comparative insights from elsewhere in Africa to point out how Christian messages often appealed to women before they did so to men. In Cooper's case, it was only after the evangelical mission had embarked on medical work from the 1940s onward that it could approach women and children directly, with fostering, marriage, and childbirth complementing conversion as a path to Christianity. Cooper details the role of ritual in the mission's effort to lay claim to children. Apart from the ritual—itself a public event during which the child is displayed to a wide audience, Christian and non-Christian—Cooper discusses the radio announcements of Christian naming ceremonies and weddings as important conduits for making public the success of Christian reproduction. Her view on mediation thus combines insights into ritual and broadcasting and alerts us to the perils of considering the electronic media in isolation from older performative modes.

The infusion of Christian idioms into the politics of community survival and reproduction is also a central theme in chapter 5, by Ruth Prince. Her analysis of debates about widow inheritance among the Luo of western Kenya situates highly intimate and personal experiences in a range of interventions extending from mission and revivalist Christianity to traditionalist assertions of patriarchy to campaigns against the spread of HIV/AIDS. Within this complex field of argument and intervention, Prince identifies a spectrum of Christian responses that include support for the practice by some African-instituted churches, recent efforts to reshape it by the Anglican and Catholic Churches, and outright opposition against it by the Pentecostal and evangelical churches. Material considerations shape these arguments as opposition against widow inheritance is buttressed by well-funded alliances between Christians, human rights activists, and feminists, and as those women who succeed in opposing it have often achieved a measure of economic security. At the same time, Prince shows how claims voiced in Christian idioms can be more compelling than those expressed in terms of rights. Recalling Kamau-Goro's observation on the capacity of Christian imagery to provide tools for critique, the debate in western Kenya does not so much pit Christians against non-Christians as involve Christians of various persuasions in reflecting on tradition and morality.

When participants in a debate are all Christians, Christianity's contribution to a critique of public culture is not best described as resistance against dominant discourses. In chapter 6 Damaris Parsitau examines the entry of Pentecostal pastors and prophets into electoral politics and various charitable enterprises. What makes Parsitau's study unusual is her focus on female leaders whose achievements have offered inspiration and mentorship to countless women in Kenya, a country where women's participation in public life has long faced considerable obstacles. Drawing on biblical references to exceptional women, these female leaders have confounded their male critics through business acumen and a commitment to raising children without a husband. However, Parsitau shows how their involvement in Kenya's public culture is a complex mix of empowering and illiberal standpoints. For example, their promotion of hope and ambition among women is in tension with their preaching against abortion and premarital sex. The pride they wish to instill in single mothers can be diluted when the aspiration to become a respectable member of Parliament makes them want marriage. Their critique of corruption and tribalism among politicians, moreover, coexists with their intolerance toward Islam and homosexuality.

A Plurality of Pentecostal Publics

The entry of Pentecostal clergy into mainstream political competition is a relatively new phenomenon in Africa. It is also a controversial development, both for many Pentecostals themselves and for their academic observers.[51] Whereas Pentecostals debate among themselves the extent to which party politics is fundamentally divisive and un-Christian, some observers can barely conceal their contempt for this overtly emotional and personal form of Christianity. Although Pentecostalism has had a presence in Africa since the early twentieth century, including in rural Africa,[52] Paul Gifford was one of the first to identify a new and more intense phase of proselytization from the 1980s onward.[53] Focusing particularly on southern Africa, he emphasized the negative effects of this trend on African liberation, distressed as he was by the conspicuous role played by conservative American evangelists at a time when the Christian church was being decolonized in Africa. Gifford has since explored the theological and social dimensions of the so-called faith gospel in, among other African countries, Ghana and Kenya.[54] Although he has been able to produce more nuanced accounts of Pentecostal diversity and African initiative, he has continued to find Pentecostalism problematic in its impact on public debates about the need for structural change in Africa's governance and economies.

Other liberal academics in Europe and the United States have sometimes been able to pronounce alarmist views on Pentecostalism in Africa without referring to any empirical study in particular. As recently as in 2009, Patrick Chabal deplored Pentecostalism's individualist ethos, which promotes personal self-improvement and internationalism: "Worthy as they may seem to the American churches that sponsor Pentecostalism, these priorities are disruptive of received notions of identity, reciprocity, and even nationality. In ways that are not always discernible today, they could pose a greater challenge to the African polity than is presently envisaged."[55] An unsubstantiated impression is created that African Pentecostalism depends on American churches and that the entire African polity is threatened by the way in which its priorities contradict identity, reciprocity, and nationality. The lack of references to any actual Pentecostal practitioners makes this comment particularly revealing of the ease with which this form of Christian practice lends itself to generalizations that would hardly be acceptable in relation to other religious orientations.

Generalizations of this kind, often accompanied by pronouncements about the "spectacular rise"[56] and "enormous sweep"[57] of Pentecostalism in contemporary Africa, can be refuted on several grounds. Overall, religious and spiritual complexity has not been reduced by the undeniable mushrooming of Pentecostal churches across the continent during the past thirty years. African-instituted churches do not belong to the past but are a powerful presence in many countries,[58] while, according to David Maxwell, "the historic churches remain enormously influential, still staffed by expatriate missionaries who work in tandem with and usually under the authority of African clerics."[59] Moreover, during the rise of Pentecostalism, the African religious scene has witnessed another, less dramatic but equally significant, phenomenon in the increase of faith-based organizations that provide development and humanitarian aid.[60]

Perhaps the most devastating blow to generalizations is dealt by the sheer diversity of Pentecostal approaches and practitioners. The effect is particularly evident when scholars link Pentecostalism with Charismatic movements. Theological affinities can be obvious enough, arising from nineteenth-century revivalism in the Methodist and Holiness movements in North America, Europe, and even elsewhere, and revolving around the gifts of the spirit such as prophecy, healing, and speaking in tongues. Yet Allan Anderson, for example, advocates definitions that can be adapted to particular contexts, bearing in mind that charismatic experiences and fellowships are not the prerogative of Pentecostal-type churches but form an influential element within the Catholic Church and some Protestant denominations.[61] When resulting in staggering statistics about church growth, the linking of Pentecostals with charismatics can, therefore, serve triumphalism among Pentecostal missionaries rather than analytical purposes.[62] Part III of this volume contributes to the view that is less concerned with definitional niceties thrown up by unwarranted generalizations than with exploring doctrinal malleability and membership fluctuations in congregations and movements that identify themselves as Pentecostal.[63]

The diversity that the chapters in part III seek to demonstrate is particularly poorly served by the impression that the faith, or prosperity, gospel is the quintessential feature of African Pentecostalism. The impression obscures the range of topics that Pentecostalism has enabled scholars, particularly anthropologists, to explore with regard to contemporary Africa, topics such as commodification,[64] transnational connections,[65] African diasporas,[66] mass media,[67] and responses to the crisis in public health.[68] In chapter 7, Birgit Meyer, who does here use *Pentecostalism* and *prosperity gospel* interchangeably, shows how this type of Christian orientation is embedded in wide-ranging reforms that, often informed by neoliberal economics, have sought to enhance free markets and pluralist democracy across Africa since the late 1980s. She points out that the process of "making public," of exposing the secrets of non-Christian worship, has a long history in African Christianity and is by no means reducible to Pentecostalism. However, Meyer argues that the current process of "going public" by Pentecostal and charismatic preachers and prophets suggests a range of new questions for research, not least because of their skillful use of media such as television, videos, radio, and Web sites. This process, Meyer emphasizes, revolves around style rather than community, casting doubt over the congregational model of religious life that has informed the study of Christianity in Africa as elsewhere. Addressing Eurocentric theorizing about the public sphere, Meyer also contends that the contemporary public sphere in Ghana is a hybrid of critical public discussion and religiously motivated consumerism.

The conflation of Pentecostalism with the prosperity gospel may betray the pull of megachurches in cities among those scholars whose linguistic and methodological limitations leave them ill equipped to face the diversity of Pentecostal practice in poor townships and rural villages. It is these settings that form the background for Harri Englund's exploration of spiritual warfare in Malawi (chapter 8). Building on fieldwork among impoverished township dwellers and born-again radio journalists, Englund shows how the quest for security rather than for prosperity animates the Pentecostal imagination. The issue of spiritual warfare, especially when it engages Muslims as its key adversaries, also bears notable public significance in a country marked by inequalities and polarization between Christians and Muslims. When the rhetoric and practice of spiritual warfare is studied in a specific historical and ethnographic context, Englund argues, unexpected insights into the rights and obligations of membership can emerge. Spiritual warfare here turns born-again Christians' gaze as much inward to demonic forces within one's own congregation, if not oneself, as outward to those who openly oppose baptism in the Holy Spirit. Central to the essentially peaceful and civil effects of spiritual warfare is the expansion of trust through spiritual kinship that embraces anyone regardless of their religious and ethnic provenance. The experience that the Holy Spirit works in and through human relationships gives the lie to the unvarnished association of Pentecostalism with individualization. The role played by testimonies broadcast in the Chichewa language is explored in detail, from the viewpoints of both their born-again editors and their narrative contents and idioms.

Chapter 9, by Ilana van Wyk, is no less unflinching in its challenge to the stereotypes and generalizations that plague the study of Pentecostalism's impact on public culture. Here the focus is on a big urban church and its apparent prosperity gospel. The Universal Church of the Kingdom of God would seem to realize the worst nightmares of Pentecostalism's critics. The sense of a community assisting each other materially and spiritually—a sense so easily attributed to African Christianity—is demolished by the distrust among participants in the South African congregation that van Wyk has studied. Distrust is actively promoted in the church, whose pastors never stay long enough with the same congregation to develop personal attachments, whose congregations scarcely notice funerals and weddings in their midst, and whose pews are filled more with lone individuals than with couples and families. However, as in the rest of this volume, neither contempt nor endorsement is the result of analysis. Van Wyk shows how the one-off "contracts" with God that confound some observers' expectations of denominational loyalty and doctrinal rigor take place within troubled lives that involve moves from church to church and from one prophet or healer to another in search of blessings. At the heart of van Wyk's contribution lies a challenge to anthropologists and other scholars who have come to question the notion that belief is a propositional attitude (see above). An alternative notion, she suggests, is not Christian practice as trust or commitment but as a kind of technology inextricably linked to pragmatic pursuits.

Despite their divergent perspectives on Pentecostalism, the chapters by Meyer, Englund, and van Wyk all indicate dissatisfaction with the conventional models of churches and congregations as stable, bounded communities. Style, spiritual kinship, and technology are some of the conceptual alternatives these three authors, respectively, put forward instead to capture the sense in which Pentecostal publics are in the process of becoming rather than simply addressed. However, Michael Okyerefo (chapter 10) completes this volume's exploration of Pentecostal diversity by analyzing two Ghanaian churches' search for public respect and legitimacy. The key means by which they attempt to go mainstream is through the provision of health and orphan care and educational facilities. Okyerefo thereby documents a trend that liberal critics' consternation has not been able to foresee. Along with participation in electoral politics, developmental activities have seemed a distant prospect in Pentecostals' self-indulgent ways. Okyerefo expands, however, the issue of public legitimacy and respect to address the manner in which development has been envisioned, not only by Africa's foreign masters but also by Pentecostalism's liberal critics. Rather than seeing in Pentecostals' interventions in development work another cynical ploy to attract followers and money, Okyerefo asks whether the very concept of development has to be revised in light of these interventions. Do they not bespeak a desire to unite the economic and spiritual dimensions of life into one concept of development?

This volume comes full circle with Okyerefo's chapter describing in a contemporary context the indivisibility of the material and the spiritual that Pritchett's account of medical missionaries as miracle workers demonstrated for historical encounters. In a broader sense, this insight is but an aspect of the perspective this volume seeks to put forward. The relationship between Christianity and public culture in Africa is not so much an instance of religion determining some people's approach to apparently secular institutions as an invitation to rethink the manner in which influential academic and popular theories, with the secularization thesis *and its inversions* at the helm, have partitioned society into subsystems. What publics as constituted and not merely as addressed demonstrate is that we cannot know the significance and form of such divisions in advance of empirical research. A closer attention to the claims African Christians make warrants a contextual and historical approach to the boundaries that separate the religious and the secular, the private and the public, the liberal and the illiberal.

Notes

1. The journalistic and academic writing along these lines has grown into a veritable industry, and the decontextualized approach is particularly evident in discussions about so-called jihadism and Islamic extremism. A flavor of book-long interventions, often including prescriptions for the West's response, can be gained, for example, from Will Marshall, ed., *With All Our Might: A Progressive Strategy for Defeating Jihadism and Defending Liberty* (Lanham, MD: Rowman and Littlefield, 2006).

2. A defense of the secularization thesis is given in Steve Bruce, *God Is Dead: Secularization in the West* (Oxford: Wiley-Blackwell, 2002). Much debate was provoked by Bruce's

earlier book, *Religion in the Modern World: From Cathedrals to Cults* (Oxford: Oxford University Press, 1996). A more wide ranging—and less tendentious—intellectual history is provided by Charles Taylor, *A Secular Age*, (Cambridge, MA: Harvard University Press, 2007). The idea that religion can be abstracted as a separate system goes further back in intellectual history than the works of Durkheim, Marx, and Weber, at least to the Enlightenment. Among contemporary sociologists, José Casanova put forward the argument that although society may be functionally differentiated, religion has not ceased to have public significance, as events in many parts of the world since the 1980s attest. See Casanova *Public Religions in the Modern World* (Chicago: University of Chicago Press, 1994).

3. Crusading atheists such as Richard Dawkins and Christopher Hitchens were an inevitable by-product of this panic over religion in public life. See, for example, Richard Dawkins, *The God Delusion* (London: Bantam Press, 2006); Christopher Hitchens, *God Is Not Great: How Religion Poisons Everything* (New York: Atlantic Press, 2008). Their arguments have been ably demolished by Terry Eagleton, *Reason, Faith, and Revolution: Reflections on the God Debate* (New Haven: Yale University Press, 2009).

4. See, for example, Lara Deeb, *An Enchanted Modern: Gender and Public Piety in Shi'i Lebanon* (Princeton: Princeton University Press, 2006); Charles Hirschkind, *The Ethical Soundscape: Cassette Sermons and Islamic Counterpublics* (New York: Columbia University Press, 2006); Saba Mahmood, *Politics of Piety: The Islamic Revival and the Feminist Subject* (Princeton: Princeton University Press, 2005). See also Talal Asad, *Formations of the Secular: Christianity, Islam, Modernity* (Stanford: Stanford University Press, 2003).

5. Deeb, *Enchanted Modern*.

6. Hirschkind, *Ethical Soundscape*, 106.

7. Mahmood, *Politics of Piety*, 39.

8. Bruno Latour, *We Have Never Been Modern* (New York: Harvester Wheatsheaf, 1993); Marilyn Strathern, "Cutting the Network," *Journal of the Royal Anthropological Institute* 2, no. 3 (1996): 517–35.

9. Stephen Ellis and Gerrie ter Haar, *Worlds of Power: Religious Thought and Political Practice in Africa* (London: Hurst, 2004), 6. For a critique, see Maia Green, "Confronting Categorical Assumptions about the Power of Religion in Africa," *Review of African Political Economy* 33, no. 110 (2006): 635–50. See also the response by Ellis and ter Haar to some of their critics in "Religion and Politics: Taking African Epistemologies Seriously," *Journal of Modern African Studies* 45, no. 3 (2007): 385–401.

10. A sweeping and therefore ill-informed indictment on Western scholars' choice of research topics in African studies can be found in Jemima Pierre, "Anthropology and the Race of/for Africa," in *The Study of Africa*, vol. 1, *Disciplinary and Interdisciplinary Encounters*, ed. Paul Tiyambe Zeleza (Dakar: CODESRIA, 2006), 39–61.

11. Paul Tiyambe Zeleza, *Rethinking Africa's Globalization*, vol. 1, *The Intellectual Challenges* (Trenton, NJ: Africa World Press, 2003), 282.

12. For an alternative to the piety literature, see Magnus Marsden, *Living Islam: Muslim Religious Experience in Pakistan's North-West Frontier* (Cambridge: Cambridge University Press, 2005); Marsden, "Talking the Talk: Debating Debate in Northern Afghanistan," *Anthropology Today* 25, no. 2 (2009): 20–24. Mahmood, among others, has noted how contemporary Islamist discourses presuppose the practical and conceptual conditions of the secular-liberal world they criticize. See Mahmood, *Politics of Piety*, 191–92. This point is, however, separate from the observation that the same persons may subscribe to both religious and liberal dispositions.

13. Adrian Hastings, *The Church in Africa, 1450–1950* (Oxford: Clarendon Press, 1994).

14. Ibid., 7.

Introduction

15. Terence Ranger, "Religious Movements and Politics in Sub-Saharan Africa," *African Studies Review* 29, no. 2 (1986): 1–69.

16. For example, Johannes Fabian, *Jamaa: A Charismatic Movement in Katanga* (Evanston, IL: Northwestern University Press, 1971); James W. Fernandez, *Bwiti: An Ethnography of the Religious Imagination in Africa* (Princeton: Princeton University Press, 1982); Bennetta Jules-Rosette, *African Apostles: Ritual and Conversion in the Church of John Maranke* (Ithaca: Cornell University Press, 1975); J. D. Y. Peel, *Aladura: A Religious Movement among the Yoruba* (Oxford: Oxford University Press, 1968); Bengt Sundkler, *Bantu Prophets in South Africa* (Oxford: Oxford University Press, 1948).

17. For example, Nicholas B. Dirks, ed., *Colonialism and Culture* (Ann Arbor: University of Michigan Press, 1992).

18. The literature is vast and varied, but see, for example, T. O. Beidelman, *Colonial Evangelism: A Socio-historical Study of an East African Mission at the Grassroots* (Bloomington: Indiana University Press, 1982); Jean Comaroff and John L. Comaroff, *Christianity, Colonialism, and Consciousness in South Africa*, vol. 1 of *Of Revelation and Revolution* (Chicago: University of Chicago Press, 1991); Richard Gray, *Black Christians and White Missionaries* (New Haven: Yale University Press, 1990); Dorothy Hodgson, *The Church of Women: Gendered Encounters between Maasai and Missionaries* (Bloomington: Indiana University Press, 2005); Paul Landau, *The Realm of the Word: Language, Gender, and Christianity in a Southern African Kingdom* (London: James Currey, 1995); David Maxwell, *Christians and Chiefs in Zimbabwe: A Social History of the Hwesa People, c. 1870s–1990s* (Edinburgh: Edinburgh University Press, 1999); Birgit Meyer, *Translating the Devil: Religion and Modernity among the Ewe in Ghana* (Edinburgh: Edinburgh University Press, 1999); Peter Pels, *A Politics of Presence: Contacts between Missionaries and Waluguru in Late Colonial Tanganyika* (Amsterdam: Harwood Academic, 1999).

19. Jean Comaroff and John L. Comaroff, *The Dialectics of Modernity on a South African Frontier*, vol. 2 of *Of Revelation and Revolution* (Chicago: University of Chicago Press, 1997). The Comaroffs' turn to a culturalist historical anthropology had been prefigured by Marshall Sahlins, *Islands of History* (Chicago: University of Chicago Press, 1985).

20. J. D. Y. Peel, "'For Who Hath Despised the Day of Small Things?': Missionary Narratives and Historical Anthropology," *Comparative Studies in Society and History* 37, no. 3 (1995): 581–607. See the response in Comaroff and Comaroff, *Dialectics of Modernity*.

21. Landau, *Realm of the Word*; Derek R. Peterson, *Creative Writing: Translation, Bookkeeping, and the Work of Imagination in Colonial Kenya* (Portsmouth, NH: Heinemann, 2004).

22. Karin Barber, ed., *Africa's Hidden Histories: Everyday Literacy and Making the Self* (Bloomington: Indiana University Press, 2006).

23. See, for example, George A. Shepperson and Thomas Price, *Independent African: John Chilembwe and the Origins, Setting and Significance of the Nyasaland Native Rising of 1915* (Edinburgh: Edinburgh University Press, 1958); Landeg White, *Magomero: Portrait of an African Village* (Cambridge: Cambridge University Press, 1987). The rising led by John Chilembwe in present-day Malawi can be seen as an instance of the wider phenomenon of Ethiopianism, whose varieties deployed from the late nineteenth century onward Christian idioms to advance the cause of African liberation and independence. See James T. Campbell, *Songs of Zion: The African Methodist Episcopal Church in the United States and South Africa* (Chapel Hill: University of North Carolina Press, 1998); Hastings, *Church in Africa*, 478–87.

24. Karen Fields, *Revival and Rebellion in Colonial Central Africa* (Princeton: Princeton University Press, 1985).

25. Jean Comaroff, *Body of Power, Spirit of Resistance: The Culture and History of a South African People* (Chicago: University of Chicago Press, 1985).

26. One example of changing perspectives on power and resistance is the work of James C. Scott, notably *Weapons of the Weak: Everyday Forms of Peasant Resistance* (New Haven: Yale University Press, 1985). See also Scott, *Domination and the Arts of Resistance: Hidden Transcripts* (New Haven: Yale University Press, 1990). Another influence, particularly apparent in Jean Comaroff's work, was the cultural studies school initiated in Birmingham in the United Kingdom by, among others, Stuart Hall. See, for example, Hall and Tony Jefferson, eds., *Resistance through Rituals: Youth Subcultures in Post-war Britain* (London: Hutchinson, 1976).

27. See, for example, Lila Abu-Lughod, "The Romance of Resistance: Tracing Transformations of Power through Bedouin Women," *American Ethnologist* 17, no. 1 (1990): 41–55; Sherry Ortner, "Resistance and the Problem of Ethnographic Refusal," *Comparative Studies in Society and History* 37, no. 1 (1995): 173–93.

28. Mahmood, *Politics of Piety*, 15.

29. Matthew Schoffeleers, "Ritual Healing and Political Acquiescence: The Case of the Zionist Churches in Southern Africa," *Africa* 61, no. 1 (1991): 1–25.

30. See, for example, Barbara Bompani, "African Independent Churches in Post-apartheid South Africa: New Political Interpretations," *Journal of Southern African Studies* 34, no. 3 (2008): 665–77; Joel Cabrita, "Isaiah Shembe's Theological Nationalism, 1920s–1935," *Journal of Southern African Studies* 35, no. 3 (2009): 609–25; Liz Gunner, *The Man of Heaven and the Beautiful Ones of God: Writings from Ibandla lama Nazaretha, a South African Church* (Leiden: Brill, 2002).

31. Richard Werbner, "The Political Economy of Bricolage," *Journal of Southern African Studies* 13, no. 1 (1986): 151–56.

32. Jean Comaroff and John Comaroff, introduction to *Modernity and Its Malcontents: Ritual and Power in Postcolonial Africa*, ed. Jean Comaroff and John Comaroff (Chicago: University of Chicago Press, 1993); Comaroff and Comaroff, "Occult Economies and the Violence of Abstraction: Notes from the South African Postcolony," *American Ethnologist* 26, no. 2 (1999): 279–303. Among the many critiques of the Comaroffs' argument about witchcraft, see esp. Adam Ashforth, *Witchcraft, Violence, and Democracy in South Africa* (Chicago: University of Chicago Press, 2005), 116–21.

33. Ruth Marshall, *Political Spiritualities: The Pentecostal Revolution in Nigeria* (Chicago: University of Chicago Press, 2009), 29.

34. Ibid., 28.

35. A remarkable precedent for such rethinking can be found in Talal Asad's critique of the category of religion in anthropology. See Asad, *Genealogies of Religion: Discipline and Reasons of Power in Christianity and Islam* (Baltimore: Johns Hopkins University Press, 1993), 27–54.

36. As the above discussion has indicated, the Comaroffs' work has represented religious resistance as both cognitive and nonverbal.

37. Karin Barber, *The Anthropology of Texts, Persons, and Publics: Oral and Written Culture in Africa and Beyond* (Cambridge: Cambridge University Press, 2007), 139–40.

38. Michael Warner, *Publics and Counterpublics* (New York: Zone Books, 2002), 56.

39. For example, Harri Englund, "Pentecostalism beyond Belief: Trust and Democracy in a Malawian Township," *Africa* 77, no. 4 (2007): 477–99; Thomas G. Kirsch, "Restaging the Will to Believe: Religious Pluralism, Anti-syncretism, and the Problem of Belief," *American Anthropologist* 106, no. 4 (2004): 699–709; Galina Lindquist and Simon Coleman, "Against Belief?" *Social Analysis* 52, no. 1 (2008): 1–18; Joel Robbins,

Introduction

"Continuity Thinking and the Problem of Christian Culture: Belief, Time, and the Anthropology of Christianity," *Current Anthropology* 48, no. 1 (2007): 5–38.

40. Malcolm Ruel, *Belief, Ritual and the Securing of Life: Reflexive Essays on a Bantu Religion* (Leiden: Brill, 1997), 36.

41. Wilfred Cantwell Smith, *Belief and History* (Charlottesville: University Press of Virginia, 1977); Smith, *Faith and Belief* (Princeton: Princeton University Press, 1979).

42. Ruel, *Belief*, 36–59.

43. Dale F. Eickelman and Jon W. Anderson, eds., *New Media in the Muslim World: The Emerging Public Sphere* (Bloomington: Indiana University Press, 1999); Rosalind I. J. Hackett, "Charismatic/Pentecostal Appropriations of Media Technologies in Nigeria and Ghana," *Journal of Religion in Africa* 28, no. 3 (1998): 258–77; Birgit Meyer and Annelies Moors, eds., *Religion, Media, and the Public Sphere* (Bloomington: Indiana University Press, 2006); Dorothea A. Schulz, "'Charisma and Brotherhood' Revisited: Mass-Mediated Forms of Spirituality in Urban Mali," *Journal of Religion in Africa* 33, no. 2 (2003): 146–71; Hent de Vries and Samuel Weber, eds., *Religion and Media* (Stanford: Stanford University Press, 2001); Marleen de Witte, "Altar Media's *Living Word:* Televised Charismatic Christianity in Ghana," *Journal of Religion in Africa* 33, no. 2 (2003): 172–202.

44. Meyer and Moors, introduction to *Religion and Media*, 7. See also Harri Englund, "Witchcraft and the Limits of Mass Mediation in Malawi," *Journal of the Royal Anthropological Institute* 13, no. 2 (2007): 295–311; Jeremy Stolow, "Religion and/as Media," *Theory, Culture and Society* 22, no. 4 (2005): 119–45; Hent de Vries, "In Media Res: Global Religion, Public Spheres, and the Task of Contemporary Comparative Religious Studies," in Vries and Weber, *Religion and Media*, 3–42.

45. Jürgen Habermas, *The Structural Transformation of the Public Sphere: An Inquiry into a Category of Bourgeois Society* (Cambridge, MA: MIT Press, 1989).

46. Ibid., 23.

47. An excellent guide to the critique of Habermas remains Craig Calhoun, ed., *Habermas and the Public Sphere* (Cambridge, MA: MIT Press, 1992).

48. For example, Nick Crossley and John Michael Roberts, eds., *After Habermas: New Perspectives on the Public Sphere* (Oxford: Blackwell, 2004); Jon Elster, ed., *Deliberative Democracy* (Cambridge: Cambridge University Press, 1998); Luke Goode, *Jürgen Habermas: Democracy and the Public Sphere* (London: Pluto Press, 2005); Christina Tarnopolsky, "Platonic Reflections on the Aesthetic Dimensions of Deliberative Democracy," *Political Theory* 35, no. 3 (2007): 288–312.

49. Comaroff and Comaroff, *Dialectics of Modernity*; Hastings, *Church in Africa*, 277; Markku Hokkanen, *Medicine and Scottish Missionaries in the Northern Malawi Region, 1875–1930: Quests for Health in a Colonial Society* (Lewiston, NY: Edwin Mellen Press, 2008).

50. J. D. Y. Peel, "Christianity and the Logic of Nationalist Assertion in Wole Soyinka's *Ìsarà*," in *Christianity and the African Imagination: Essays in Honour of Adrian Hastings*, ed. David Maxwell with Ingrid Lawrie (Leiden: Brill, 2002), 127–50.

51. Harri Englund, "The Dead Hand of Human Rights: Contrasting Christianities in Post-transition Malawi," *Journal of Modern African Studies* 38, no. 4 (2000): 600; David Maxwell, *African Gifts of the Spirit: Pentecostalism and the Rise of a Zimbabwean Transnational Religious Movement* (Oxford: James Currey, 2006), 218–21.

52. Maxwell, *African Gifts*, 38–59.

53. Paul Gifford, *The New Crusaders: Christianity and the New Right in Southern Africa* (London: Pluto Press, 1991).

54. Paul Gifford, *African Christianities and Public Life: A View from Kenya* (London: Hurst, 2009); Gifford, *Ghana's New Christianity: Pentecostalism in a Globalising African Economy* (London: Hurst, 2004).

55. Patrick Chabal, *Africa: The Politics of Suffering and Smiling* (London: Zed, 2009), 102.

56. Birgit Meyer, "Christianity in Africa: From African Independent to Pentecostal-Charismatic Churches," *Annual Review of Anthropology* 33, no. 1 (2004): 448. Unlike Chabal, Meyer indicates familiarity with Pentecostal diversity.

57. Chabal, *Africa*, 102.

58. See, for example, Matthew Engelke, *A Problem of Presence: Beyond Scripture in an African Church* (Berkeley: University of California Press, 2007); Thomas G. Kirsch, *Spirits and Letters: Reading, Writing and Charisma in African Christianity* (New York: Berghahn, 2008); Isabel Mukonyora, *Wandering a Gendered Wilderness: Suffering and Healing in an African Initiated Church* (New York: Peter Lang, 2007).

59. David Maxwell, introduction to *Christianity and the African Imagination: Essays in Honour of Adrian Hastings*, ed. David Maxwell, with Ingrid Lawrie (Leiden: Brill, 2002), 21.

60. Erica Bornstein, *The Spirit of Development: Protestant NGOs, Morality, and Economics in Zimbabwe* (New York: Routledge, 2003).

61. Allan Anderson, *An Introduction to Pentecostalism: Global Charismatic Christianity* (Cambridge: Cambridge University Press, 2004), 13–14.

62. See Gary B. McGee, "Pentecostal Missiology: Moving beyond Triumphalism to Face the Issues," *Pneuma* 16, no. 2 (1994): 276–77.

63. David Martin, *Pentecostalism: The World Their Parish* (Oxford: Blackwell, 2002); Donald E. Miller and Tetsunao Yamamori, *Global Pentecostalism: The New Face of Christian Social Engagement* (Berkeley: University of California Press, 2007).

64. Birgit Meyer, "Commodities and the Power of Prayer: Pentecostalist Attitudes towards Consumption in Contemporary Ghana," *Development and Change* 29, no. 4 (1998): 751–77.

65. André Corten and Ruth Marshall-Fratani, ed., *Between Babel and Pentecost: Transnational Pentecostalism in Africa and Latin America* (London: Hurst, 2001).

66. Rijk A. van Dijk, "From Camp to Encompassment: Discourses of Transsubjectivity in the Ghanaian Pentecostal Diaspora," *Journal of Religion in Africa* 27, no. 2 (1997): 135–59; Dijk, "Negotiating Marriage: Questions of Morality and Testimony in the Ghanaian Pentecostal Diaspora," *Journal of Religion in Africa* 34, no. 4 (2004): 438–67.

67. De Witte, "Altar Media"; Hackett, "Charismatic/Pentecostal Appropriations"; Birgit Meyer, "'Praise the Lord': Popular Cinema and Pentecostalite Style in Ghana's New Public Sphere," *American Ethnologist* 31, no. 1 (2004): 92–110.

68. Hansjörg Dilger, "Healing the Wounds of Modernity: Salvation, Community, and Care in a Neo-Pentecostal Church in Dar es Salaam, Tanzania," *Journal of Religion in Africa* 37, no. 1 (2007): 59–83; Frederick Klaits, *Death in a Church of Life: Moral Passion during Botswana's Time of AIDS* (Berkeley: University of California Press, 2010); James Pfeiffer, "Condom Social Marketing, Pentecostalism, and Structural Adjustment in Mozambique: A Clash of AIDS Prevention Messages," *Medical Anthropology Quarterly* 18, no. 1 (2004): 77–103.

PART ONE

Missionary and Nationalist Encounters

ONE

Christian Mission Stations in South-Central Africa
Eddies in the Flow of Global Culture

JAMES A. PRITCHETT

THE CLICHÉ that early missions attracted the African outcast, the vulnerable, and the marginal obscures the reality of mission stations as complex hierarchies of individuals, collectively constructing novel institutions.[1] Africans residing at a rural mission station could have been teachers, lay preachers, schoolchildren, carpenters, bricklayers, mechanics, craftspersons, cooks, cleaners, launderers, seamstresses, farmhands, herders, buyers, clerks, accountants, stockers, or day laborers. In many instances these were occupational categories that had not long existed, whose gender assignment remained unclear, and whose relative hierarchical rankings had yet to be sorted out. Clearly the individuals recruited to these categories had not all been equally marginal characters in the societies from whence they came, if at all. Clearly they exercised differing levels of influence on the functioning of the mission station. And clearly their individual relationships with the missionaries varied from possibly intimate and meaningful daily interaction to only occasional and rather incidental contact.

African chiefs and headmen routinely sent family members or trusted subjects to live at mission stations, to report back on their operations, to assess the threats or opportunities contained therein.[2] Disadvantaged social or ethnic groups routinely ensconced themselves at mission stations seeking escape and protection, a fresh start under a new dispensation. Some early mission stations, with their array of sacred and secular aims, their occupational and ethnic diversity, their daily experimentations with new forms of cultural and economic intercourse, and the concomitant possibilities for social friction, could easily have been the most complex social aggregates on the African landscape. Thus, to discuss the impact of mission stations in terms of generalized narratives about the tenets of particular ecclesiastical orders juxtaposed to so-called traditional African belief systems, or the political configuration of particular European nations juxtaposed to traditional African social structures, is to overlook the complexity and contingency of everyday life, the power of circadian interaction to generate new modes of thought and action for both Africans and missionaries alike.

An opening caveat: while this chapter may appear as one more study of the "encounter" that transforms African consciousness, I nevertheless agree wholeheartedly with Derek Peterson's assertion that we "must discard the idea that colonialism was an 'encounter' between a textual, rational European world of modernity and an oral, negotiated African world of experience. Framing colonial history in this way forecloses investigation into the hard work that colonized people did within their own intellectual traditions."[3] Complex conversations about change, otherness, and social reorientation in Africa did not begin with the coming of Europeans. Nor did such conversations begin with decoding the contingencies of urban life. Engaging and negotiating colonialism did not produce the first cultural, aesthetic, or epistemological bricolage on the African continent. Life in south-central Africa has long been characterized by the movement of people, ideas, forms of social organization, and ritual practices whose multiple intersections required constant social and psychological adjustments.[4] The arrival of Europeans may have required somewhat greater adjustment, but frameworks and models for thinking about such adjustments already existed.

In this chapter, I will first illustrate a bit of the local character of the epistemological tête-à-tête that characterized the African-European encounter in Mwinilunga, Zambia. I will also present a few vignettes from daily life on and around mission stations that buttress my view of them as early, and continuing, sites for the development of African popular culture. Finally, I will tilt the analytical lens slightly to show how the same material could contribute to emerging discourses on public culture that draw our attention to new forms of imagined communities, mediated by a range of communicative technologies, linked and underpinned by distinctive imagery, rhetorical modes and performative styles. This chapter is much too short to explore these topics in any depth but simply aims to suggest some of the rich possibilities of approach. The material is derived from longer case studies of two mission stations in the Mwinilunga District of northwestern Zambia: one, Kalene Mission, organized by an evangelical Protestant group, the Christian Missions in Many Lands (CMML), who settled in Central Africa in the 1890s; the other, Lwawu Mission, founded by Catholics of the Franciscan order, who extended their reach into Mwinilunga in the 1950s. The aim is not a denominational comparison. Rather, the two mission stations were selected simply because of my familiarity with the history and personnel of each, having spent considerable time at both since the early 1980s.[5] The degree of continuity between the colonial and postcolonial roles of these mission stations is astonishing. Four decades after Zambian independence, each mission remains the largest provider of health care and educational services in its respective area, the largest employer of both skilled and unskilled labor, the preferred point of dispersal for a host of government services, the standard place of assembly for major social and political events, the most sought after destinations by refugees fleeing war and poverty in surrounding countries, and the favored places of rest and relaxation for any important person passing through the district. Operational funds continue to come largely from overseas. The leadership remains mostly European.[6]

Lexicons and Landscapes

Walter Fisher, the man who would become widely known as Ndotolu (the doctor), moved his CMML mission operation from Angola to the extreme northwestern corner of Zambia in 1906.[7] In doing so he founded Kalene Mission a year before troops of the British South Africa Company arrived to lay claim to the territory. Lacking a wealthy home organization capable of totally funding overseas activities, CMML mission stations were responsible for their own economic viability. Thus Kalene Mission pursued a wide range of economic strategies. The solicitation of overseas donations was complemented by local cash cropping, cattle rearing, craft production, trade in consumer goods, as well as exporting honey, wax, and various tropical commodities. But medical work was Fisher's principal passion. With the judicial use of local labor, much of it from former patients and their families, combined with volunteers and material contributions from abroad, Fisher built the largest and best-staffed medical complex in Central Africa.

At Kalene Mission, medicine was the major domain from which the Christian assault was launched. Dr. Fisher's medical cures and his painless surgery may have boggled the mind. But Fisher was first and foremost a missionary. Healing bodies was simply a device for gaining access to souls. The CMML seized every opportunity to publicly announce their faith, to spread their version of God's tenets and to bring Africans into the Christian fold. Patients were enjoined to pray before receiving treatment, subjected to frequent sermons while convalescing, and enticed to attend Bible study groups upon recovery. As Walima Kalusa has noted, "Medical evangelists at Kalene hoped that by relocating African healing to clinical settings and launching an onslaught on Lunda etiological beliefs and practices, they would weaken the ideological foundations that underlined local medicine. Once the Lunda came to appreciate the rationality, efficacy and superiority of biomedicine over indigenous medicines, they would . . . reject their 'fetish remedies' predicated on 'heathen' belief systems."[8]

On the one hand, missionaries claimed superior knowledge. They put forward biomedicine as scientific and universally applicable, and disease as a phenomenon standing apart from spirits and social relations. On the other, in seeming contradiction, missionaries regularly spoke of the power of prayer, and of God's intercession in the healing process as indispensable. Fisher was said to have routinely urged his African patients to place more faith in the curative and prophylactic power of God than in the actual medicines being dispensed at his hospital. Thus, ironically, some Africans came to place mission medicine in the same category as their own spirit medicine rather than accept it as a strictly biological phenomenon.[9] Furthermore, Africans not only creatively engaged and reconceptualized mission medicine, transforming it into a local idiom, they successfully led European medical missionaries to alter their own discourse to appeal to Africans in that idiom. Over time, hospitals came to resemble ritual sites, with predictable daily rounds of prayer, preaching, and the vibrant singing of hymns. Even those not particularly ill at a given moment might show up and participate in hospital rituals as a prophylactic measure.

Kalene Mission attempted to create a coterie of African medical elites, local medical auxiliaries who would be the champions of modernity among their own people. Trained in the rudiments of biology, lab analysis, simple diagnostic procedures, and the dispensation of pharmaceutical drugs, they were expected to be the vanguard in the war against African "superstition," taking the battle, if need be, to its physical source in the African village, or to its mental source in the uncultivated African mind.

Yet it was these same medical auxiliaries who played a key role in Africanizing, or Lundaizing, mission medicine. It was they who were most deeply engaged in translation, in the construction of a local medical lexicon. It was an endeavor that ultimately coined few new terms but rather tended to bring in terms from the preexisting Lunda medical lexicon. For example, the missionaries came to adopt the Lunda word *yitumbu* for the English *medicine*. Yet to Lunda consciousness *yitumbu* connoted not only curing substances but also incantations, spells, and rituals. *Musongo* became the accepted gloss for *disease*. Yet to the Lunda *musongo* not only meant physical disorders but could also imply bad luck or bewitchment. *Kusolola* became the accepted term for diagnosis. Yet it is a term locally saturated with notions of uncovering and revealing (witches and spirits), that is, divination. Hence, instruments such as microscopes and stethoscopes became recognized locally as "little metal diviners." Through this exercise of translation, mission medicine—and Christianity itself—became saturated with Lunda metaphors and meanings, Lunda traditional assumptions, and Lunda metaphysical associations.

The initial set of African medical auxiliaries tended to be young males with the highest fluency in English. Lunda sensibility, however, tended to prefer more elderly medical practitioners (males or females), who had received their knowledge and power through long apprenticeship with well-known practitioners from the even more senior generation. Over time, Kalene Mission felt compelled to emulate this pattern of recruitment and began to select younger family members of extant auxiliaries as trainees.

The Africanization, or Lundaization, of mission medicine was in many ways a response to its initial ineffectiveness in treating even the most common African diseases such as malaria, sleeping sickness, and river blindness. Concomitantly, the mission's entrance into local African life was coterminous with the area's incorporation into the new colonial regime, with its harsh reality of taxation, migrant labor, debilitating poverty, devastating epidemics of new diseases (tropical ulcers, Spanish influenza, tuberculosis) that collectively produced rising mortality and morbidity rates. These profound challenges contested and decentered the explanatory authority of missionaries. Missionaries, in turn, responded by experimenting with local pharmacopoeias and allowing some Lunda practitioners a limited range of operation on mission premises.

Medical material moved two ways, however.[10] Shortly after the European arrival, some Lunda traditional practitioners added white lab coats to their regalia and "little metal diviners" to their paraphernalia. Some began giving "injections." Some added prayer and bits of biblical verse to their traditional incantations. Indeed, the anthropologist Victor Turner working in Mwinilunga in the 1950s draws our attention to a piece of local innovation. At least two new rites of affliction, *tukuka* and *masandu*, had emerged to appease the European spirits that caused illness. "These two rituals are becoming very popular and are often performed for persons suffering from tuberculosis. The shades (spirits) who cause the disease are said to be those of Europeans or of members of other tribes like the Lwena and part of the treatment consists of giving the patient European foods, served by a 'houseboy,' miming European dancing in couples, wearing European dress, and singing up-to-date songs such as 'We are going in an airplane to Lumwana.'"[11]

As Wim M. J. van Binsbergen detailed in *Religious Change in Zambia* (1981), Central Africa has a long history of being swept by religio-medical movements.[12] Territorial cults, shrine cults, cleansing cults, antiwitchcraft movements, prophetic movements, healing rites of all sorts rapidly emerge, gain a huge following if they appear efficacious, or disappear equally rapidly if not. The famous "microcosm" that is foundational to Robin Horton's notion of African conversion has long been shattered in Central Africa.[13] The realization that disease could emanate from people outside the lineage has led local practitioners, inspired by foreign diviners and healers, to continually reformulate existing cosmologies of disease and healing, to conceptualize the ancestors of neighboring peoples, refugees, or foreign traders as new etiological agents. The resulting cultural exchange entails more than simply appropriating the ideas and objects of others. It involves refashioning and reassigning meanings and uses to symbolic resources originally belonging to cultural others in order to fit them into existing medical knowledge and treatment repertoires—in essence, creative recontextualization. Accordingly, at Kalene Mission a new bricolage emerged, not simply a synthesis of African and European medical knowledge and procedures but an expanded repertoire of meanings and actions for addressing old and new epidemiological and socioeconomic concerns. Some might say postmodernity happened. It was a rejection of the universalistic, absolutist assertions of mission medicine, not by African retreat to conservative traditions but through incorporation, reconfiguration, and transcendence of mission offerings. The process of creative recontextualization would also be manifested in other social domains and in other places.

Fifty miles to the south of Kalene lies Lwawu Mission, established in 1951 by Franciscan friars from the United States. Here, education and agricultural innovation, rather than medicine, were the targeted domains of the African-European engagement.[14] Indeed, the Franciscans brought with them to Mwinilunga a distinctly midwestern American sensibility about the relationship between people and land. They had grown to maturity observing a fertile landscape, with immaculately maintained rows of corn, soybeans, and wheat extending to the horizon. It was land that had sustained extended families for generations, nourished a nation, and launched the American economic miracle. The intense greens of the Mwinilunga rainy season led the Franciscans to overestimate the fertility of local soils. The bleak arid browns of the dry season, they reasoned, could be easily overcome with irrigation. With generous support from home, the Franciscans were able to buy tractors, hire local labor gangs to remove rocks and tree stumps, and level a significant area, readying it for plowing by tractor. They experimented with hybrid seeds and newly developed chemical fertilizers, pesticides, and herbicides. It was a determined effort to demonstrate the superiority of modern farming practices, indeed to initiate an agricultural revolution in Mwinilunga that presumably local Lunda youth would lead, and that would concomitantly lead those youth into sustained engagement with Catholicism. The mission's agricultural thrust received such a continual infusion of overseas cash and materials that it is difficult to ascertain if it could ever have been sustained on local resources alone. Nevertheless, Lwawu Mission did manage to create an astonishing visual effect. Its grounds were increasingly covered with a neatly trimmed Kentucky bluegrass hybrid, with stands of swaying pine and eucalyptus trees, and sprays of red poinsettias and purple bougainvillea. Fruit orchards and irrigated vegetable gardens generated locally novel produce. And just beyond view, rows of maize saturated with chemicals managed to overcome all obstacles and sprout their golden ears.

Each set of Franciscan friars residing at Lwawu Mission over the years would leave its own imprint on the landscape. One set of friars began experimenting with fishponds in the late 1960s. In the early 1970s another set took up game ranching with the gift of fifteen impalas from the government game department. Still others would add pineapples, sugarcane, and sunflowers to the local cropping inventory. The early 1980s saw the expansion of cattle rearing. Again, Lwawu Mission, with dozens of friars and young novices, hundreds of workers, ringed by an ever thickening cluster of African villages, was a visually unique spectacle, attracting many visitors who merely wished to gaze upon it.

The initial success of Lwawu Mission, however, was mostly illusory. Fish and animals were under constant assault from unknown pathogens, whereas crop yields tended to decline rapidly from one year to the next, if they grew at all. Since the 1950s, much has been learned about the fragility of tropical and subtropical soils. Mwinilunga, additionally, is part of a geological region that suffered cataclysmic upheavals eons ago, convoluting the substrata and bringing to the surface oscillating bands of black, red, brown, and gray soils—alluvial, clay, loam, and sandy soils that switch places every few yards.[15] The land is rugged and rocky with heavy metallic content. The humus layer is generally thin and overall soil fertility varies from poor to extremely poor. It rains nearly every day for half the year and virtually not at all the other half. Little about midwestern American farming is applicable to local conditions.

The mission took to renting or loaning out one of its two tractors to local farmers to allow them to conduct their own experimentation. The mission also purchased an electric mill to grind local maize into flour and a seed press to extract oil from sunflowers, further encouraging the production of those crops. The missionaries also made small loans to select young Christian men to purchase agricultural inputs, saplings for orchards and fingerlings for stock ponds. Much innovation took place under these conditions.

Missions were somewhat unique among local social groups in actually having secured formal title to their property. Over time, however, Lwawu Mission would come to realize what the Lunda had long known: movement and segmented land holdings were the most effective tools for dealing with highly variable soil fertility. The mission found itself planting maize on one spot for two or three years and then, after declining yields, sought out fresh soils. Likewise, mission personnel began to pay closer attention to the specific attributes of the red, black, brown and gray soils that invariably comingled in every garden plot. In due course, the precisely measured, Cartesian grid–like borders of the mission station became increasingly fuzzy, increasingly Africanized, as specific crops followed ribbons of fertility and soil types across the landscape. Hence, in many ways the gap between mission and tradition narrowed. The universalistic principles of agronomy and agricultural science developed in the temperate zone met the reality of the tropics.

As had been the case up north at Kalene Mission, African response to European innovation around Lwawu mission was not a simple acceptance or rejection of the totalizing mission package. The multifaceted reaction was more that of observation, experimentation, deconstruction, reconfiguration, and partial incorporation into the local world of actions and meanings in ways that defy, challenge, or transcend initial meanings. Entirely new forms of agricultural and land management practices emerged—equally modern and scientific, equally incorporating "traditional" knowledge of local soil characteristics and plant preferences. The fragmented holdings of villages around Lwawu increasingly included maize following erratic bands of dark alluvial soils, pineapples following bands of gray sandy soils, sunflowers on bands of brown loamy soils, each intercropped with traditional varieties of pumpkins, groundnuts, and mixed greens. Hundreds of fishponds were carved out of red clay soil between the fields. Conversations about timing and density of seed dispersal, weed and pest control for novel plant sequences, as well as possible food sources for pond-raised fish became nightly affairs. The results of such deliberations could later be seen carved into the physical landscape.

Interestingly, as I have written elsewhere, Lunda landscapes have long been readable topographies of power and knowledge.[16] Villages, as well as forests, hills, valleys, rivers, and plains tend to be named after the most famous chief, headman, or big man who lives or has lived nearby. Ambitious men vie for such honors. Lineage segments, political factions, and cohort groupings squabble over the rights to name particular geographical features after their leaders. The landscape can indeed be read as an ever-changing map of power, frequently pitting the fame of living males against the renown of their predecessors. Likewise the complexities of the African-European encounter in Mwinilunga can be read on the landscape around Lwawu; the visible scars of failed agricultural initiatives, and the lush greens of successful new syntheses. Up north, around Kalene Mission, the encounter could best be read in the medical lexicon that emerged thereabouts. In both instances we witness creative recontextualizations of formerly alien ideas and practices in ways that reveal a cultural milieu long accustomed to engaging new people and new ideas. The Lunda, and Central Africans more broadly, have long demonstrated eagerness, and indeed a flair, for cultural synthesis and the capacity to hold complex conversations and make continual adjustments to local ways of being.

JAMES A. PRITCHETT

Fashion, Drama, Music: Missions and Popular Culture

According to Karin Barber,

> popular "cultural productivity" ... has emerged in Africanist scholarship only as a residual category: a vague, shapeless, undefined space, demarcated only by what it is not. It is not wholly "traditional"—in the sense given to this term by much Africanist scholarship, that is purely oral, expressed in exclusively indigenous African languages or images, and coming from or alluding to the pre-colonial past. On the other hand it is not "elite" or "modern," "Westernized" culture—in the sense of inhabiting a world formed by higher education, full mastery of European languages and representational conventions, defined by its cultural proximity to the metropolitan centres, and addressed to a minority but "international" audience. It is rather defined by its occupation of the zone between these two poles.[17]

Mission stations were not simply sites where the relative superiority of European and African medical and productive systems were evaluated, or where cosmic battles raged between competing metaphysical worlds. Mission stations were also living, breathing residential agglomerations where the stresses and strains of daily life had to be mitigated, where people grew up, fell in love, and got married, where creative impulses percolated to the surface seeking new modes of expression. The occupational, educational, class, and, sometimes, ethnic diversity that comprised mission stations proved to be fertile ground for the production of popular culture. Mission stations, and the concomitant contact with European missionaries and their accoutrements, frequently gave rise to distinctive fashion, theatrical, and musical styles.

For example, long before the emergence of the current global system for dumping tons of *salaula* (second-hand clothing) in Zambia and elsewhere, missionaries had used donated attire from their home countries as their own local currency.[18] Missionaries grew accustomed to acquiring food and construction materials, labor and loyalty through the systematic barter of clothing. The topographical elevation of Mwinilunga produces frigid temperatures during portions of the year. This combined with limited local opportunities for earning cash and the virtual absence of retail stores in the district to accentuate the value of ready-made clothing. But clearly clothes are desired not simply as protection from the elements, but also as markers of style and class and as evidence of privileged connections to the places from which those clothes originated. Lwawu Mission, for example, cultivated a support network back in the United States that provided a steady stream of used clothing and factory irregulars. Young schoolboys, cowhands, laborers, clinic workers, and catechists at the mission dressed essentially like their American counterparts. At worst, Lwawu youngsters might have been a season or two out of fashion by U.S. standards. In their own heads, however, they were perhaps at the cutting edge of assigning meaning to heretofore unavailable items of clothing. In either case they were trendsetters without equal on the local stage.

The circulation of foreign cloth and clothing in Mwinilunga did not originate with the Protestant CMML or the Catholic Franciscan missionaries. Cloth was the major European export to Africa during the entirety of the slave trade and colonial eras. Furthermore, Swahili and Arab traders had brought cloth and clothing into Central Africa from the Indian Ocean long before the appearance of Europeans.[19] During the seventeenth and eighteenth centuries Central Africa was the point of intersection and overlap between the Indian Ocean and Atlantic trade worlds, where the relative value of European linens and wools, and the silks and satins of the East were determined. The subsequent colonial discourse on the African body and the appropriate mode of its coverage was extensive. The Mwinilunga record is replete with early examples of concerns about Africans "acting European" by attempting to emulate the latter's style of dress. Much of the attention was focused on the absurdity of that African effort as men, for example, sometimes wore female intimate apparel as outerwear, or as women converted window drapes and table cloths into wrap skirts.[20]

Colonial suppositions about uninformed imitation, however, could not have been further from the truth. The amount of Lunda exposure to European styles of dress has been immense. Explorer David Livingstone and his entourage passed through Mwinilunga in the mid-1800s. Dr. Fisher at Kalene, a host of European CMML missionaries and volunteers, and their differentially clad spouses and children, were constant fixtures on the northern Mwinilunga landscape from the early 1900s onward. Lwawu Mission, to the south, played host to a progression of young American, German, Swiss, and Irish friars. Each would be the subject of village fireside commentaries about his individual style and relative coolness vis-à-vis the others.[21] Movies, magazines, and elite politicians on tour were standard visual fashion fare on display at mission stations. The intensity of local interest in fashion is apparent in the program guides of Mwinilunga District agricultural and craft fairs starting in the early 1940s, which included African fashion shows and best-dressed-baby contests.[22] The overall effect might appear in some instances to be entirely mimetic. Yet for many a creative Lunda mind the aim was never imitative but rather a reworking of new materials, new sources of inspiration within an existing set of aesthetic parameters, with the intent of expanding on local fashion sensibilities. The dense concentration of Europeans at mission stations provided a set rich of material for stimulating creativity more so than a limited set of ideals for emulation.

Secondhand clothing became incorporated into a local system of economic reckoning that could easily convert units of labor into articles of clothing, or baskets of food into pieces of attire. Even today, in exchange for complete outfits, teams of young males travel about Mwinilunga negotiating to clear and stump plots of land in preparation for cash crop cultivation. The negotiated dimensions of the plots vary in accordance with the size and density of trees on the land or the quality of clothing being offered for the work. The youth proceed at their own pace, viewing the promised attire whenever they wish for added incentive, but in accordance with local custom, the garments do not change hands until the entire task has been completed. But, again, as Karen Tranberg Hansen has ably shown, wearing secondhand clothing is about much more than simply imitating Western styles.[23] It is about taking a garment and transforming it into something local, something that partially adheres to and partially expands on local aesthetic parameters. It is serious business on the one hand. On the other hand it is about play and performance, about creativity and persuasion. It is about "pulling it off" and "playing to the crowd." Missionaries, by literally providing the raw material, have given generations of Mwinilunga youth an edge over some of their urban contemporaries in the cultural practice of acquiring, appropriating, reworking, and thereby commenting on global fashion trends.

Lacking cheap sources of illumination, the Lunda are accustomed to finishing most essential tasks by sunset. In this land near the equator, the sun sets year round at roughly six o'clock; the remainder of the waking hours, which can extend to midnight or later, finds large groups gathering to entertain themselves around bonfires. Indeed, the desire to save on firewood pushes people to amass in large numbers in regular locations. The Lunda possess an extensive and ever-evolving repertoire of stories, songs, poems, riddles, and dramatic presentations. Youth, in particular, excel at improvising skits about the *muzungu* (white person). A standard theme has long been the humorous contrasts between the European and African modes of doing very basic things. "Africans walk like this," a narrator might say as his confederate glides by with a smooth, elegant, and well-balanced gait. "Muzungu walks like this," he then intones as the village clown rambles into view with jerky motions, head bobbing out of control and ultimately tripping over a barely visible twig, in Charlie Chaplin fashion.[24] Some skits comment on comparative work habits: "Africans wake up early, go straight to the field, sweat—then go home and eat." "Europeans wake up late, take a warm bath, eat warm food, sweat—then call 'lazy' Africans to do their work." Such skits are generally accompanied by such carefully crafted vocal inflections and bodily movements that the audience might well be aware of a particular muzungu being parodied at the moment. Other skits spoof food preferences, table manners, sexual practices, and even standard toilet behavior.

Some of these skits are quite old, passed along with great pride, but reinvigorated by each generation with the addition of contemporary flourishes. Some emerge spontaneously to quickly capture the ludic quality of some recent event or to memorialize some recent cultural realization. At one level, these skits serve to chronicle and satirize the differences between African and European comportment and worldviews. At another level, these skits sustain an ongoing dialogue about the meaning and relevance of particular social categories. Exposure to the ever-changing array of European individuals at mission stations, each with his or her own temperament, preferences, and peccadilloes, begs the question, what are the essential elements of being European? Furthermore, what does it mean to be an African? With demographic shifts in the ethnic composition of particular areas due to government policies, economic opportunities, and entrepreneurial impulses, previously unrelated African individuals and groups are brought into daily juxtaposition. The category African takes on new meanings. The establishment of acceptable rules of engagement, extending from agreement on social norms and etiquette is a necessity. Amusing fireside skits are forums for experimenting with such cultural meanings in an environment that defuses the potential for antagonism. But above all else, fireside dramas are fun; fun to enact, fun to show off to friends and strangers alike. Some skits transcend their local specificity and achieve widespread fame, the performance of which on special occasions is eagerly awaited.

Lastly, missions and music are virtually inseparable. Although CMML missionaries officially eschewed the accretion of rituals within their churches, they nevertheless became widely known for their vibrant hymns. Many, if not most, of the hymns were either entirely composed or at least translated into the Lunda language, by African converts. Hymns thus represent a new cultural form, neither entirely Lunda nor entirely European. Lunda words, and all the metaphorical baggage they contained, were marshaled to compose messages of European origin. The results were novel texts that challenged the exegetical acumen of Europeans and Lunda alike. Additionally, a new musical signature emerged that reflected neither a pure European nor a pure Lunda musical sensibility, but rather reflected, to some degree, the attempt by each to engage, accommodate, or appropriate the musical style of the other.[25]

Lwawu Mission is likewise justly famous for its music, particularly its choir. Africans who make up the Lwawu Mission choir spend perhaps more time in the church building than the Franciscan friars themselves. The acoustics within the grand cathedral are fantastic. Rehearsal is a daily event. There are always new songs to be composed, new arrangements to be scored, new musical instruments to be mastered. Indeed, it might be difficult to disentangle the choir's love of music from its acceptance of Christianity. In some respects the choir is conducting its own musical ministry, only nominally under the authority of the Catholic Church. Many youth, in particular, attend Sunday services primarily to hear the choir perform. Afterward, each song is endlessly critiqued, memorized, resung, or perhaps even rearranged until the following week's performance provides new musical material for rumination.

On one well-remembered occasion, the African choirmaster at Lwawu Mission was publicly scolded by the European head priest for making unauthorized plans for a choir performance off-site. The choirmaster promptly left the Catholic Church and became choirmaster at a local Protestant church, carrying a sizeable number of Catholic youth with him. He was quietly enticed back within a couple of weeks.

The Catholic Church has assembled the largest collection of musical instruments in the district: drums, keyboards, brass horns, guitars, harmonicas, and even an accordion. The church provides a framework for the steady improvement of musical skills among its members and provides the largest local stage for carrying out performance impulses: Sunday Mass. But again, as with the CMML, the music that has emerged is a new genre. It may have borrowed from both European and African musical traditions, but it reflects an altogether new sensibility. It is as much infused with musical signatures heard on the radio as with elements heard at a Protestant performance or with entirely new arrangements that spring from the minds of inspired choir members.

Church music, be it Catholic or Protestant, has not stayed in the church. Church musicians are in great demand at boys' circumcision camps, girls' maturation rites, local weddings, curing-cult enactments, and even exorcisms and other rituals performances aimed at conjuring up and making appeals to the ancestors. Despite the best efforts of European Catholic and Protestant missionaries to mark out absolute differences between their two faiths, to use "church music" as a tool of ecclesiastical purity and a recruitment device, the music has nevertheless transcended its church roots. In a sense, it has become genuinely popular music, music that straddles and yet dissolves any distinctions between traditional and elite, African and Western musical forms.

Mail, Movement, and *Maconferenci*

According to emergent theses on public culture, a public is a distinct social entity, increasingly characteristic of the contemporary world, comprising individuals who may or may not ever meet face to face. A public thus is at least partially brought into existence through mediated encounters. Correspondingly, modern or postmodern societies are invariably composed of many publics. These could include religious communities, political action committees, professional associations, special-interest groups, perhaps even Facebook and MySpace social networks, and other groupings that escape the categorization of the dominant political public culture. The study of public culture need necessarily engage the medium of mediation (digital, broadcast, print, and so on), the use of social memory and collective accounts of the past to assert connectedness, performances to animate those connections, and rhetorical content and styles used to recruit, persuade, and move the collectivity in particular directions.

Much of the discourse about public culture is associated with urbanism, cosmopolitanism, and global citizenry.[26] Its participants, typically, are individuals who have transcended the need to be totally, or exclusively, encased in local ascribed groupings such as family, lineage, clan, or ethnic groups. They occupy positions in the globalized division of labor in which the sources of their livelihood are minimally contingent upon social relations with the group of acculturation. That position affords them a range of choices of personal association, particularly outside the workplace. They can assemble with one group for recreational purposes, another for worship, another to move forward political agendas, or yet another to quietly subvert the political agendas of others. Mission stations, as sites of innovation, were likewise incubators of new public cultures.

Missionaries were the bringers of new forms of long-distance communication. Rural Catholic mission stations that proliferated in Zambia in the 1950s and 1960s, for example, were linked to one another via ham radios. Generally twice a day, morning and evening, each mission station would power up and via an open channel, report in, signal safe operations, and inquire about the health and welfare of others. It was also an opportunity to announce travel plans, make arrangements for ecumenical gatherings, petition for supplies, inquire about prices and market conditions in town, and so forth. Needless to say, the African house staff—cooks and cleaners, steady conduits of European-centered information back to the villages—always listened intently to these conversations. The more trusted ones, on occasion, were allowed to forward messages of their own. Additionally, Lwawu Mission erected a thirty-foot radio antenna, bringing shortwave broadcast from the world over within range of the mission.

Additionally, the advent of mission schools and the literacy that it produced resounded across the landscape as flows of mail; letters from locals working in town, stuffed perhaps with a few banknotes, but certainly with a tale or two about life elsewhere; letters from headman to headman, from chief to chief discussing weighty matters of village or state politics; letters between young lovers perhaps planning their next tryst. Literacy also stimulated a flow of magazines, newspapers, religious tracts, textbooks, government department announcements, agricultural and veterinary extension service pamphlets, and even novels about people and places barely imaginable. Missions were central nodes in these flows, as a disproportionate amount of this written material would arrive first at the mission station before secondary redistribution throughout the district. In Mwinilunga, both Kalene and Lwawu Missions, by design or default, were used as quasi-federal post office stations, routinely listed by villagers from miles around as their personal post office box of record.

Concomitantly, mission stations invariably possessed mechanical modes of movement; motorcycles, cars, and trucks, along with sets of reasons and rounds of activities that kept those vehicles constantly on the road and filled with bodies. The transportation links between mission stations, and between mission stations and town, combined with radio broadcasts and print materials to fundamentally alter local African perceptions of time and space. Distances once considered vast could now be bridged with the flick of a switch or the turn of a dial, with the posting of a letter or with a perch on the back of a mission truck.[27] Correspondingly, new productive strategies, new coteries of economic partners, and new social collectivities became imaginable in this world of greatly expanded reach.

Constructing community, however, was nothing new for the Lunda. Embeddedness in social units, as in much of Africa, is not a given. The household, the village, the kin group, the ethnic group, the affinal group, the curing group, and the cohort group may serve as units rich with possibilities for affiliation. However, full membership in such groups requires activation and periodic reinforcement through participation, performance, and exchange. Groups offer the individual material from which to sculpt a life of connections. But the individual must take the initiative to actually do so. Social groups may vary widely in the claims they make on individual members, and the rights and privileges they confer in return. The social field among the Lunda offers flexibility, the freedom to pick and choose where and when to make social investments, and which benefits are worthy of the effort. The breadth of possibilities for social connections tends to mediate against the perceived need for rigid conformity to particular patterns of behavior, thought, or action. The individual is free to develop his or her own unique personal style while simultaneously able to pursue productive and comfortable connections.

Mission stations gave rise to an array of new opportunities, new equations for calculating cost-benefit ratios, and a greatly enriched set of symbolic material for commenting on one's interpretation of, and strategic thrust, vis-à-vis the new possibilities. Mission stations bring eddies of global cultural flows to the rural area. They serve as places and offer occasions where cultural, social, and political differences emerge as public phenomena. Choir members, for example, join kin and village mates as significant social units that can achieve both affective and economic importance over time. Other unrelated individuals might coalesce simply as *maguys* (the guys); enduring groups of friends whose relationships emerged from shared mission-related experiences such as work or study. Concomitantly, Christian youth are fond of organizing *maconferenci* (conferences); retreats where youth from throughout the district camp out for days and nights of singing, lay preaching, and social networking. The lack of formal mission support and, indeed, genuine mission ambivalence about such gatherings in the woods has not dampened youthful enthusiasm for constructing extralocal Christian communities. In each case, be it a cohort of choir members, friends, or conference associates, new rituals of intensification emerge; new ways of manifesting and animating relationships are constructed that often rely heavily on Christian symbolism.

Clearly not everyone is equally astute at imagining the possibilities, nor is everyone equally positioned to seize opportunities. Yet many locals have become quite proficient at manipulating the mission-provided array of symbolic material to signal their intent to engage or construct new worlds. The missionaries, of course, viewed such actions principally through a religious lens, interpreting them as signs of religious conversion. While the Lunda seem to have had little difficulty historically merging the substance of tradition and Christianity, mediating the symbolic distance between the two was a different and far trickier matter. The European view of an apocalyptic struggle between good and evil required clearly drawn lines between "us" and "them," between "converts" and "heathens." Symbols as markers of affiliation had to be overt and unambiguous. Conversion to Christianity had to have more than intellectual, philosophical, and emotional implications. It had to have its visual, material, and behavioral components as well. Lunda Christian converts, for example, were encouraged to broadcast their status through residential architecture. Christians were to build square or rectangular houses rather than the traditional round dwellings. Christians were supposed to eschew eating with the fingers, favoring instead European utensils. Good Christians used English, no matter how poorly, somehow managing to introduce God, Jesus, or biblical themes into the most prosaic conversation. European clothing, no matter how tattered, was a Christian symbol preferred over the traditional loincloth, no matter how elegant.[28]

Missions and the Creation of New Publics

It has not been my aim here to comment on the quality of African conversion experiences. It has certainly not been my aim to suggest that such experiences were merely strategic exercises designed to gain access to European-controlled resources rather than being deeply transformative events. But often, as Maia Green reminds us, "The image of conversion as a miraculous transformation in the consciousness of an individual is not a sociological account of the historical process of conversion, but a rhetorical device of evangelical Protestantism."[29]

An accurate account would foreground the role of colonial conquest in creating the political and economic contexts within which missionaries were allowed to operate relatively unchallenged in specific and well-protected niches. Here I will merely suggest that conversions can be polysemic, polyvocalic events. They may signal a willingness to entertain a host of new ideas about the nature of the metaphysical world. They may also signal more pragmatic set of hopes for this world as well: perhaps a desire that one's children can attend school at the mission, that one's wife can earn a bit of money providing food to the mission, that one's cousin can secure a job as a cook or one's brother a job as a driver.

Conversion is also a signal among Africans themselves about the construction of, and membership in, a particular public. It announces one's new vision of the world, one's willingness to engage rather than retreat from modernity (however defined locally), one's desire for experimentation with new social forms and productive processes. This adoption of new architectural, sartorial, culinary, rhetorical, and performative styles need not, however, signal a desire to break with the old community or communities, as European missionaries would have wished. It is not about replacing one totalizing paradigm with another. Quite the contrary, conversion, in a true postmodern fashion, is a signal about the courage to live with fragmentation, multiplicity, and contingency. As noted earlier, Christians can frequently be spotted in leading roles in traditional affairs, such as securing ritual practitioners for a healing ceremony, sponsoring a boys' circumcision camp, providing gifts for girls' puberty rites, or paying for a divination session to ferret out witches. Christians' claim to fame is their participation in, and mastery of, multiple worlds rather than their withdrawal from one to another. Missionaries are quick to frame such complex behavior as examples of "primitive recidivism," simple proof that African Christians have not been immersed in the gospel long enough, the teachings have not sunk in deeply enough, faith has not blossomed broadly enough, for Africans to resist the primal call of ancient traditions.

Yet there are two threads of local culture that do appear to run unwaveringly through the Lunda's hundred-year engagement with Christianity that help to frame such behavior. First, while there has been constant experimentation with forms and functions of community, every configuration that has emerged is underpinned by the assumption that ancestors, particularly the recently departed, must be reckoned with. The Lunda traditionally believed that spirits of the dead remained in the areas they frequented during life. Their happiness was contingent upon the performance of symbolic acts that acknowledged their contributions to, and continued association with, the world of the living. The frequent mention of their deeds, propitiating them at mealtimes, and passing on their names to children and topographical features were the standard means of honoring the deceased. Spirits insufficiently venerated would vent their wrath via disease and misfortune. Social relationships developed in life continued on into the afterlife. The binding nature of promises and obligations does not cease with death. These basic presumptions remain as salient today as they were a hundred years ago.

The second, and related, thread is ritual as a form of communication. Ritual is neither exclusively a set of curative practices for ameliorating spirit-induced ailments nor a method for addressing life crises, a set of practices for moving people from one stage of life to another. Ritual is technology, a set of cutting-edge techniques for communicating with unseeable members of the community. It is a tool of inclusion, a social device for speaking across the divide, a periodically needed exercise in consensus building. Ritual is an essential social device for the construction of community through time and space, across physical and metaphysical realms. Yet much remains unresolved today. For example, in which communities can the departed maintain membership? Need deceased choir members and maguys be propitiated? Need the names of maconferenci associates be passed along? Just as the imprint of local ideations about the spirits of deceased Europeans found it way into curing rituals of the 1950s, so too one might expect reformulated connections between ancestors, rituals, and newly configured communities today. Thus, in brief, the emergent theoretical discourse on public cultures in Africa need be infused with local sensibilities about the inseparability of the living and the dead, and with the never-ending drive for tools of communications with the unseen realm.

IN THIS chapter I have urged, rather than fully demonstrated, the utility of reframing some of our anthropological insights on rural Africa.

Cultural heterogeneity and hybridity have increasingly become the norm everywhere. Anthropologists working in urban Africa have rightly identified meaningful social groupings that extend the anthropological object of analysis beyond our traditional focus on elements of ascription, such as family, clan, lineage, and ethnic groups. Instead, we now analyze the role of occupational groupings, unions, political parties, market associations, sport clubs, and so forth. The analytical lenses of popular culture and public culture have proven useful in heuristically tying together the myriad and seemingly disconnected social, economic, and political strands of contemporary life in urban Africa. Yet when anthropology turns its analytical gaze back to rural areas, it often likewise reverts back to a focus on old ascriptive categories, overlooking local heterogeneity and hybridity and the role of missions in enriching that context. Space prevents a detailed discussion here of the many and convoluted ways that the modernity-postmodernity nexus has been configured, or the conceptual nuances that could lead one to ponder the equivalence of popular culture and mass culture, or the discourse about which intersection of communicative technologies and rhetorical practices are requisite to the emergence of public cultures. I simply encourage that these discussions be moved back in time, and outward in space, to include the early and continuing impact of Christian mission stations in rural areas.

Notes

1. For descriptions of early mission converts as marginals or outcasts, see Robert W. Strayer, *The Making of Mission Communities in East Africa: Anglicans and Africans in Colonial Kenya, 1875–1935* (London: Heinemann, 1978), 11, 52–55; Jean Comaroff and John L. Comaroff, *Christianity, Colonialism, and Consciousness in South Africa*, vol. 1 of *Of Revelation and Revolution* (Chicago: University of Chicago Press, 1991), 238–40, 247. For the counterargument, see Justin Willis, "The Nature of a Mission Community: The Universities' Mission to Central Africa in Bonde," *Past and Present* 140, no. 1 (1993): 127–28.

2. James A. Pritchett, *Friends for Life, Friends for Death: Cohorts and Consciousness among the Lunda-Ndembu* (Charlottesville: University of Virginia Press, 2007), 34; Willis, "Mission Community," 127.

3. Derek R. Peterson, *Creative Writing: Translation, Bookkeeping, and the Work of Imagination in Colonial Kenya* (Portsmouth, NH: Heinemann, 2004), 242.

4. See esp. David Birmingham and Phyllis M. Martin, eds., *History of Central Africa* (London: Addison Wesley Longman, 1983), vol. 1; Jan Vansina, *Kingdoms of the Savanna: A History of Central African States until European Occupation* (Madison: University of Wisconsin Press, 1966).

5. In addition to periods of residence and research in Mwinilunga District in 1982, 1984–87, 1994, 1995, 1998, and 2005, I have been in continual written contact with mission staff and local residents.

6. Following local convention, the term Europeans also includes Americans.

7. For the most comprehensive account of Dr. Walter Fisher, his wife Anna, and the development of the CMML mission station at Kalene Hill, see W. Singleton Fisher and Julyan Hoyte, *Africa Looks Ahead: The Life Stories of Walter and Anna Fisher of Central Africa* (London: Pickering and Inglis, 1948).

8. Walima Kalusa, "Disease and the Remaking of Missionary Medicine in Colonial Northwestern Zambia: A Case Study of Mwinilunga District, 1902–1964" (PhD diss., Johns Hopkins University, 2003), 85.

9. Ibid., 97.

10. Ibid., 76, 123.

11. Victor W. Turner, *The Forest of Symbols: Aspects of Ndembu Ritual* (Ithaca: Cornell University Press, 1967), 15.

12. Wim M. J. van Binsbergen, *Religious Change in Zambia* (London: Routledge and Kegan Paul, 1981).

13. Robin Horton, "African Conversion," *Africa* 41, no. 2 (1971): 85–108.

14. I gathered information on Lwawu Mission through personal observations while living there periodically as a guest since 1982, as well as through personal communications with dozens of resident Franciscan friars, including the founder of the mission. While onsite I had access to bundles of letters, diaries, and newsletters that reflect on the history of the mission.

15. Colin Trapnell and J. N. Clothier, *The Soils, Vegetation and Agricultural System of North Western Rhodesia: A Report of the Ecological Survey* (Lusaka: Government Printer, 1937).

16. James A. Pritchett, *The Lunda-Ndembu: Style, Change, and Social Transformation in South Central Africa* (Madison: University of Wisconsin Press, 2001), 142; Pritchett, *Friends for Life*, 107.

17. Karin Barber, introduction to *Readings in African Popular Culture*, ed. Barber (Bloomington: Indiana University Press, 1997), 1.

18. Karen Tranberg Hansen, *Salaula: The World of Secondhand Clothing and Zambia* (Chicago: University of Chicago Press, 2000).

19. On the historical importance of imported cloth in Central Africa, see Joseph C. Miller, *Way of Death: Merchant Capitalism and the Angolan Slave Trade, 1730–1830* (Madison: University of Wisconsin Press, 1988), 78–83.

20. For a summary of colonial discourse on the relationship between African clothing needs and desires, see Hansen, *Salaula*, chap. 2.

21. Audrey Richards has commented on the tendency of rural Central African peoples to intently scrutinize the clothing styles of all who entered their purview. I noted the persistence of that tendency from the early 1980s well into the current century. Richards, *Land, Labour and Diet in Northern Rhodesia: An Economic Study of the Bemba Tribe* (London: Oxford University Press, 1939).

22. Original program guides are preserved in the Zambian National Archives, Mwinilunga District Notebook, KSE 4/1.

23. Hansen, *Salaula*.

24. Pritchett, *Friends for Life*, 70–71.

25. The CMML collection of hymns was ultimately published locally and circulated in the district as *Tumina: Chuma chachiwahi chakusakilila Jehova* (Songs: Wonderful Things for Thanking God). The Franciscans would later counter with their own published hymnal *Malombelelu ni tumina* (Prayers and Songs).

26. *Public Culture*, the journal published by Duke University Press since 1990, describes its editorial policy thus: "*Public Culture* reports and reflects current research

on the cultural transformations associated with cities, media and consumption, and the cultural flows that draw cities, societies and states into larger transnational relationships and global political economies."

27. For a fuller discussion of the local discourse about mediating great distances while maintaining local relationships, see Pritchett, *Friends for Life*, 59–91.

28. Christian communities in most villages in Mwinilunga are overseen on a daily basis by African lay leaders, with periodic visits from European Protestant preachers or Catholic fathers. Even today there remains a conspicuous concern for the display of appropriate symbols of affiliation, which become even more exaggerated when Europeans visit.

29. Maia Green, *Priests, Witches and Power: Popular Christianity after Mission in Southern Tanzania* (Cambridge: Cambridge University Press, 2003), 12.

TWO

Debating the Secular in Zambia
The Response of the Catholic Church to Scientific Socialism and Christian Nation, 1976–2006

MARJA HINFELAAR

IN DECEMBER 1991 the newly elected president of Zambia, Frederick Chiluba, made the following announcement: "On behalf of the nation I have entered into a covenant law with the living God. And therefore I want to make the following declaration. I declare today that I submit myself as president to the lordship of Jesus Christ. I likewise submit the government and the entire nation of Zambia to the lordship of Jesus Christ. I further declare that Zambia is a Christian nation that will seek to be governed by the righteous principles of the Word of God."

Some scholars have described Chiluba's political victory and the subsequent Christian nation declaration as the inevitable outcome of the rise of charismatic Christianity in Zambia. While Isabel Phiri appraises the declaration as a triumph for the holistic African worldview,[1] David Maxwell contends that born-again Christianity played a key role in the events leading to Kenneth Kaunda's downfall, paving the way for this type of declaration.[2] But to what extent should we stress the triumph of Christianity in the public domain and explain Chiluba's victory purely in religious terms? In this regard, academics seem caught between two extreme positions—between the celebration and the outright rejection of the public role of religion, with proponents of the latter view maintaining that religious influence over political life can only indicate the general backwardness of society.

The reifications of religion in Africa have been under attack before. In 1982, Karen Fields observed that Africanist scholars regarded religious revival and protest as a phase in the evolutionary march toward perfected "modern" forms, namely secular workers' organizations and political parties, thereby understating the impact of the religious movements themselves.[3] Crucially, these evolutionary assumptions have influenced the way in which Zambian history has been represented. It is important in this context to remind ourselves that throughout the period from the 1920s to the early 1970s, it was indeed tempting to compare Zambia's historical trajectory to that of Europe, especially insofar as the processes of urbanization and industrialization were concerned. Technology in the mining industry was considered to be cutting edge. Moreover, Zambia was one of the highly urbanized countries in sub-Saharan Africa.[4] Not surprisingly, much research focused on the Copperbelt, with numerous studies produced on labor and migration, urbanization and social change.[5] Most of these studies were underpinned by the notion that "urbanization ... seemed to be a teleological process, a movement towards a known end point that would be nothing less than a Western-style industrial modernity."[6]

While successfully challenging this notion and the simplistic "metanarrative of modernization" in which it resulted, James Ferguson's ethnography of the Copperbelt in the 1980s overlooked an essential component of modernist accounts, namely the expected onset of a secularization process.[7] His disregard for religion can perhaps be explained by the narrow focus of his fieldwork, during which he mostly interviewed young male mineworkers. Interestingly, Ferguson has more recently come to stress the shortcomings of the Eurocentric evolutionary narrative about secularization: "Christian mission organizations are arguably more important today in Africa than ever ... but are strangely relegated to the colonial past in the imagination of much contemporary scholarship."[8]

In this respect, I concur with Talal Asad, who has resisted identifying either virtues or vices of secularism or religiosity, proposing instead to describe "the forms that articulate them, the powers they release or disable."[9] This chapter will therefore explore the lively and very public discussions surrounding important constitutional changes, mainly from the Catholic point of view. Less than a decade after the influential debate on scientific socialism, Zambia's public discourse shifted from dissecting the potential establishment of a Marxist state to arguing about the actual declaration of Zambia as a Christian nation. These debates on secularity (and religiosity) illuminate the diversity of views in Zambian society. Additionally, these deliberations give us precious insight into the forces and processes that shape these debates. As Maia Green has recently suggested, "Closer study of mainstream religious communities and of less totalizing involvements would reveal enormous differentiation in the extent to which people are religiously engaged, not only between different social categories and locations, but between different genders, life stages and religious affiliations."[10]

The reason to focus on the Catholic Church is its continued influence on Zambian society, which, in part, is the result of its membership in a powerful transnational institution.[11] Numerically it is the country's single largest church, with an estimated 20 to 25 percent of the population claiming to be Catholic. After it has enjoyed a high profile in public matters since independence, Zambians, Catholics and non-Catholics alike, have come to expect a nonpartisan Catholic Church to speak out on urgent matters affecting society and to act as a mediator in times of crisis. While Pentecostal-charismatic churches have most definitely made serious inroads into the Catholics' statistical and public predominance, with the establishment for instance of commercial television and radio stations such as Trinity Broadcasting Network and Radio Christian Voice, it is possible conclude that "organizations like the Catholic Church and Western neoliberal aid organizations have cornered the private and community-based media networks in Zambia."[12]

From an Antimodern to a Modern Roman Catholic Church

Shortly after Zambia gained its independence, in 1964, Pope Paul VI received the president of the Republic of Zambia with the following words:

> We welcome Your Excellency as a distinguished representative of the vigorous young Christianity of the new Africa, which We extolled at the canonization of the glorious Martyrs of Uganda. In your speeches and writings, Mister President, you have always proudly pronounced yourself a Christian, and proclaimed the benefits which the Gospel message has brought to your country and to all Africa. To you, We need not underline the distinction We drew, in that homily, between evangelization and colonization. Rather do We pledge to you anew the renewed efforts of all Our Catholic children in the building up of the *Christian Nation of Zambia*, by their ever more generous

contributions towards the religious, social and cultural progress of its citizens.[13]

This address is remarkable in two ways. First, it recognizes, self-servingly perhaps, the Christian character of the state and its leader and, second, it commends a type of church involvement in the state which was to be soon rejected by the Second Vatican Council.[14] Zambia's independence coincided neatly with the proceedings of the council, where the church moved from being a proponent of a state church to a defender of a modernist state in which both spheres would be strictly separated. As José Casanova has rightly observed, the ideological shift that found expression in the council is crucial in order to understand the Catholic Church's subsequent appropriation of a new public role: "Catholicism served as the focus point in the Enlightenment critique of religion. It fought capitalism, liberalism, the modern secular state, socialism, the sexual revolution ... in brief, it had been the paradigmatic form of anti-modern public religion. In the mid 1960s, however, the RC church inaugurated a process of official *aggiornamento* to secular modernity and accepted the legitimacy of the modern age. Yet, it refuses to become a private religion. It wants to be both modern and public."[15]

The council also laid a new emphasis on the human condition in the present, as opposed to human fulfilment in the afterlife. It had looked at what it called the "full integrity" of human beings, declaring that the church shared the "joy and hope, the grief and anguish of contemporary humanity, particularly of the poor and afflicted."[16] The modernist Catholic Church rode on the wave of this development and of the human rights ideology that was informed by the papal encyclical of 1967 called *Populorum progressio* (On the Development of Peoples).[17] This, together with a body of other doctrines of Catholic social teachings, signaled the beginning of the influential Justice and Peace movement.

It is not surprising, therefore, that on the eve of independence the developmentalist Catholic Church insisted on "coming down to earth," thereby challenging the promise of a "heaven on earth" as proclaimed by Zambia's main nationalist party, the United National Independence Party (UNIP). In one of their first pastoral statements the Zambian bishops said,

> Today we are celebrating the birth of a Nation. Now, birth is only a beginning. After birth come the difficulties of growth and further

> development. There was a time when some people thought that when the great goal of Independence was reached, everything would be different immediately; that poverty, disease and ignorance would in some wonderful fashion disappear. No one any longer thinks this way and the leaders of the Country have made it clear that Independence is not a magic medicine to cure all ills, but an incentive and a call to work, to dedication and service.[18]

The radical nature of Vatican II's proposals undeniably influenced the mindset of European missionaries. As one contemporary observed, the postwar generation of missionaries lost confidence in the superiority of Western culture and started to have doubts about their evangelical mission.[19] This "confusion of mission" can be seen as the start of what some have called the trend of NGO-ization, or the transition from a Christian to a secular eschatology.[20] In this period, Karl Marx's writings seemed to have gained a great significance in Christian thought and, particularly, action. This was in a great contrast to the outright hostility previous popes had displayed toward communism.[21]

Indicative of the impact and consequences of this transformation is the direction taken by Catholic education and media after independence. It can be briefly characterized as a move from a confessional to a professional and from a denominational to an ecumenical Christian practice. The move from confessional to professional religious education in primary schools was the outcome of a common syllabus meeting set up by the Zambian Ministry of Education in 1972. The new syllabus has been described as life centered, rather than Bible or catechism centered. At the secondary level, the so-called joint religious education syllabus covered all world religions but also incorporated Zambian humanism (as propounded by Zambia's first president) and had a distinctive socialist orientation.[22] A second syllabus, however, was developed under pressure from evangelical churches, which insisted on a Bible-centered curriculum. In practice, schools could choose either option, as the two syllabi coexisted. With the rise of evangelical and Pentecostal movements in the 1980s, a paradoxical situation arose in which Catholic missionaries taught a secular curriculum, while being challenged by their (far more confident) evangelically oriented students, who openly resisted secular teachings. Not the least significant feature of the paradox was that students were not only drawn to mission education as a "civilizing process" yet also resisted many of the lessons that the official institution offered, particularly with respect to claims of "true" Christian identity.[23]

The media of the mainstream churches similarly altered their approach toward journalism. The *National Mirror*, a joint communication of all mainstream churches, stated clearly that it was not to be a pious newspaper. Rather it aimed at "propagating Christian principles based on the Gospel message in the fields of politics, economics, education and the whole social and industrial range of the country's life," and it endeavored "to co-ordinate the political thinking of all parties so as to bring about the maximum amount of intelligent co-operation of all for the general good of the community," in addition "to exercis[ing] diligent scrutiny on public affairs at all levels."[24] This independent newspaper proved to be an important forum for public debates on issues such as scientific socialism and for articulating a general critique of the one-party state.

From Religious Humanism to Secular Scientific Socialism

Shortly after independence, Kenneth Kaunda introduced humanism,[25] a philosophy that, according to Megan Vaughan, is a mixture of "Fabian socialism, nineteenth-century liberalism, Christian morality and idealization of the communal values of Zambia's pre-capitalist past."[26] After independence, the clergy were generally attributed high respect, as could be witnessed during events of national importance, when "representatives of both realms, spiritual and temporal, would sit side by side in the official celebration, always accompanied by a thanksgiving service."[27] The quest of the church for status was mirrored by the ruling party's desire to involve the church in national affairs. This ideological trait informed the tendency to promote clergymen to high public office. At the same time, Kaunda publicly encouraged the church to act as a watchdog: "We have allowed the Church and Judiciary to act as a mirror to the nation so that the Government and the Party might see what sins they are committing."[28] However, when the Catholic Church spoke out in 1972 following the government's decision to legalize abortion, the church's moral stand was translated into an act of political subversion. Religious freedom was seen to come under threat with the institution of citizenship-training programs from the early 1970s onward. These included the Zambia Youth Service, which aimed to promote national consciousness, patriotism, discipline, and leadership. At the Youth Service camps religious expressions or services were explicitly forbidden.

The introduction of the national anthem and the raising of the national flag in schools led to a long-running conflict with the Jehovah's Witnesses, who refused to take part in this ceremony and were consequently dismissed from schools in large numbers. In this case, the *National Mirror* defended the rights of the Jehovah's Witnesses.[29]

The first open confrontation between the government and all the country's mainstream churches, however, was the result of the announced introduction in 1976 of a syllabus for "political education" in primary and secondary schools.[30] The syllabus was rumored to include the discussion of "the missionaries and the Church as fore-runners of imperialism and colonialism in Zambia."[31] In fact, with the establishment of the ruling party's research bureau in 1974, Henry Meebelo, a prominent historian, and others planned to introduce political education as a school subject with a view to instructing children in different types of socialism, comparing *ujamaa* in Tanzania with Maoism and Marxism-Leninism.[32] A group of selected teachers were trained at the President's Citizenship College for this purpose, preparing them to disseminate their knowledge at various teacher-training colleges. The churches complained that religious education was left out of the draft statement on educational reforms.[33] In 1978 the ruling party initiated the Union of the Working Class, one of its purposes being to acquaint the youth with scientific socialism or, in the words of its leader, Njekwa Anamela, "to arm the working class youths with revolutionary theory founded on the basis of Scientific Socialism."[34]

In 1979, in response to these events, the three main church bodies (the Zambia Episcopal Conference, the Christian Council of Zambia, and the Evangelical Fellowship of Zambia) published a statement entitled "Marxism, Humanism and Christianity: A Letter from the Leaders of the Christian Churches in Zambia to All Their Members about Scientific Socialism." The church leaders stated they did not dismiss socialism as such. In fact, as has been seen, many priests at the time flirted with socialism and were experts on Marxism in their own right. However, they saw themselves forced "to reject those forms of socialism which did not respect the dignity and religious dimension of man and which, therefore, can never lead to real humanism. Scientific Socialism is one of these."[35] During an encounter with the National Council of Catholic Women, the director of the ruling party's research bureau sought to defend the party's ideological stance by pointing out that the teaching of the syllabus was not presently well coordinated and, as a result, one would find teachers denying the existence of God.[36] Archbishop Emmanuel Milingo, however, blamed Zambians for this development: "If Christians failed to uplift the poor, one could hardly complain if communists came and took their place."[37]

Zambian political leaders put up a strong defense, elaborated in a series of articles and debates in national newspapers. They argued that scientific socialism did not necessarily pose a threat to Christianity. When Mainza Chona, the then prime minister and a staunch Catholic, was asked why scientific socialism should be introduced, he replied, "This is like asking why we should have Christianity in the country. It is the way to heaven."[38] He explained that the only difference between Christianity and scientific socialism was the "denial of the existence of God."[39] At the same time, politicians' counterattack also took the form of an attempt to call into question the legitimate boundaries of churches' public role. "Should churches be involved in politics?" demanded some government newspapers.[40] The position of the churches was, however, strengthened by the involvement of the trade unions that had stepped into the debate and used it, not only as a means to voice their discontent with the government, but also to defend the freedom of religious expression. Frederick Chiluba, the prominent leader of the Zambia Congress of Trade Unions, signaled its opposition to scientific socialism by "going to church almost every day."[41]

It was direct church intervention that forced the government to retract scientific socialism. Following a two-day seminar in March 1982 entitled "Humanism for Religious Leaders in Zambia" and a number of other meetings with church leaders—some rumored to have been private meetings between Archbishop Milingo and Kaunda—scientific socialism was suspended.[42] Not surprisingly, Kaunda felt compelled to publicly reconcile with the churches. His speeches were consequently full of praise for the missionaries, stating, for instance, that "in the missionary days the sight of one missionary in the remotest village was the strongest hope for good health, education and an approaching bright future for men and women" and that "without missionaries we could not have waged the liberation struggle of our country."[43]

What would have been the chances of Zambia becoming a Marxist state? Reuben Kamanga, then the chairman of the political and legal subcommittee of the ruling party's central committee, questioned the severity of the response, calling the pastoral letter "alarmist and ill-intentioned."[44] It could be argued that church leaders were alarmed by the introduction of Marxist regimes in Ethiopia, Mozambique, and Angola[45] and that their fear of communist penetration might have been heightened by the fact that several Marxist liberation movements were based in Zambia. Pro-communist radio stations like Radio Freedom (voice of the African National Congress), Voice of Namibia, and Zimbabwe People's Revolutionary Voice were transmitted via Zambia.[46]

The strong reaction by the churches must, however, be regarded as a response to the increasingly repressive nature of the postindependence regime. They were concerned with the ruling party's move from a so-called participatory democracy to a state run by a vanguard party that claimed to know what was good for the people and proceeded to give it to them whether they liked it or not. The call of the churches was therefore to protect political and civil liberties.[47]

A Christian Nation versus a Secular State

One reason why churches never left the public domain after Independence was thus the growing authoritarianism of the Zambian political system.[48] As elsewhere in Africa, the introduction of a one-party state in Zambia meant that the Christian churches came to be among the few formal organizations "with the capacity to mobilize large sections of the population without recourse to government resources or control."[49] In Zambia, where the overwhelming majority of the population adheres to Christianity, it was not entirely surprising that, in the words of John McCracken, "with secular ideologies like Marxist Socialism discredited, the search [was] on to discover Christian examples which might provide the basis for a new and more acceptable political culture."[50] This happened quite literally in Zambia when President Chiluba declared Zambia a Christian nation in December 1991, only a few months after coming to power.

In order to analyze public debates surrounding the Christian nation declaration and subsequent constitutional controversies, changes within the media in the context of political and economic liberalization must be understood. The power of the state over the media radically diminished under the Movement for Multiparty Democracy led by Chiluba. As a result, church publications such as the *National Mirror* lost their erstwhile monopoly of independence to other newspapers such as the *Post* and a whole range of other newspapers and publications. The airwaves were similarly liberalized, a move that resulted in the proliferation of a wide range of radio stations, both religious and nonreligious, and an additional television channel. Catholic vernacular publications such as *Icengelo* kept their appeal, especially during politically volatile times. Whereas church cooperation in the media and in Justice and Peace continued, it was severely shaken by the emergence of a new political divide between the supporters and opponents of president Chiluba. The diversification and expansion of religious movements led to disunity, and the churches were no longer able to speak with one voice. Their divergent views came out clearly in the Christian-nation debate.

Perhaps as a result of the euphoria that surrounded the political transition in 1991, a process the churches clearly believed was attributable to their support, the Christian-nation declaration was initially welcomed. On January 16, 1992, the Christian Council of Zambia, the Evangelical Fellowship of Zambia, and the Zambia Episcopal Conference released a statement on the declaration. While criticizing "the lack of consultation with the churches" they nonetheless showed their support. "In view of the fact that Christianity is the main religion in Zambia, and of the assurance that the rights of those practicing other religions will be respected, we endorse the President's declaration of Zambia as a Christian Nation and we accept his challenge to rededicate ourselves to the Glory of Almighty God."[51] Crucially, the fact that the declaration was not lawfully enacted prevented the Catholic Church from rejecting it outright. However, in the Catholic pastoral letter that followed in February 1992 and was read out in all churches during the Sunday Mass, the bishops specifically warned of the dangers of religious intolerance and referred to the Second Vatican Council's 1965 Declaration on Religious Freedom (*Dignitatis humanae*), which says that "the right to religious freedom has its foundation in the very dignity of the human person as this dignity is known through the revealed Word of God and by reason itself. This right of the human person to religious freedom is to be recognized in the constitutional law whereby society is governed."[52]

The most tangible consequences of the Christian nation declaration before its constitutional enshrinement have been described elsewhere.[53] But it was the consequent partitioning of Christians and "pseudo-Christians," of those who declared their loyalty to Chiluba and those who criticized him, that soon led to disunity among denominations and various church bodies. Most Pentecostal churches embraced the Christian nation declaration. The rise of President Chiluba steered them, for the first time, into the inner circle of political power.[54] Their criticism centered on what they considered to be the imperfect implementation of the declaration. For instance, Bishop Tom Msiska, of the Christ Gospel Church Fellowship of Zambia, charged, "There is divorce and adultery among our leaders and they cannot be disciplined because there is no Christian law. If we legalise the declaration, then biblical principles will be followed when dealing with offenders."[55]

Not surprisingly, when it was proposed that the declaration was to be enshrined into the preamble of the 1996 constitution, the leaders of two church bodies, both Protestant and Catholic—but excluding the Evangelical Fellowship—made their opposition clear by emphasizing their belief in a plural society. "The constitution of the country belongs as fully to these citizens [who profess other faiths] as it does to those who profess Christianity." Moreover, they claimed that the majority of Zambians would not support this legal enactment.[56] The Catholic Church, in an open letter to the president and members of Parliament, further argued that the declaration needs considerably more legal debate and theological clarification. Additionally, the bishops felt that on the whole "the constitutional debate has not in fact reached the grassroots and ordinary people, especially those in rural areas."[57]

However, the heated debate and the divisions that had accompanied the declaration faded away in the late 1990s. Chiluba's growing unpopularity, largely a consequence of corruption in his regime and the social costs of the neoliberal economic policies it implemented, led the churches to take a united political stand. Since 2001, the Zambia Episcopal Conference, the Zambia Christian Council, and the Evangelical Forum of Zambia have been united by the Oasis Forum, a loose coalition initiated with a view to opposing Chiluba's decision to stand for a third term in office. The Oasis Forum also included the Law Association of Zambia and an umbrella organ for women's organizations in what has been called "an auspicious wedding of the legal authority of the lawyers, the moral authority of the Church, and the popular authority of the women's movement."[58] After Chiluba's demise, the Oasis Forum continued its operations, partly to promote a culture of constitutionalism and the doctrine and practice of the separation of powers.

These divergent views on Zambia's status as a Christian nation reemerged after the installation of the Mung'omba Constitutional Review Commission, in 2003. The commission had initially stated that "an overwhelming number of those who made submissions on the subject called for the retention in the Constitution of the Declaration of Zambia as a Christian nation."[59] The subsequent removal of this particularly clause from the draft and its replacement with the statement that Zambia was a secular country, underscored by the argument that "Christianity or any religion could be safely secured without any form of declaration," were met with a public outcry. Challenging the Constitutional Review Commission's recommendation to remove the clause, Rev. Peter Ndhlovu of the Bible Gospel Church said Zambia could not revert to being a secular state, because doing so would be tantamount to handing over the country to the devil.[60]

Catherine Mukuka, in her published submission to the Constitutional Review Commission (CRC), stated that she was driven by the desire to challenge "a move to assert the Secular Humanist agenda on Zambia. As the people of God we must act together to stop this conspiracy against our nation."[61] She submitted that the Christian-nation declaration should be maintained in the constitution. Again, we can observe the equation of secular humanism with Satanism, for Mukuka wondered, "What is the god of secularism? Its tenets are not of biblical origin and thus it can only be concluded that it is a religion of Satan. Clearly the god of secular humanism is Satan."[62]

The Catholic hierarchy initially supported the proposed inclusion of the caveat about the secular nation. In 2003, in the pastoral letter entitled *Let My People Go,* which was read out during Sunday Mass, Catholic Church leaders stated that "our understanding, from the Catholic Church's social teaching, that emphasizes freedom of religion and respect for individual conscience, makes us cautious of the contentious provision in the constitution that 'Zambia is a Christian Nation.'" The letter therefore wholeheartedly supported the initial recommendation to remove the clause, citing Pope Benedict XIV's call for a "positive secularity" that guarantees "each citizen the right to live his or her own religious faith with a genuine freedom, including in the public realm." Seemingly cautioned by the heated debate, the Catholic hierarchy changed its position in 2005, making the admission that "because the phrase 'secular' has become so disputed and confused in the current constitutional discussions, the Jesuit Centre for Theological Reflection (JCTR) recently included in its formal submission to the CRC the recommendation that the phrase simply be dropped from the Part II, Article 8 of the Draft Constitution. Thus Article 8 (1) would not read, 'Zambia is a secular State without a state religion,' but 'Zambia has no state-endorsed religion.'"[63]

The controversy surrounding the insertion of "secular nation" led the Constitutional Review Commission in 2005 to provisionally retain the

Christian nation clause, arguing that "considering that the subject is emotive and contentious, the Commission is of the view that the matter should be subjected to further debate and a decision by the people through the institutions and processes recommended by the Commission, that is, the Constituent Assembly and national referendum. In the meantime, the declaration of Zambia as a Christian nation as contained in the current Constitution should be retained."

It had become clear, however, that the long-winded debate between the leaders of the churches, civil society, and politicians on the technicalities of the constitutional process had alienated the general public. The public debate was, as a result, infused with a growing skepticism about the ability of civil society leaders, including church movements, to speak on behalf of their constituencies. An example of this type of discontent is illustrated by the following excerpt from a letter coming from a leading Zambian commentator posted on his Web site:

> When the same civil society leaders started to claim that [the constitutional submissions] show that the people of Zambia do not want Zambia to remain a Christian nation, the Christian leaders were annoyed and organized their church members to aggressively protest this. The civil society leaders have since stopped making that claim and have quietly allowed the Mung'omba CRC to sneak the pro-Christian nation clause into their final draft of recommendations, in spite of the fact that "the people" said they did not want it to continue ... everyone is determined to "win" this debate no matter how contradictory their position is and that's a dangerous state for a civilized nation to find itself in.[64]

Evolutionary assumptions about the direction of social change in postcolonial Zambia have militated against a full understanding of the public role of religion and religious institutions. A presentist analysis of the Christian-nation declaration would have easily contradicted the modernist narrative of secularization. However, by isolating this episode from its immediate past, we risk accepting the idea that the introduction of multiparty democracy and the Christian-nation declaration constitute a break with the past. By following a Pentecostalist interpretation of Zambia's history—reading it as a progression from a secular, satanic past to a glorious Christian future—we ignore the steady public influence of churches since independence. The significant influence of the churches in the scientific socialism debate substantiates this argument. While I can confirm the rise and authority of Pentecostal movements in the Zambian Third Republic, the public role of so-called mainstream churches has endured.

Notes

1. Isabel A. Phiri, "President Frederick J. T. Chiluba of Zambia: The Christian Nation and Democracy," *Journal of Religion in Africa* 33, no. 4 (2003): 402.

2. David Maxwell, "Post-colonial Christianity in Africa," in *World Christianities c. 1914–c. 2000*, ed. Hugh McLeod, vol. 9 of *The Cambridge History of Christianity* (Cambridge: Cambridge University Press, 2006), 415.

3. Karen Fields, "Charismatic Religion as Popular Protest: The Ordinary and the Extraordinary in Social Movements," *Theory and Society* 11, no. 3 (1982): 324.

4. Deborah Potts has recently shown that Zambia's urbanization rates have been systematically overstated. Potts, "Counter-urbanization on the Zambian Copperbelt? Interpretations and Implications," *Urban Studies* 42, no. 4 (2005): 583–609.

5. A. L. Epstein, *Politics in an Urban African Community* (Manchester: Manchester University Press, 1958); H. S. Meebelo, *African Proletarians and Colonial Capitalism: The Origins, Growth and Struggles of the Zambian Labour Movement to 1964* (Lusaka: Kenneth Kaunda Foundation, 1986); J. Clyde Mitchell, ed., *Social Networks in Urban Situations: Analyses of Personal Relationships in Central African Towns* (Manchester: Manchester University Press, 1969); Jane L. Parpart, *Labor and Capital on the African Copperbelt* (Philadelphia: Temple University Press, 1983).

6. James Ferguson, *Expectations of Modernity: Myths and Meanings of Urban Life on the Zambian Copperbelt* (Berkeley: University of California Press, 1999), 5.

7. Ibid.

8. James Ferguson, *Global Shadows: Africa in the Neoliberal World Order* (Durham, NC: Duke University Press, 2006), 98.

9. Talal Asad, *Formations of the Secular: Christianity, Islam, Modernity* (Stanford: Stanford University Press, 2003), 17.

10. Maia Green, "Confronting Categorical Assumptions about the Power of Religion in Africa," *Review of African Political Economy* 33, no. 110 (2006): 642.

11. Other missionary churches in Zambia became "localized" churches. For instance, the Dutch Reformed Church became the Reformed Church of Zambia. The international character of the Roman Catholic Church translates into a strong presence in education, health, media, development projects, and refugee work.

12. B. Phiri and D. Powers, "Plurality and Power Relations in Zambian Broadcasting," http://www.waccglobal.org/wacc/publications/media_development/archive/2001_2/plurality_and_power_relations_in_zambian_broadcasting.

13. Pope Paul VI, "Address of Paul VI to The President of the Republic of Zambia, Saturday 7 November 1964" (emphasis mine), http://www.vatican.va/holy_father/paul_vi/speeches/1964/documents/hf_p-vi_spe_19641107_president-zambia_en.html.

14. Vatican II was a series of meetings of the bishops of the entire world which began on October 11, 1962, and concluded on December 8, 1965.

15. José Casanova, *Public Religions in the Modern World* (Chicago: University of Chicago Press, 1994), 9.

16. James Hennesey, "Second Vatican Council: General Information," http://mbsoft.com/believe/txs/secondvc.htm.

17. Pope Paul VI, "On the Development of Peoples," *Papal Encyclicals Online*, http://www.papalencyclicals.net/Paul06/p6develo.htm.

18. Fr. J. L. Calmettes, founder of the Justice and Peace movement in Zambia, has questioned the extent to which these pastoral statements, written at a national level by a European hierarchy and strongly informed by this modernist thinking, actually represented the views of the laity in the church. Calmettes to A. Ipenburg, Maisons Alfort, February 4, 1988, Zambia White Fathers Archives, Lusaka, 1-M-hi-137.

19. Hugo Hinfelaar, *History of the Catholic Church in Zambia, 1895–1995* (Lusaka: Bookworld, 2004), 167. See also Anthony Simpson, *"Half-London" in Zambia: Contested Identities in a Catholic Mission School* (Edinburgh: Edinburgh University Press, 2003).

20. Stephen Plant, "Freedom as Development: Christian Mission and the Definition of Well-being," paper presented at the Henry Martyn Centre, Cambridge, UK, October 24, 2002. See Henry Martyn Centre, Understanding Mission and World Christianity, http://www.martynmission.cam.ac.uk/CPlant.html.

21. Michael Walsh, "The Religious Ferment of the Sixties," in McLeod, *World Christianities*, 318.

22. Bendan Carmody, "Religious Education and Pluralism in Zambia," in *Religion and Education in Zambia*, ed. Carmody (Ndola: Mission Press, 2004), 80–81.

23. Of the forty-one secondary church schools, twenty-seven were run by the Catholic Church. Primary schools had all become government schools in the early 1970s.

24. Francis P. Kasoma, *The Press in Zambia: The Development, Role, and Control of National Newspapers in Zambia, 1906–1983* (Lusaka: Multimedia Publications, 1986), 117.

25. The heading of this section comes from Isabel A. Phiri, "Why African Churches Preach Politics: The Case of Zambia," *Journal of Church and State* 41, no.2 (1999): 334.

26. Megan Vaughan, "Exploitation and Neglect: Rural Producers and the State in Malawi and Zambia," in *History of Central Africa: The Contemporary Years since 1960*, ed. David Birmingham and Phyllis M. Martin (London: Longman, 1998), 178.

27. Gerrie ter Haar, *Spirit of Africa: The Healing Ministry of Archbishop Milingo of Zambia* (London: Hurst, 1992), 202.

28. *National Mirror*, November 1972.

29. Kasoma, *Press in Zambia*, 120.

30. Here I rely on Marja Hinfelaar, "Legitimizing Powers: The Political Role of the Roman Catholic Church, 1972–1991," in *One Zambia, Many Histories: Towards a History of Post-colonial Zambia*, ed. Jan-Bart Gewald, M. Hinfelaar, and Giacomo Macola (Leiden: Brill, 2008).

31. Joseph C. McKenna, *Finding a Social Voice: The Church and Marxism in Africa* (New York: Fordham University Press, 1997), 195.

32. *Africa Confidential*, May 12, 1980.

33. *National Mirror*, August 1976.

34. *National Mirror*, February 1979.

35. Joseph Komakoma, *The Social Teaching of the Catholic Bishops and Other Christian Leaders in Zambia: Major Pastoral Letters and Statements 1953–2001* (Ndola: Mission Press, 2003), 111.

36. Mr. K. Nsingo, Director of the Research Bureau and Principal Advisor to the Secretary General of UNIP at Freedom House, notes on an address to the National Council of Catholic Women, Annual General Meeting at Natural Resources Development College, Lusaka, August 14, 1982, Kasama Archdiocese Archives, R01.00, Church and State Controversies.

37. Haar, *Spirit*, 208.

38. *National Mirror*, February 1979.

39. *Times of Zambia*, September 17, 1979.
40. Some of the headlines read: "Should Churches Be Involved in Politics?" *Times of Zambia*, June 10, 1979; "Marxism Panic: Scientific Socialism Won't Ban Religion, Vows Chona," *National Mirror*, February 1979; "Nkhoma Explodes Myth on Marxism," *National Mirror*, July 1979.
41. *Africa Confidential*, May 12, 1980.
42. *National Mirror*, October 29, 1989. The issue briefly raised its head again in 1989, when it was said by the Zambian Episcopal Conference and the Evangelical Fellowship of Zambia that the ruling party had reintroduced a political education syllabus at schools that included Scientific Socialism
43. *National Mirror*, April 20–May 3, 1984.
44. *Daily Mail*, May 28, 1982.
45. Maxwell, "Post-colonial Christianity," 406–7.
46. QTH Africa and Miki Vcelar, "Clandestine Stations of Southern Africa," *Southern Africa Clandestines of the 1970's*, http://www.intervalsignals.net/countries/african_clandestines.htm.
47. The frustration of church leaders, moreover, was compounded by the fact that they felt sidelined by Kaunda, who had abolished his meetings with religious leaders at State House. As Rev. John Mambo observed at the time, "The church in Zambia has long been left because there is no longer a religious advisor to the President." Kaunda's earlier Christian advisors had, in fact, been replaced by an Indian guru, Dr. M. A. Ranganathan, in 1976. *Daily Mail*, May 27, 1982.
48. The heading of this section comes from Catherine Mukuka, *A Christian Nation versus a Secular State: The Making of a Constitution* (Lusaka: Abiyah Publishing House, 2006), 11.
49. Maia Green, *Priests, Witches and Power: Popular Christianity after Mission in Southern Tanzania* (Cambridge: Cambridge University Press, 2003), 8.
50. John McCracken, "Church and State in Malawi: The Role of the Scottish Presbyterian Missions, 1875–1965," in *Christian Missionaries and the State in the Third World*, ed. Holger B. Hansen and Michael Twaddle (Oxford: James Currey, 2002).
51. Komakoma, *Social Teaching*, 266.
52. Ibid., 282.
53. For instance, the reestablishment of diplomatic ties with Israel (and the breaking of ties with the Palestinian Liberation Organization, Iraq, and Iran) and the opening of a Department of Christian Affairs within the president's office. See Phiri, "President," 407.
54. Ibid., 408.
55. *National Mirror*, February 3–9, 2001. The Frontline Fellowship sees the "Christian Reconstruction of Zambia" as a marked break with the past, because "during these dark years, Zambia played host to a bewildering assortment of Marxist terrorists—the MPLA, Frelimo, ZANU, ZAPU, SWAPO, the PAC and the ANC." Brian W. Abshire, "'Those Who Walk in Darkness, Will See a Great Light . . .': The Christian Reconstruction of Zambia," http://www.swrb.com/newslett/actualNLs/Zambia.htm.
56. "Church Leaders' Statement on the Constitutional Debate," signed by Bishop T. G. Mpundu, chairman (Zambia Episcopal Conference) and Bishop Clement H. Shaba (Christian Council of Zambia), December 1, 1995. Reproduced in Komakoma, *Social Teaching*, 236.
57. "Open letter to the President and Members of Parliament," signed by all Catholic bishops, April 26, 1996. See Komakoma, *Social Teaching*, 340.
58. Joseph Komakoma, quoted in Jeremy Gould, "Subsidiary Sovereignty and the Constitution of Political Space in Zambia," in *One Zambia, Many Histories: Towards a*

History of Post-colonial Zambia, ed. Jan-Bart Gewald, Marja Hinfelaar, and Giacomo Macola (Leiden: Brill), 278–80.

59. The quotation further reads, "A majority of these said that the declaration should be reflected in the preamble whilst a minority said that it should be in the main body. The major reason cited for the retention of the declaration was that the majority of Zambians are Christians. . . . a number of petitioners called for the repeal of this provision . . . they found the declaration discriminatory and a violation of the freedom of worship and conscience." Mukuka, *Christian Nation,* 11.

60. *Times of Zambia,* 2005, http://www.times.co.zm/news/viewnews.cgi?category=6&id=1125253262.

61. Mukuka, *Christian Nation,* 113.

62. Ibid., 23.

63. P. Henriot, "Let's Say No to a Christian Nation and Yes to a Nation of Christians," *Post* (Lusaka), Nov. 8, 2005.

64. Chanda Chisala, "The Zambian Constitution Debate, part 1: Who Are the People?" http://www.zambia.co.zm/articles/constitution1.html.

THREE

Rejection or Reappropriation?
Christian Allegory and the Critique of Postcolonial Public Culture in the Early Novels of Ngũgĩ wa Thiong'o

NICHOLAS KAMAU-GORO

IN 1986 the Association Member Episcopal Conferences of Eastern Africa, representing Ethiopia, Kenya, Malawi, Sudan, Tanzania, Uganda, and Zambia, observed, "The African creative writers usually exhibit a social conscience, although, rightly or wrongly, they have become alienated from the Church.... The Church should see them as a challenge where matters of peace and social justice are concerned and should not continue to ignore them. The faith of future generations of Africans depends to some extent on a dialogue with their literary spokesmen. Ultimately, the pen is mightier than the sword."[1]

This statement is significant because it acknowledges that African writers have a moral vision and capacity to intervene in public culture in ways not always coincident with the church's mission. Because of their status as public spokespersons, pioneering writers like Ngũgĩ wa Thiong'o, Chinua Achebe, Wole Soyinka, Kofi Awoonor, and Ayi Kwei Armah have a large public who take them as moral beacons. If the writers become "alienated" from Christianity, it is easy to see why the church should see them as a challenge.

How did the African writer acquire the image of a public spokesperson? As Achebe has explained, the African writer models himself on the artist in African traditional society.[2] As the "sensitive needle" of his community, the artist is at once the custodian of moral values and an arbiter in his society.³ This interfacing of art, morality, and notions of the artist's public role suggests that literary studies should pay closer attention to ethical issues. T. S. Eliot's call for a literary criticism that takes a definite "ethical and theological standpoint" has, however, been overshadowed by ahistorical methods of analysis that have tended to disassociate texts from their social context.⁴ African literature—its public role, its field of concerns, and its forms of representation—has been shaped by tradition. However, this was not the only influence. Writers had their consciousness indelibly marked by Christianity. This is because for most of them their first encounter with Western culture was through the mission school. As a part of the emergent African elite with a Western-style education, an element of historical accident cast the pioneer African writer to the forefront, where issues of national formation and development were being debated as Africa decolonized from the 1950s onward. In a sense, this historical conjuncture had predetermined the writers' public role.

A product of the mission school, Ngũgĩ started his literary career as a Christian but later developed into a radical critic of Christianity. Despite this, Christian idioms and allegories remained prominent features of his aesthetic praxis. Of all African writers, Ngũgĩ has perhaps most consistently used the Bible as a frame of aesthetic reference. When he began to write, he was a Christian novelist who, in his own words, "used to go to Church at 5 o'clock in the morning" and was "quite sure my destiny lay in heaven, not hell."⁵ Ngũgĩ's home area was adjacent to a Church of Scotland mission station. Not surprisingly, he could not separate his Christian calling from his other calling as a writer. Ngũgĩ sees the two roles melding together in an aesthetic whose goal is the total liberation of the human person: "I am a writer. Some have even called me a religious writer. I write about people: I am interested in their hidden lives; their fears and hopes, their loves and hates . . . how, in other words, the emotional stream of the man interacts with the social reality."⁶

An understanding of the forces behind the formation of Ngũgĩ's literary consciousness is important if we are to appreciate the uses of Christianity in his fiction. Ngũgĩ had a typical childhood in a household in which home education was through the traditional verbal arts of storytelling and riddling. His early education was in independent and mission schools. This was also a time of intensified nationalist agitation against colonialism in Kenya. Gĩkũyũ nationalists had fallen out with the Christian missionaries in the controversy of 1929–30 over the issue of female circumcision. African-instituted churches and schools stressed the necessity of cultural purity and mental liberation as a prerequisite for liberation from colonialism.[7] If colonialism was disruptive of the institutions and values by which people had hitherto ordered their lives, missionary education held for Ngũgĩ the promise of personal success in the new colonial dispensation. This became a reality when he was admitted to Alliance High School in 1955, which offered a British public school education to a "future ruling African elite."[8] Alliance exemplified the subtle link between colonial-missionary education and the colonizing mission. The school alienated the students from their peasant roots and cultures with its Christian ideology and the exclusively English curriculum. It was at Alliance that Ngũgĩ converted to Christianity. In an essay Ngũgĩ wrote at this time, "I Try Witchcraft," he depicted witchcraft as a metonym for Africa's cultural backwardness. He saw Christianity as "without doubt the greatest civilising influence" that held the promise of emancipating the African from cultural darkness and "superstition."[9]

Ngũgĩ proceeded to Makerere University, where he discovered his vocation as a writer and wrote the short stories included in the anthology *Secret Lives* (1975) along with his first two novels—*The River Between* (1965) and *Weep Not, Child* (1964). At Makerere, lecturers' attempts to induct students into English middle-class mannerisms and critical methods that avoided relating texts to their social context reinforced the Christian-imperial model inculcated at Alliance. Despite this, the English department played a crucial role in nurturing writers. But Ngũgĩ was also confused about his identity as a writer in the postcolonial situation.[10] With these anxieties on his mind, Ngũgĩ proceeded to the University of Leeds for postgraduate studies, following in the footsteps of four former Makerere students who were later to become important writers and literary critics in East Africa—Peter Nazareth, Grant Kamenju, Pio Zirimu, and Elvania Zirimu.

Ngũgĩ initially enrolled for a diploma in English before transferring to the MA-by-thesis program, with the idea of studying West Indian literature.[11] He identified with what he regarded as a shared historical experience between the West Indies and Africa—the experience of colonialism, the persistence of the "African consciousness" in the West Indian literary imagination, and the quest for an identity in a colonial world. He lost his Christian faith and found an alternative in Frantz Fanon's critiques and Marxist theory. The appropriation of these secular frames of reference reflected the radicalization of Ngũgĩ's political consciousness. Yet despite Ngũgĩ's rejection of Christianity, in the novel he wrote at that time, *A Grain of Wheat* (1967), these secular Fanonist and Marxist tropes complemented rather than superseded his earlier Christian-inspired vision. Like *A Grain of Wheat* whose title is derived from the First Epistle to the Corinthians,[12] the titles of many of Ngũgĩ's texts—*The River Between* (originally *The Black Messiah*), *Weep Not, Child,* and *Devil on the Cross* (1982)—have unmistakable biblical resonance, reflecting the prominence of biblical tropes in Ngũgĩ's discursive strategies.

Ngũgĩ, a Christian and a writer, came to cast himself as an actor in Kenya's postcolonial public culture. His writing and its public role intertwined; both had been overdetermined by the politics of colonial and neocolonial oppression. Also important were early memories of colonial deprivation and even resistance. Ngũgĩ talks of his childhood in a family that lived as "tenants-at-will on somebody else's land" and contrasts this with the expansive settler farms just next to his village, on which he sometimes worked as a child.[13] These memories made it difficult for him to reconcile the realities of the colonial situation with the message of missionary Christianity and inclined him, like many other intellectuals of his time, to nationalism.[14] From the very start, Ngũgĩ's works located themselves in the public culture of postcolonial Kenya and participated in the complex politics of imagining the nation. His early novels offer a perspective on the complex appropriation of Christianity in African public cultures, even when it is ostensibly rejected or relegated to the status of a religion in an otherwise secular society.

Toward a New Christendom: Nationalist Imagination and the Indigenization of Christianity

The integral use of biblical references and Christian mythology in Ngũgĩ's early novels has sometimes been seen as a sign of a writer who is alienated from an authentic African mythology.[15] I contest this reading for the way in which it ignores the location of Ngũgĩ's fictions in the tradition of local efforts to appropriate Christianity. Ngũgĩ's novels are works of the political imagination, involved in the process of forging a group consciousness as people debated on how to respond to the reality of colonial subjugation.[16] They help readers understand the reality of colonial subjugation but, even more important, imagine deliverance from the colonial legacy in the postcolonial public sphere. As many

African Christians before him,[17] Ngũgĩ appropriated Christianity and other missionary texts and assigned them a radically different role in the contested public culture of colonial Kenya. The draft of his first novel (though the second to be published), *The River Between*, for instance, was originally entitled *The Black Messiah*. The title signals not just the influence of the Bible on Ngũgĩ's consciousness but also an awareness of the black man's disadvantaged position in the colonial dispensation. The notion of Messianism captured the nationalist dream of liberation from colonial oppression. Similarly, the weeping-child motif in *Weep Not, Child* has unmistakable biblical resonances.[18] This novel focuses on the Mau Mau liberation struggle and expresses optimism that ultimately all will be well despite the social disruption the struggle engenders.

The River Between begins with colonialism looming, threatening traditional notions of land ownership and self-rule. Christian missionaries have already established a station at Siriana, and there are rumors of colonial administrators building posts all over the country. People must seek ways of dealing with the prospect of colonial conquest and a threatening modernity. This threat compels them to recall the prophecy by the Gĩkũyũ seer Mũgo wa Kĩbiro, who had warned, "There shall come a people with clothes like butterflies" (*TRB*, 2).[19] However, speaking in a distinctly Christian idiom, Mũgo had also told the people, "Salvation shall come from the hills. From the same blood that flows in me, I say from the same tree, a son shall rise. And his duty shall be to lead and save the people" (*TRB*, 20). Ngũgĩ mobilizes traditional prophecy in Gĩkũyũ nationalist discourse "which is refracted through a Christian eschatological narrative."[20] The Gĩkũyũ seer, Mũgo, spoke before the great hunger (*ngaragu ya rũraya*, the famine of Europe), which occurred around 1899 when a Maina generation's authority had been weakened "by the recent cattle plagues of pleura-pneumonia and riderpest [*sic*], by locust infestation and smallpox, and when a candidate of Mwangi generation was impatient for recognition."[21] His prophecy is interpreted by Gĩkũyũ nationalists in Ngũgĩ's fictions as espousing a political strategy of reconciliation and negotiation.

Ngũgĩ's recourse to Gĩkũyũ gnosis—to the past, local history, and the oral tradition—plays a most important role. The Gĩkũyũ myth of origin and the ancient prophecy are the icons of Ngũgĩ's narrative. It is through these religious myths that precolonial history is constructed. According to this myth, God (*Murungu*) told the original parents of the Gĩkũyũ, "This land I give to you, O man and woman. It is yours to till, you and your posterity" (*TRB*, 2). This myth gives sacred entitlement to local people's ownership of their ancestral lands. While the myth of origin is specific to Gĩkũyũ culture, its deployment in Ngũgĩ's writing carries a double meaning. It naturalizes the birth of the Gĩkũyũ and, by extension, the Kenyan nation, while subverting the conventional idea of the nation as a recent construct. Since myth predates the colonial notion of African historicity, the narrative asserts the nation as a natural phenomenon. This notion of the nation has roots in Gĩkũyũ ontology, in which a spiritual link exists between the people and their land; a link that goes back to the mythical beginnings. Christianity provides the other part of what is essentially a syncretic language of contestation with the myths of the colonizing ideology.

The novel symbolically captures the Manichaeanism of the colonial world in the portrayal of two antagonist ridges, Makuyu and Kameno, facing each other across the Honia River "like two rivals ready to come to blows over the leadership of this isolated region" (*TRB*, 2). By fanning this intra-Gĩkũyũ conflict, the coming of the white missionaries provides new fronts for ancient conflicts. The river that divides the two ridges signifies two contesting ideological positions, prefiguring two political theories of responding to colonial subjugation. On the one hand, there are those led by Joshua, the Christian priest, who invest their hope of salvation in Christianity and the efficacy of the colonial system. On the other hand, there are the traditionalists, led by Kabonyi, a regressed Christian, who are convinced that to accept Christianity is to forfeit national pride. On the surface, the rivalry is framed in the idiom of tradition, invoking the sacred myth of origins and arguing over where exactly the mythological first parents—Gĩkũyũ and Mumbi—stood when God showed them the land that was to be their heritage. The religious grammar of the debate masks issues of power and political supremacy that are being contested. But the re-creation of such myths is also central to Ngũgĩ's textual strategies and to the nationalist discourse in his fictions. The local knowledge rooted in myth, remembered histories, local geography, and the flora and fauna stands in stark contradistinction to the white stranger's ignorance. We get a glimpse of this authorizing knowledge when Cege the elder, who is depicted as the custodian of the deepest secrets of the tribe, takes his son, Waiyaki, the hero of the novel, to the hills to show him the sacred site. It is here that Waiyaki learns from his father about the myth of origin and the ancient prophecy (*TRB*, 17–20). By mapping an alternative public that lies beyond the colonial domain, the knowledge of place embedded in the Gĩkũyũ sacral myths acquires a nuanced secular authority. That knowledge helps counteract the colonial mythologizing of the land as an untamed wilderness, hence undermining one of the key pillars of the colonial occupation.

Ngũgĩ's writings of the 1960s have traditionally been read as narratives of cultural conflict. The extent to which Ngũgĩ melds both cultures and tries to forge an aesthetic of liberation out of their contesting tropes has largely been ignored, although this in fact is the way the Gĩkũyũ tried to deal with the hegemonic claims of colonial modernity and to imagine a future beyond colonial control. However, by positioning Ngũgĩ's early fictions in the confluence of Gĩkũyũ cultural discourses, Gĩkũyũ religion, and Gĩkũyũ nationalist discourses, "a far more nuanced view of Ngũgĩ's relation to religious and nationalist discourses emerges."[22] Beneath the narratives of Gĩkũyũ appropriation of colonial culture is a metanarrative of resistance. The original title of his first novel, *The Black Messiah*, signals not just the influence of the Bible on Ngũgĩ's consciousness but also an awareness of the African's disadvantaged position in the colonial dispensation. It expresses a tacit longing for the African's liberation. In fact, the Gĩkũyũ prophet Mũgo uses the biblical language of salvation for what is essentially political liberation. Ngũgĩ's failure to develop the political theme tends to foreground cultural conflict and explains the failure of Waiyaki's messianic mission.

The Christian and yet ostensibly secular curriculum that Ngũgĩ followed as a student of English explains the prominence of Christian idioms and allegories in his novels. English literature itself had been influenced by the authorized translation of the Bible—one of the most "revolutionary events in the history of English style" and the chief means by which Protestant England "sought the recovery of the original spirit of Christianity."[23] This had a significant impact on literary style in the postcolonial world. An influential text in this regard was Bunyan's *Pilgrim's Progress*.[24] Widely read in missionary schools, *Pilgrim's Progress* was one of the most important texts missionaries used to spread the gospel in the colonies. They found that its portability and simple linear style made it more authoritative and less theologically problematic than the multiple narratives of the life of Christ in the gospels. Ngũgĩ deployed the style of *Pilgrim's Progress* to reconfigure Christianity. In *The River Between* and *Weep Not, Child*, he replicates Bunyan's simple linear plot to write an African story of pilgrimage through the trials of colonial bondage and the hope for eventual salvation. Salvation for Ngũgĩ, however, is understood in the sense of liberation from colonial oppression.

The failure of Waiyaki's mission in *The River Between* is central to understanding Ngũgĩ's reappropriation of Christianity. As a product of missionary education, Waiyaki has internalized the ethos of Western individualism. He finds it difficult to subordinate his individual will to the demands of a communal polity that has its own ancient rules of belonging. He persists in his love for Nyambura, the daughter of the Christian priest Joshua. The problem is that as a Christian, Nyambura is uncircumcised and therefore completely unacceptable to the traditionalists. This puts Waiyaki in a difficult situation where he is rejected by both the traditionalists led by the Kiama (council of elders) and the Christians (led by the priest), who see him as a heathen. Between these two extreme positions, Waiyaki suggests a reconciliatory project that molds a new culture out of aspects of tradition and those of modernity—hence his obsession with education. In fact, he, Nyambura, and her sister, Muthoni, who dies in a botched circumcision, represent a youthful generation that pays dearly for trying to find a middle ground between Joshua's fundamentalist Christianity and the cultural intransigence of the elders. The new culture must of necessity be synthetic, embracing both tradition and modernity. In defying her father and opting for circumcision, Muthoni embraces tradition, but it is a reconfigured tradition that also includes Christianity. Her vision of the way forward out of the crisis of values that colonialism has engendered is expressed in her message to her sister. It is significant that Waiyaki, the messianic figure, is the bearer of this message: "Tell Nyambura I see Jesus. . . . I am still a Christian, see, a Christian in the tribe. . . . Look, I am a woman and will grow big and healthy in the tribe" (*TRB*, 12). The traditionalists who coalesce around the Kiama represent a similarly reconciliatory project, as do the Christians in the Gĩkũyũ Karĩng'a Independent Church. The Kiama embrace tradition and education. They may be opposed to missionary Christianity, but it is clear that they reject Christianity only to the extent that it denigrates Gĩkũyũ tradition. In other words, their ideology is similar to that of the Karĩng'a Church, which advocates for a Christianity that is rooted in Gĩkũyũ culture.

Njoroge in *Weep Not, Child* is another—and the last—of Ngũgĩ's heroes in this mode. The parallels between the modernist conception of the fictional hero are strikingly reminiscent of the messianic notion in the Bible where we see Jesus—another outstanding individual—crying out on the cross, wondering why his father (God) has forsaken him. It is this sense of abandonment and hopelessness that drives Njoroge to attempt suicide when he is expelled from the mission school. *Weep Not* exhibits the same dialectics between tradition and colonial culture as the first novel. The difference is that in this novel, Ngũgĩ develops the theme of colonialism and the anticolonial struggle in a more nuanced political vocabulary. The accent here falls not on Christianity per se but on missionary education. Njoroge's is a story about the individual and communal investment in education, which is seen as a form of passive, long-term resistance to colonialism in line with Mūgo's prophecy. Like Waiyaki before him, Njoroge experiences bouts of messianic fervor in which he sees himself as the one who would eventually save his people from colonialism (*WNC*, 92–95). After he passes his exams, the people see him "no longer as the son of Ngotho but of the land" (*WNC*, 105). This insistence on Njoroge's communal identity is at odds with the Protestant ethic of individualism inculcated by the mission school and Njoroge's Western-style education. It shows how the people continue to view education through the prism of traditional communal consciousness. Njoroge's self-casting as the messiah who would save the people from colonialism responds to this traditional vision. But as in the case of Waiyaki, this is shown to be mere romanticism.

Njoroge's messianic delusions are brought to a rude end when the colonial police pick him from school and accuse him of having taken the Mau Mau oath, leading to his expulsion from school (*WNC*, 117). This is a false accusation, but it also serves to expose the shallowness of Njoroge's messianic aspirations. He contemplates running away to Uganda with his childhood friend Mwihaki, but she refuses, pointing out very significantly that they cannot run away because they are no longer children and have responsibilities to other people (*WNC*, 134). Feeling abandoned by God and by Mwihaki, Njoroge attempts suicide but even that fails when his mother saves him in the last minute. Ngũgĩ closes all options to force his character to face the reality of the colonial situation and in the process bring into sharp focus the discrepancy between the promise of missionary Christianity and colonial modernity on the one hand, and the state of African dispossession on the other. In the process, colonial education is exposed as one of the tools colonialism uses to control the African mind. Njoroge is another case of a failed would-be messianic figure.

Mark Mathuray contends that "it is unclear if the fantasies of the self-proclaimed Messiahs are empty delusions of alienated individuals, or if they fulfil they role as prophets."[25] I think the tragedy of Ngũgĩ's messiahs is precisely that they are alienated and thus out of sync with the real aspirations of their community. This is principally an aesthetic and ideological problem. Writing against the backdrop of a volatile colonial context, in which African agency can only assert itself in political terms, Ngũgĩ is engulfed in the aesthetic of the Western modernist novel. Consequently, where the logic of narrative context suggests a political theme, Ngũgĩ, the young novelist, does not know how to reconcile this with the aesthetic principles of the great tradition of English literature he had learned in mission school and at Makerere. This is a tradition that espouses an aesthetic that eschews political commentary as demeaning in art. Consequently, by imagining his messiahs as outstanding, lone individuals in the modernist mode, Ngũgĩ compromises their capacity to meet the demands of a community that emphasizes a relational rather than individualist ethos.

Ngũgĩ and the Postcolonial Public Culture: The Secular Reappropriation of Christianity

A Grain of Wheat is significant as the first of Ngũgĩ's works after he dropped his Christian name—James—and denounced Christianity as a personal faith. According to Wamulungwe Mwikisa, "It is not possible to speak in precise terms of the significance and the kind of conversion implied by [Ngũgĩ's] change of names."[26] However, if we keep in mind Ngũgĩ's attempts in the earlier novels to reconnect his praxis with a continuous cultural tradition, the change can be understood as a more radical and fundamental return to the sources of indigenous identity in African culture. It had been one of the glaring contradictions of Ngũgĩ's practice that while criticizing the Bible and Christianity for their complicity in the colonial project, his own persona remained inscribed by Western culture and Christianity. Dropping the Christian name was, for Ngũgĩ, one way of reasserting the primacy of the African perspective in his authorial ideology. The change reflects Ngũgĩ's more radical posture toward Christianity and an ideological shift in his perspectives on how to combat the culture of colonialism and its continuing legacy in postcolonial Kenya. It is this impulse to resist colonial hegemony that underlies his attempts to privilege African culture as the principal means through which Western culture is appropriated and relativized in his fictional world.

Some critics talk of a rupture between Ngũgĩ's treatment of Christianity in the earlier novels and the more recent works originally composed in Gĩkũyũ.[27] However, the easy division that Mwikisa sees between Ngũgĩ's earlier works and those that come from *A Grain of Wheat* onward exists, I submit, only on the surface. Ngũgĩ's literary oeuvre is best read in the context of what Simon Gikandi describes as his "long and agonized search for the narrative forms that might best represent the complex culture of postcolonial Africa."[28] In other words, Ngũgĩ's writing is a project of experimentation with various aesthetic strategies and forms. Christianity remains a consistent source of aesthetic tropes and idioms—a fact that valorizes the influence of missionary education on his consciousness but also the trauma of colonialism and almost unconscious quest for a liberator in the mold of the messianic figure. Hence, in the earlier works an indigenized Christianity presented one model of engagement with colonial culture and seemed to hold real regenerative potential as Ngũgĩ actively explored the possibilities of melding African culture with Christianity. But Ngũgĩ is also a writer whose works are extremely sensitive to what is happening in the public sphere in which they are produced.

In the case of *A Grain of Wheat* and *Petals of Blood* (1977)—the last novel Ngũgĩ wrote in English before renouncing the language and opting to write all his subsequent imaginative works in Gĩkũyũ—the Kenyan and African political scenario was the most important formative reality behind his fictions. The crisis of consciousness that assailed the African writer in the first decade of independence mirrored the political crisis engendered by the strong feeling that the political elite were inclined to betray the high ideals, the hopes, and the aspirations that had driven the nationalist struggle for independence. The situation called for a reevaluation of "formal and artistic priorities and political tactics."[29] Frantz Fanon's *The Wretched of the Earth*, a diagnostic and prophetic study of the transition from colonialism to neocolonialism in the postcolonial world, was instrumental in helping Ngũgĩ focus his critique of public culture in Africa around the failure of independence to initiate a decisive break with the colonial past.[30] Still, the vocabulary and tropes of Christianity remain important frames of reference in Ngũgĩ's critique of postcolonial public culture. My reception of *A Grain of Wheat* is shaped by two significant epigraphs—one from the Bible about a grain that must wilt and die in order to give new life (1 Corinthians), and the author's note about peasants who fought for independence but now see all they fought for put aside. The epigraphic texts echo Fanon's critique of decolonization as a failed project and his representation of the postcolonial state as an edifice collapsing in the "process of regression."[31] For the writer, the political crisis also represents an aesthetic challenge.

If indeed the writer is a public spokesperson, as African writers claim to be, what is his or her public? In the face of Africa's postcolonial crisis, how does the writer ensure that he or she reaches the public with his or her message? In his earlier works, Ngũgĩ wrote largely from the perspective of a cultural insider informing a foreign public about African culture and the issues fought out in the nationalist struggle. From *A Grain of Wheat* on, he constructs a more specific public. He is keen to articulate the interests of a subaltern, peasant audience who he feels have been betrayed in the new postcolonial dispensation. The challenge is how to aesthetically—not just ideologically—identify with the masses for whom he presumes to speak. Although it was not until ten years later that Ngũgĩ was able to finally jettison the English language, his aesthetic anguish expresses itself in the form of an acute sense of the unsuitability of English for his aesthetic and political project.[32] As Mwikisa rightly observes, Ngũgĩ's views on African culture and religiosity cannot be divorced from his decision to stop using English and switch to Gĩkũyũ, because he does not "compartmentalize language, religion, politics etc. into separate categories."[33] He taps into these resources for a less intellectualized aesthetic register for his writing.[34] The Bible is an important element of Ngũgĩ's literary imagination and a popular cultural tradition that the author mines to forge a counterdiscourse against neocolonialism. Rather than being a means by which indigenous culture was overwritten, Christianity in an appropriated and modified form becomes in Ngũgĩ's fictions a vehicle for secular political expression. Another important influence is the Mau Mau liberation struggle, which provides a model of how the exploited might recapture their agency in the postcolonial period.[35] Ngũgĩ's commitment to revolutionary change enmeshed with the powerful influence of his Protestant mission education is crucial to an understanding of how he reconfigures the Bible in his fiction.

Despite the failure of the messianic-savior model explored in *The River Between* and *Weep Not, Child*, Ngũgĩ's analysis of the postcolonial crisis in Kenya and Africa and the predicament of his putative public lead him to reconsider the messianic notion. Not surprisingly, in view of the significance he attaches to the Mau Mau as a model for radical change, the reconfiguration of this notion in *A Grain of Wheat* is effected through Kihika, a Mau Mau combatant. This was a moment of ideological reappraisal for Ngũgĩ,[36] and it is important to note that in the novel, Ngũgĩ finds it necessary to revisit the themes he had treated in the earlier works. The difference is that *A Grain of Wheat* expresses a more radical vision and critique of the colonial and postcolonial sphere. In the earlier novels, Waiyaki and Njoroge uncritically embraced missionary education as a pathway to liberation. In *A Grain of Wheat,* Kihika actually runs away from the mission school to join the Mau Mau liberation struggle. Unlike Waiyaki and Njoroge, for whom the messianic closure that would culminate in liberation lies somewhere in the future, for Kihika the future is implicated in the present moment of struggle.

In the novel, the sacred myths of the past, like that of origin and even Mũgo's prophecy, are recovered in a way that imbues urgency to the struggle for freedom. This radicalism is reflected in the way Kihika appropriates Christianity to articulate a vision of secular political liberation. Ngũgĩ conceives liberation in ways that resonate with biblical allegory. The muted theme of sacrifice in *The River Between* is here foregrounded. As the earlier novels show, Ngũgĩ is, however, also aware that Christianity has been deeply implicated in propagating ideologies that sanctified the hierarchical dichotomies of slave and master, native and colonizer, African pagan and Christian European—the multiple ways in which the Bible was used to entrench colonialism. The way Ngũgĩ uses Christianity in *A Grain of Wheat* is indicative of how his praxis intertwines with Western texts, including the Bible. This relationship is subversive and stems from a conviction that it is quite possible to read colonial texts in ways that undermine colonizing ideologies.

A Grain of Wheat is, in the view of numerous critics, the most aesthetically accomplished of Ngũgĩ's early novels, but it is in fact a parody of Joseph Conrad's *Nostromo* and *Under Western Eyes,* two of the iconic texts of English literature. Ngũgĩ rewrites Conrad's novels into a political tale of Kenya by contextualizing Conrad's moral aesthetic within the struggle against colonialism. In the same vein, Ngũgĩ uses the precolonial past, the colonial present, and the neocolonial future to contextualize his appropriation of the Bible. The emphasis is not on what the missionaries say but on the ways in which African interpreters make sense of Christianity in their own context. Ngũgĩ is simply making aesthetic use of a hermeneutical tradition that is characterized by a proactive use of the African context as resource for biblical interpretation. This tradition is dominated by the inculturation-evaluative method and liberation hermeneutics. African culture and religion are crucial in the project, because the tradition emphasizes the interpreter's perspective.³⁷ Christianity provides the vocabulary of Kihika's attempts to mobilize and inspire people to higher resolve in the struggle against colonialism. Ngũgĩ's reconfiguration of the Bible is in line with the radical aesthetic taught at Leeds, where he wrote the novel, an aesthetic that encouraged students to relate texts to their social context and to try and change the world. But it is also informed by the author's close observation of the scene in late-colonial Kenya filtered through the prism of Fanon's politics of decolonization in *Wretched of the Earth*, where decolonization is seen as an inevitably violent phenomenon. Interestingly, in Ngũgĩ's novel, decolonization is not apprehended in the vocabulary of Fanon's secular analysis, but in the Christian idiom of sacrifice and salvation. Kihika, the Mau Mau and Christian hero of the novel, explains, "But a few shall die that many shall live. That's what crucifixion means today. Else we deserve to be slaves, cursed to carry water and hew wood for the white man for ever and ever. Choose between freedom and slavery and it is fitting that a man should grab at freedom and die for it" (*AGW*, 167).

"Today" reifies the immediate context in which Kihika is rereading the Bible. One cannot fail to notice the allusion to Joshua's curse to the Gibeonites during his conquest of Canaan in the phrase "carry water and hew wood for the white man"³⁸—an allusion that reflects Kihika's appreciation of the link between the Christian discourse and oppression through history; a connection that is being reenacted in colonial Kenya. This is a link that the oppressed can only sever by de-ideologizing the Bible (and Christianity in general) to make it speak the language of the oppressed. In the hands of the postcolonial subjects, the Bible is no longer an agent but an object, subject to the inscriptions of the Other, whose story it must be forced to tell. Kihika achieves this with uncanny creativity. We see this, for instance, in the way he reconfigures the biblical notion of the messiah, investing it with new meaning. However, in Ngũgĩ's earlier novels the messianic hero is the outstanding, lone individual who, like Waiyaki, carries the burdens of the whole world on his shoulders. In *A Grain of Wheat*, the messianic notion is relativized in a shift that also signals Ngũgĩ's abandonment of notions of the fictional hero as known in the Western tradition, where the hero is a variant of the Christ figure. In Ngũgĩ's new conception, the hero and messiah is every oppressed person who takes up arms to fight foreign domination. This is the true meaning of redemptive sacrifice.

Kihika envisions a radical role for Christianity as a channel of the political aspirations of the oppressed. Christianity melded with Fanonist critique of decolonization yields a new register for Ngũgĩ's increasingly radical political consciousness. In Kihika, the messianic figure becomes the martyr who is ready to answer the call of a nation in turmoil. He exhibits none of the moral oscillations we see in Waiyaki and Njoroge. He is a man of action, not romantic dreams, who is ready to translate his political consciousness and his nuanced understanding of the Bible into a program of liberation. He is the organic politicized Christian, still in touch with his peoples' deepest aspirations for freedom, even if it means giving up his life in the process (*AGW*, 15). From this perspective, the biblical notion of sacrifice seems superficial. Kihika explains the logic of his more radical use of the biblical theme of sacrifice and redemption thus,

> Yes—I said he [Jesus] had failed because his death did not change anything, it did not make his people find a centre in the cross. All oppressed people have a cross to bear. . . . In Kenya we want a death which will change things, that is to say, we want a true sacrifice. But first we must be ready to carry the cross. I die for you, you die for me, we become the sacrifice for one another. So I can say that you, Karanja, are Christ. I am Christ. Everybody who takes the Oath of Unity to change things in Kenya is a Christ. (*AGW*, 83)

To devalue the significance of Christ's death as Kihika does is to rock one of the most fundamental pillars of Christianity. What we see here, however, is not a rejection of Christianity as such. Kihika is simply insisting on a culturally and politically relevant biblical interpretation, a contextual understanding of Christianity. In the process, he offers a "radically innovative form of messianism"[39] that, unlike in the earlier novels, stresses the relevance of messianism and sacrifice. In the search for agents of social change, Ngũgĩ makes the point that lone martyrdom, like that of Christ, would be quite meaningless in Kenya. In a context defined by colonial oppression, Kihika declares everybody who has taken the oath to change things as part of "the community of Messiahs, a community of saviors."[40] Kihika's insistence on communal sacrifice harks back to the imaginary relational ethos of life in traditional society in which every person is his or her brother's keeper. The call to political action, though couched in biblical terms, makes sense within the context of Gĩkũyũ moral economy, and it appeals to both Christians and non-Christians.

It must sound irreverent to associate Mau Mau oathing and Christ as Kihika does. In colonial Kenya the missionaries certainly discouraged their converts from partaking of the oath and denounced those who did as morally weak, lacking the moral courage to stand up to the Mau Mau. The missionaries denounced the movement as being "savage and anti-Christ."[41] However for Gĩkũyũ nationalists, the oath was a device for binding people to a moral public duty. And in a society where the divide between civic and religious duty interweave almost seamlessly, even Christians "seem to have regarded the oath as a religious duty. . . . [They] did not make distinctions between the moral goals of Christianity and Mau Mau."[42] What we see here is the merging of Gĩkũyũ and Christian sacral discourses in a narrative that imagines liberation from colonialism as simultaneously a public, civic duty and a moral, religious duty. As John Stotesbury points out, the verses underlined in black in Kihika's Bible come from the New Testament and emphasize sacrificial martyrdom, while the verses underlined in red come from the Old Testament and are concerned with the suffering of the oppressed, alluding to the Moses messianic narrative.[43] Through these different biblical prophetic traditions superimposed on an originary Gĩkũyũ prophetic discourse, Kihika converts Christian religious discourse "into a form of political praxis."[44] In this theologically dynamic world, Kihika is, as the one who has taken the oath and as a Mau Mau fighter, also a Christ.

Through Kihika, Ngũgĩ espouses a "freedom-fighter Christology,"[45] an image of a Christ who takes sides with the oppressed. And though he might be killed in the cause of the struggle against colonialism, as indeed happens, his death, unlike that of the biblical Christ, cannot be in vain as it heralds change for the oppressed. According to John Karega, this reconfiguration of Christ is contestable, because it is justifies violence, while Christ's message was based on love: "Faced with two options, of violence and peaceful resistance, Christ opted for the later and died on the cross. Christ also stipulated clearly that his kingdom is not of this world. . . . His revolution . . . was based on the 'not yet,' the eschatological future of the Kingdom rather than the worldly Kingdom."[46] This might well be so, but the point Ngũgĩ tries to make is that interpretations like Karega's are just one way of relating with the discourse of Christianity, and, for him, not the most relevant in the postcolonial context where the forces of oppression cynically use the Bible to exploit the poor. In Ngũgĩ's case what Hugh Dinwiddy has seen as the "abusage" of the Bible in Kenyan fiction[47] in fact represents "a strategy . . . of appropriating Christian mythology to serve political and secular ends—a demythologizing impulse."[48]

NGŨGĨ STARTS his narrative of Christianity in Kenya by showing it as a culturally and socially divisive force. Its complicity in colonial oppression is implicit in the support the Christian missionaries rendered to the so-called civilizing mission of colonialism. His novels, however, focus not so much on the role of Christianity as on the creative use the colonized make of some of its theological tropes—prophecy and redemption, for instance—to argue a case for their own culture and to articulate their dreams for salvation from colonial oppression. Ngũgĩ's appropriation of Christianity is part of a more comprehensive aesthetic project in which he seizes the discursive forms of Western culture, including the English language and the novel, and uses them as tools for the liberation of his people. Indeed, in his writings, the Christian vocabulary of salvation and redemption compels Christianity—a reconfigured Christianity—to speak a radically subversive language in the context of Kenya's colonial and postcolonial public culture. This is the language of cultural and political self-determination that some of the characters in Ngũgĩ's early novels voice but is best articulated by Kihika in *A Grain of Wheat*. Apart from being a Mau Mau fighter, he is also a something of a theological thinker. The point Ngũgĩ tries to make is that in the postcolonial context it is inadequate for Christianity to preach salvation in the otherworldly sense. Christianity should be recontextualized and de-ideologized to articulate the discourses of those who suffer any form of oppression.

Ngũgĩ's early novels were written in the tradition of the classic realist novel, but the later narratives—*Devil on the Cross, Matigari* (1986), and *Wizard of the Crow* (2006)—in addition to incorporating Mau Mau and Christian mythology, also experiment with literary form. His early novels, particularly in their apparent rejection of Christianity, highlight creative writing as an important arena for contesting public culture in Africa. Rather than being estranged from each other, African writers and the Christian clergy might find ways of working together as the prophetic voice of justice and social equity in Africa.

Notes

1. Association of Member Episcopal Conferences in Eastern Africa, "Priorities and Challenges," *AFER* (Eldoret, Kenya), no. 28 (1986): 37–38.
2. Chinua Achebe, *Morning Yet on Creation Day* (London: Heinemann, 1975), 42–45.
3. Mary Ebun Modupe Kolawole, "Kofi Awoonor as a Prophet of Conscience," *African Languages and Cultures* 5, no. 2 (1992): 125.
4. T. S. Eliot, *Essays, Ancient and Modern* (London: Faber and Faber, 1936), 93.
5. James Ngũgĩ, "James Ngũgĩ Interviewed by Fellow Students at Leeds University," interview by Alan Marcuson, Mike González, and Dave Williams, in *Ngũgĩ wa Thiong'o Speaks: Interviews with the Kenyan Writer*, ed. Reinhard Sander and Bernth Lindfors (Trenton, NJ: Africa World Press, 2006), 27.
6. Ngũgĩ wa Thiong'o, *Homecoming* (London: Heinemann, 1972), 31.
7. Bildad Kaggia, *Roots of Freedom, 1921–1963: The Autobiography of Bildad Kaggia* (Nairobi: East African Publishing House, 1975), 74.
8. Christiana Pugliese, *The Life and Writings of Gakaara wa Wanjau* (Bayreuth: Eckhard Breitinger, 1995), 28.
9. Ngũgĩ wa Thiong'o, "I Try Witchcraft," *Alliance High School Magazine*, September 1957, 21–22.
10. Micere Mũgo, *Visions of Africa: The Fiction of Chinua Achebe, Margaret Laurence, Elspeth Huxley and Ngũgĩ wa Thiong'o* (Nairobi: Kenya Literature Bureau, 1978), 25; Ngũgĩ, *Homecoming*, 83, 89.
11. Carol Sicherman, "The Leeds-Makerere Connection and Ngũgĩ's Intellectual Development," *Ufahamu: Journal of the African Activist Association* 23, no. 1 (1995): 5–6.
12. 1 Corinthians 15:37.
13. Ngũgĩ, *Homecoming*, 48.
14. Simon Gikandi, "On Culture and the State: The Writings of Ngũgĩ wa Thiong'o," *Third World Quarterly* 11, no. 1 (1989): 149–56.
15. David Cook and Michael Okenimkpe, introduction to *Ngũgĩ wa Thiong'o: An Exploration of His Writings*, ed. Cook and Okenimkpe (London: Heinemann, 1997), 4.
16. John Lonsdale, "The Prayers of Waiyaki: The Political Uses of the Kikuyu Past," in *Revealing Prophets: Prophecy in East African History*, ed. David Anderson and Douglas H. Johnson (Oxford: James Currey, 1995), 241.
17. Isabel Hofmeyr, *The Portable Bunyan: A Transnational History of* The Pilgrim's Progress (Princeton: Princeton University Press, 2004), 7.
18. See, for example, Luke 23:28.
19. I use the following abbreviations for Ngũgĩ's fictional writings (all from East African Educational Publishers in Nairobi): *WNC—Weep Not, Child* (1964); *TRB—The River Between* (1965); *AGW—A Grain of Wheat* (1967).
20. Mark Mathuray, "Resuming a Broken Dialogue: Prophecy, Nationalist Strategies, and Religious Discourses in Ngũgĩ's Early Work," *Research in African Literatures* 40, no. 2 (2009): 41.
21. Lonsdale, "Prayers," 265.
22. Mathuray, "Broken Dialogue," 40.
23. Ganesh Devy, "Translation and Literary History: An Indian View," in *Postcolonial Translation: Theory and Practice*, ed. Susan Bassnett and Harish Trivedi (New York: Routledge, 1999), 182.
24. See Hofmeyr, *Portable Bunyan*.
25. Mathuray, "Broken Dialogue," 42.

26. Wamulungwe P. Mwikisa, "The Limits of Difference: Ngũgĩ wa Thiong'o's Redeployment of Biblical Signifiers in *A Grain of Wheat* and *I Will Marry When I Want,*" in *The Bible in Africa: Transactions, Trajectories, and Trends,* ed. Gerald O. West and Musa W. Dube (Leiden: Brill, 2000), 163.

27. David Maughan-Brown, "Matigari and the Rehabilitation of Religion," *Research in African Literatures* 22, no. 4 (1991): 177–79; Mwikisa, "Limits of Difference," 163.

28. Simon Gikandi, *Ngũgĩ wa Thiong'o* (Cambridge: Cambridge University Press, 2000), 2.

29. Neil Lazarus, *Resistance in Postcolonial African Fiction* (New Haven: Yale University Press, 1990), 212.

30. Gikandi, "On Culture," 152; Tirop Simatei, "Colonial Violence, Postcolonial Violations: Violence, Landscape, and Memory in Kenyan Fiction," *Research in African Literatures* 36, no. 2 (2005): 89. See also Frantz Fanon, *The Wretched of the Earth* (Harmondsworth: Penguin, 1967).

31. Fanon, *Wretched,* 149.

32. Marcuson, "James Ngũgĩ," 32–33.

33. Mwikisa, "Limits of Difference," 164.

34. Lazarus, *Resistance,* 23.

35. Ngũgĩ, *Homecoming,* 28.

36. Odun F. Balogun, *Ngũgĩ and African Postcolonial Narrative: The Novel as Oral Narrative in Multigenre Performance* (Quebec: World Heritage Press, 1997), 21.

37. Justin S. Ukpong, "Developments in Biblical Interpretation in Africa: Historical and Hermeneutical Directions," in West and Dube, *Bible in Africa,* 12–19.

38. Joshua 9:23

39. Mathuray, "Broken Dialogue," 42.

40. Ibid.

41. Ngũgĩ, *Homecoming,* 34.

42. Derek R. Peterson, "Writing in Revolution: Independent Schooling and Mau Mau in Nyeri," in *Mau Mau and Nationhood: Arms, Authority and Narration,* ed. E. S. Atieno Odhiambo and John Lonsdale (Oxford: James Currey, 2003), 87.

43. John A. Stotesbury, *The Logic of Ngũgĩ's Use of Biblical and Christian Reference in A Grain of Wheat* (Joensuu, Finland: University of Joensuu, 1985), 14.

44. Mathuray, "Broken Dialogue," 42.

45. John B. Karega, "Theology and Literature: Religions in the Works of Ngũgĩ wa Thiong'o" (PhD diss., Catholic University of Leuven, 1988), 310.

46. Ibid., 311.

47. Hugh Dinwiddy, "Biblical Usage and Abusage in Kenyan Writing," *Journal of Religion in Africa,* 19, no. 1 (1989): 27–47.

48. Mathuray, "Broken Dialogue," 43.

PART TWO

Patriarchy and Public Culture

FOUR

The Implications of Reproductive Politics for Religious Competition in Niger

BARBARA M. COOPER

"FERTILITY DIFFERENCES by religion in West Africa, when they occur," Jennifer Johnson-Hanks writes, "are neither a stable effect of the Muslim religion nor a straightforward consequence of economics but, rather, the result of an interaction between the two. We must conclude that social context and national politics mediate the association between religious affiliation and reproductive practice."[1] In her thought-provoking comparative statistical analysis of fertility and mortality rates by religion across West Africa, Johnson-Hanks goes on to argue that fertility patterns have less to do with religion directly than with the effects of belonging to a minority, the members of which are systematically disadvantaged economically. She convincingly demonstrates that when education and residence are taken into account, it is not clear that Muslims have the high fertility rates so often attributed to them in polemics about the rise of fundamentalism, Muslim male unemployment, and the coming anarchy. On the other hand, in national contexts in which Muslims are an economically disadvantaged minority, their "demographic metabolism" *is* more rapid than that of the majority population: both fertility and mortality rates are relatively high. Johnson-Hanks argues that "reproductive rates are social products, are the result of a variety of forms of cultural practice, and are deeply embedded in local politics."[2] There is, she notes, "no single, coherent Muslim reproductive pattern: the real story is local."[3]

Fertility patterns are highly local and must be interpreted in the light of national contexts, community networks, and perceptions of relative well-being. Although Johnson-Hanks does not herself address the issue of the media, her analysis invites attention to the *perceptions* of religious populations in the same nation relative to one another in the domain of reproduction and to how those perceptions may affect a variety of practices touching on fertility. While her analysis focuses on majority and minority Muslim populations, I will here pursue musings on her insights in the slightly different, but obviously related, context of the Christian minority in Muslim-majority Niger.

Arjun Appadurai has recently argued that competitive dynamics between majority and minority populations within national political contexts, in a shifting global media environment that simultaneously empowers minorities and promotes ambivalence on the part of national governments, have provoked increasingly volatile and violent interactions as a result of what he terms the "fear of small numbers."[4] In some of my own earlier work I have tried to come to terms with the very disturbing instances of violence toward Christians and *bori* spirit mediums—enacted in particular on the bodies of vulnerable single women—in a dense media environment and in the context of profound feelings of impotence on the part of Nigériens as a result of state decline and external economic intrusion.[5] As Appadurai so aptly notes,

> Given the systemic compromise of national economic sovereignty that is built into the logic of globalization, and given the increasing strain this puts on states to behave as trustees of the interests of a territorially defined and confined "people," minorities are the major site for displacing the anxieties of many states about their own minority or marginality (real or imagined) in a world of a few megastates, of unruly economic flows and compromised sovereignties. Minorities, in a word, are metaphors and reminders of the betrayal of the classical national project.[6]

Eliza Griswold, in a recent article in *Atlantic Monthly*, offers an example of precisely this kind of logic at work in the context of Nigeria. The controversial but influential Episcopal archbishop Peter Akinola comments to Griswold that what people in the West don't understand is "that what Islam failed to accomplish by the sword in the eighth century, it's trying to do by immigration so that Muslims become citizens and demand their rights. A Muslim man has four wives; the wives have four or five children each. This is how they turned Christians into a minority in North Africa."[7] Note here the slippage from religious group, to demographic group, to electoral group. The backdrop for demographic anxiety is a fear of being eventually outnumbered in a democratic context in which a majority of voters is understood to be a permanent ethnic or religious block.

Thus reproductive practice is often understood to be political practice, and the reproducing female body thereby becomes a central political battlefield. In other work I have suggested that the recent polio vaccination crisis in Niger was caused not by the ignorance and superstition of gullible Muslim populations led by fanatical Muslim leaders, but rather was motivated by the rather deep grasp on the part of local Muslim populations of the ways that their own fertility practices are under tremendous scrutiny at precisely the same moment that the state appears to show little interest or capacity to provide a genuine health infrastructure.[8] Muslim populations in Niger are far from ignorant, in fact they draw on the information they gather through the Internet, the radio, cassette sermons, and cell phones to counter the contingencies and dangers of a health environment riddled with fake vaccines, predatory medical practitioners, and unethical researchers. Muslim populations in Niger are increasingly skeptical about the claims of national and international agents to have their best interests at heart, and in particular to respect local preferences surrounding fertility and reproduction. As a result, conflicts between the state and local populations are regularly refracted through the lenses of fertility and religion, with all parties deploying a range of media to make claims on either side of the debates. The notion that there is a conspiracy to reduce the Muslim population on the part of a secular state in cahoots with international donors (themselves sometimes perceived to be Christian) is a powerful one.

Some of the contours of this complex environment have been underemphasized in discussions of religion and media. Fertility, reproduction, and population growth are obviously highly personal, embodied, intimate issues, issues that go to the core of family life and are addressed in subtle ways through quotidian practices that are on the whole unremarkable and largely invisible. Yet the reproduction of one's family, one's community, one's religious group, is critical and in the end political. By exploring some of the ways in which the minority community of evangelical Christians in Niger has historically promoted the growth of its population through conversion, marriage, migration, and reproduction, I think we can begin to get a better grasp for the subtle ways in which competing populations signal to one another their resilience and strength; how they use media to reinforce the boundaries of their communities; and how family life, public performance of ritual, and the use of media are all interconnected. Practices are very much shaped by perceptions—not realities—about the surrounding population. I will focus in particular on the history of how Christians in Maradi made visible the contours of their community, how they laid claim to the wives and children so critical to the growth of the community, and how they used public performance of rituals related to the growth of their community to "broadcast" to their neighbors and to themselves what Christianity meant and how it differed from Islam.

The Imperative of Monogamy and the Perceptions of Polygamy

Evangelical Christianity was introduced into Niger in the 1920s and 1930s by the Sudan Interior Mission (SIM[9]), an interdenominational but largely American "faith" mission impatient with the compromises and failings of an earlier wave of denominational missions focusing largely on coastal regions of Africa. There is not space here to detail the longer story of how SIM's intervention in the region has affected family and population,[10] but some of the more important dimensions of that encounter can be summarized as follows. Because SIM, like most Christian missions, rejected polygamy, it ran the risk of rejecting an older "wealth in people" model on which influence and power in the region was based. To build and protect the Christian community and to gain the prestige necessary to attract converts, the mission had to devote a fair amount of attention to questions of "church growth"— more bluntly, promoting population growth in the community through encouraging marriage, reproduction, and the immigration of potential converts into the community through child fostering. Despite the emphasis on baptism and conversion in studies of Christianity in Africa, these more demographic processes are at the heart of the emergence of a Christian community. Monogamy meant that the entire burden of reproduction was placed on the single wife of a male head of household; consequently, a man's sexual access to his wife was seen as paramount to the well-being of the couple, the family, and the community as a whole. Reducing birth spacing and restricting women's absence from the marital household became mechanisms to support higher rates of reproduction.[11] At the same time, the mission intruded into family life by encouraging a reduction in the lengthy lactation periods that coincided with the marital sexual abstinence that was perceived to be at the origin of polygamy and to be a stimulus to adultery among frustrated husbands. As we know today, alterations to nursing practices and birth spacing have important implications for childhood nutrition and infant mortality.[12] As a result, a heavy premium is placed on all living children, who are all the more precious for becoming increasingly vulnerable as birth spacing is reduced.

Christian men today, when discussing the relative size of Christian and Muslim populations in Niger—a topic of tremendous interest for which there is precious little credible data—tend to argue that when SIM first entered the Maradi region there were relatively few Muslims, which is a fair assessment given the concentration of Muslims in a limited social stratum in urban centers at the turn of the century. The rapid growth of Islam relative to Christianity, they argue (like Archbishop Akinola), is due to the advantage that Muslim men have in polygamy. The popular notion among Christian men is that if only Christians had had multiple wives, Christianity would have expanded just as rapidly as Islam and Christians would not feel so embattled in a national political environment dominated by Muslims. This argument reveals a patriarchal notion that the church was and is fundamentally produced and reproduced by men, not women. That is, the key issue is not how many children each woman has, but how many children each man has. Christian women are, in this way of thinking, largely Christian because they are married to Christian men. This perception of the significance of polygamy is of course a bit implausible (not all Muslim men are polygamous, and not all polygamous men have numerous offspring), but it does give us an idea of how male prerogatives, religious competition, and family life are all seen to be closely related.

When men tell the story of the growth of the Christian community in Maradi, they tend to name a variety of male leaders who were understood to be central founding figures of the church. But the real story of the expansion of the church is not simply one of important pastors and male missionaries, in an important way it is more significantly the story of how the church came to attract women and children who could literally reproduce and increase the followers of Jesus. Indeed, when men tell the story of the growth of the church, it is almost impossible to detect the role of women at all, despite the fact that some of the central male figures in the particular church I interviewed were to remark that, "apart from [their] mother" they were the first Christian in their family. An ideological reason for this myopia was expressed by Pastor Cherif when I asked whether women had been early converts to Christianity:

> Women, most of the time, they follow the religion of their husband, right? You could say that since it was Adam who was born first, he was called forth first, and then it was from the rib of man that woman was made. That's why God said, "You will return alongside of your husband." And so that's why it wasn't women who entered [the Protestant Church] first. It was men who were the first. Whatever a person [a man] was to become, so also his wife would become.[13]

Within a fundamentalist reading of the Bible, then, God created Adam first, and it is entirely natural that men, as heads of households, should determine the practices and beliefs of women, who are their subordinates. This is a reading that sits rather well with the local understanding of women as subordinate within Islam, and is therefore not likely to be particularly startling to many West African Muslims. This universalized, mythologized, and naturalized understanding of the process of conversion, of course, flies in the face of much of the history of Christianity elsewhere in Africa, for in many regions slave women and women in flight from unwelcome marriages were attracted to missions and the Christian message before men[14] or were simply more receptive to spiritual concerns than men.[15] In any case, this invocation of Adam and Eve presupposes that Adam can claim Eve as his bride unproblematically, which was certainly not the case with the church in Niger. The central problem for the church in Niger was how to attract women, and how to lay claim to children.

By the 1940s the growing church faced a demographic dilemma. While it had a number of influential male converts who were married or who were approaching the age of marriage, it had very few female converts. It had been far more difficult for the missionaries residing in Islamized urban areas to reach women than to reach men. Local households were very protective of women and girls and tended to prevent them from being exposed to the preaching of the Christians. Young men had a great deal more spatial mobility than women and girls. Married women were subject to the supervision of their husbands, who could physically punish them for misbehavior. Women could even find themselves divorced if their husbands became angered by their disobedience. Divorced women had no guarantee that they would continue to have custody of their children. The disincentives to flirtation with Christianity were numerous and substantial for women. Men had less to lose from exploring Christianity, but an unmarried man found that it was hard to find a suitable spouse once he had converted.

The mission's medical work, beginning in the 1940s and taking off in the 1950s, made it far easier for the mission to gain the ear of women, who sometimes had to remain at the dispensary for weeks or months at a time with their children for treatment. Later, when the mission also had a leprosarium at Danja, even more patients were exposed to Christianity. The effect of the medical work was twofold: it gave rise to a set of healed male converts who became committed evangelists fluent in local languages and conversant with local cultures, and it brought the mission into contact with women and children so that the demographic expansion of the church could proceed through fostering, marriage, and childbirth, and not simply through conversion. The community grew far more rapidly from the 1950s on as a result.

One of the most important ways women contributed to the growth of the Christian community was through the fostering of Muslim children in Christian households, an enterprise that relied substantially on the work of Christian women. Fostering could be part of a broader pattern of clientage and is a very common practice among Hausa families—often such children (*'yan ri'ko*) are treated in principle identically to birth children, and it is generally the responsibility of the woman of the house to ensure that they are well trained morally, that they have the necessary skills to become responsible adults, and that they ultimately marry and move to a home of their own. Christian households took in Muslim kin and disinherited neighbors from their farming villages and raised them, thereby exposing such children daily to Christian quotidian practices, beliefs, and mores. Because towns in Maradi and Tsibiri eventually had relatively high concentrations of Christians (who gravitated to neighborhoods where they felt comfortable among other Christians), rural families took advantage of their connections with Christian kin in town in order to help their children gain access to schooling. Some Christian families quite self-consciously recruited Muslim kin to Christianity by hosting them while they went to school in town. Obviously, however, if fostering Muslim children into Christian households was a laudable project, permitting the children of Christian men to be fostered out into potentially Muslim households was a danger that had to be countered vigorously by laying claim to such children from an early age. The project of building a Christian community entailed asymmetries in relations between Christians and their Muslim kin and neighbors.

Laying Claim to Children through the *Bikin Suna*

Children were to be the future of the evangelical Christian community, for it proved to be far easier to raise and convert children as Christians than to convert adults socialized into Islam. Very few fully grown adults appear in the lists of early professing Christians. Musa Marafa of Tsibiri and Abba Musa of Zinder are exceptions to the general pattern rather than exemplars of Christian conversion, despite their prominence in mission lore. The earliest converts were generally quite young men—even Musa Marafa was twenty-two when he first converted, meaning that in local parlance he was still a boy, or *yaro*. Most, however, were unmarried teenagers who had as yet no prospects for marriage.[16]

In order to continue to grow, the church had to seize every opportunity to train youth and children in Christian belief and practice. Small children and infants became coveted targets of missionary attention, and very early on one key test of a male convert's maturity as a Christian was his willingness to commit his own children to a Christian life. The local practice of "naming" a newborn child after seven days according to a nominally Muslim rite in which a Muslim scholar, or *mallam*, was to choose a name from the Qur'an at random—a ceremony known as *zanen suna*—became a battleground over whether and how to dedicate children to a future Christian life. The zanen suna is a very important part of Muslim social life in the Maradi region. Through the zanen suna, a man publicly recognizes a child as legitimate, enjoins kin and neighbors to celebrate its birth, and marks himself and his wife as successful producers of children. While this celebration, also known as the *bikin suna*, is understood by most in the region to be Muslim—through it a child receives his or her "official" (but generally little used) Muslim name—local practices bear many marks of pre-Islamic practice. In particular, the celebration entails the sacrifice of a ram (slaughtered by a Muslim butcher), which is accompanied by a variety of arcane practices that reformist Muslims today find highly objectionable, such as having the birth mother step over the sacrificed ram four times for a girl child and three times for a boy child. Such ritual surrounding the sacrifice of an animal calls into question traditionalist Muslim claims that the animal is a form of alms (*sadaka*) rather than pagan sacrifice to appease powerful local spirits (*sahi*).

Various ideas that Muslim women hold today related to the ceremony suggest to me that women understand the biki to "tie up" dangerous spirits that might endanger the child and the mother. It is this ritual closure that is central to the biki, not simply the act of naming. Local Maradi women almost never utter the Muslim name of a child—the name's potency opens up a vulnerability in the child that can be exploited by anyone who is jealous and hopes to harm the mother or child. Mothers almost universally refer to their children through affectionate descriptive nicknames capturing the spirit of the moment when the child was born. Thus, to choose a particularly relevant example, many girl children in Maradi are named Maday, because a woman missionary or a government nurse (or "madame") helped deliver the child. The bikin suna also served to situate newly born individuals relative to competing social groups in the region. Until the mid-1950s a baby also received at the bikin suna scarification markings identifying his or her clan and ethnic affiliations.

One can understand why such a socially and spiritually complex ritual might become critical to struggles to control Christian behavior. Would not the best practice simply be to forbid it? Interestingly, however, missionaries did not forbid the celebration of a bikin suna. What they gradually encouraged instead was the Christianization of the rite so that the event was overseen at first by missionaries and later by Christian pastors. Thus the early convert Musa Marafa earned approbation for having "the white *malam* [*sic*]" name his son Daniel in an improvised dedication ceremony in 1930.[17] The mission seized upon the ritual as a moment to force men to commit their children to the church in the future—in effect claiming the child in advance for the Christian community, but in that very act undercutting the notion of an individual choice to commit to Christ.

The ritual would eventually serve to publicly stage some of the differences between Christian conviction and surrounding religious practices. The role of destiny or chance in naming the child was eliminated. By 1945 the church had determined that the family would choose a name from the Bible because of its significance in the scriptures.[18] The biki would become an occasion to preach from passages in the Bible explaining the child's name and to commit the child to a Christian life worthy of that name. Finally, to demonstrate their lack of fear concerning the evil eye, Christians today publicly display the child in the doorway of the home of the parents and pronounce the name of the child out loud. The complex and slippery practice of slaughtering a ram was debated in 1946, but in the end the elders' council of the emerging church determined that the attraction that meat distribution presented to kin, neighbors, and friends, and its festive connotations, made the ram an integral part of any bikin suna. Christians were not to permit a Muslim to slaughter the animal and were to emphasize that this is for the pleasure of it (*don wasa*), not a form of sacrifice.[19] Having made such an argument about the nature of their own rams, Christian converts could hardly object to the distribution of meat among their Muslim kin and neighbors. Despite the reservations of missionaries, who raised the issue in the agenda for an elders' meeting in 1946, church elders insisted that there was no sin in attending the naming ceremonies of Muslims.[20] Clearly both missionaries and church elders micromanaged the matter of bikin suna, ever vigilant in case it should slip toward Islam or toward idolatry. One unfortunate Christian claimed to be the Malamin Almasihu (the mallam of the Savior), evidently attempting to carve out a niche for himself as the Christian counterpart of Muslim mallams who are paid to oversee bikin suna. He named the child of a church member Issa (the Qur'anic name for Jesus), provoking such ire among the elders that he was disciplined. It was not appropriate, they opined, to name a child Jesus or Emmanuel in the way that Muslims name their children Muhammed.[21] But in effect an avenue toward creating an income-generating "work of God" was abruptly closed down, and the monopoly of Christian missionaries, and later of pastors, on the performance of the bikin suna was established.

These debates and struggles over the bikin suna as the evangelical Christian community emerged in the 1930s and 1940s are interesting partly because many of the missionaries who joined SIM did not come from denominations that emphasized infant baptism. The centrality of an individual public commitment to Christ as savior to evangelical Protestantism has meant that for many evangelical missionaries infant baptism verges on heresy, and within Protestantism more broadly the status and meaning of infant baptism has been hotly debated. Within the Christian context of the United States, the notion of individual choice to be "reborn" is perhaps easier to reconcile with a rejection of infant baptism, since Christian models and ideas are readily available to most children in such a setting without the dedication of the child to Christianity and to a Christian upbringing through infant baptism. However, in a preemptive attempt to lay claim to the attentions of impressionable children before they become inculcated with Islam, the mission and early church sacrificed to a certain degree the emphasis on individual choice and commitment to Christ as it might have been understood in the sending countries of the missionaries. The mission went to great lengths to stake a claim to children who were young enough to be socialized into Christianity.

Horo, or church discipline, was one crucial weapon in this war to gain control of children. One of the earliest records of horo I can find for the Tsibiri community occurred in 1934, when the report for October to December notes, "During this quarter we had to discipline another of the young Christian workers. Nanaya let Malams 'christen his first born child' and will be under discipline."[22] In other words, as early as 1934 male members of the church were expected to deliver their children to the mission for upbringing. There is no discussion in any of the incidents I found in the church records of any recognition that the mother of the child might have some say in this issue. The paternal pattern within local Islamic practice, which held that a man could dispose of small children as he wished, particularly once they were weaned, was in effect co-opted by the mission in the service of Christian expansion. Since so few women were Christians whose husbands were not also Christian, the implicit danger in supporting this local patriarchal pattern was not perhaps appreciated by either the church or the mission. Rather than support the notion that a mother should have control over the disposition of her children, regardless of her civil status as Christian or Muslim, the mission chose to support the principle of absolute patriarchal authority for its own ends.

The mission came to raise small children through a variety of means. However, one of the most important was the dedication of a child by converted men—missionaries made special requests to their prayer partners to pray that more such children would make their way into mission hands. In the case of the following request, the emphasis was on access to impressionable girl children to become brides for the young male converts now reaching the age to marry: "We thank the Lord for each of these little ones who are being taught in the Christian life at this early, impressionable age. In a special way do we feel the need for girls to be brought up under christian [*sic*] teaching in order that they may be the help to their future husbands which they ought to be. We want you to pray with us that the Lord will continue to send us girls, that they may help in the furtherance of the Gospel, after they have come to know the way of salvation."[23]

The exhortation to turn over children—in particular girls—to the mission was so powerful that by 1945 church elders were asked to ponder whether it was appropriate to have church members dedicate their children to the church on the same day that they brought their obligatory tithe, known in Hausa as *zakka*.[24] The elders determined that it might be better to separate the two "gifts"—children would be presented shortly after Christmas instead.[25] But the slippage toward the objectification of children is rather striking here.

The Contemporary Bikin Suna as Public Performance Event

So far I have argued that the growth of the minority Christian community from the 1950s to the 1970s depended critically on the capacity of the mission to lay claim to young children susceptible to socialization into Christianity, and that the foundations for that expansion were laid in the 1930s and 1940s through the regulation of child-fostering and -naming ceremonies. However, the Christian bikin suna today is far more than a simple ritual transaction between a Christian convert and the mission. It is a highly public event that provides an occasion for public preaching. SIM was not technically permitted under French colonial rule to evangelize in public, in fact it was in theory forbidden to evangelize at all. But in practice the French administration generally understood that the mission would take little interest in Niger if it did not have the potential to attract converts and therefore turned a blind eye to the mission's evangelism so long as it did not involve public preaching. The bikin suna provided a rare opportunity to preach openly and publicly, ostensibly in a sermon directed at the Christian community. The bikin suna was seized upon as the ideal vehicle for broadcasting the significance of Christian scriptures and for making public the Christian community's claim on particular children.

At present, Christians of the Maradi region take advantage of the reality that in Niger, any event, such as a bikin suna, that breaks the monotony of life in a provincial city or village will draw a large crowd of young and curious onlookers. Muslim families hold a ceremony eight days after the birth of a child outside the father's home. Muslim scholars will be invited as well as friends, neighbors, and kin. The

The Implications of Reproductive Politics

ceremony occurs very early in the morning before the work of the day has begun. Women gather inside the compound, crowding the mother and baby in a room decorated with heavy wall hangings, smoky with incense. Men sit on mats in front of the home, and it is they who actually listen to the speech of a Muslim scholar who will choose a name. Within about five minutes the name has been chosen, and there will be noisy ululations as the women inside receive the news. Everyone will share a meal together and a ram will be sacrificed as alms and the meat are distributed. Muslim men regard the purchase of such a ram as an absolutely necessary expense and will borrow money at high rates of interest to meet this obligation.

The evangelical Christian variant on this serves a function, as I mentioned, somewhat akin to infant baptism. However, unlike a real baptism, which is not treated as an event suitable for the participation of Muslims, this ceremony is intended to include and attract non-Christians in the audience. The men gather outside the home of the couple, the women inside, and the bikin suna is carried out early in the morning. At first the event seems indistinguishable from a Muslim ceremony. But the naming event among Muslims occurs very quickly, and in reality the name chosen often has little social significance by comparison with the highly evocative nicknames more commonly used in ordinary life. Christians have a very different relationship to the name itself. The parents choose a biblical name, and they invite a pastor to offer a sermon reflecting on the meaning of that name for the gathered Christian community. The child is not kept hidden inside the compound, but is brought out to the doorway and joyously displayed to the crowd, as if to demonstrate a lack of fear of the evil eye—the Christian God will protect this child. When describing the difference between Christian and Muslim bikin suna, Christians never fail to note that the child is brought out for public viewing. The display is one way of establishing the community's claim on the child. In effect Christians use the name as an occasion to preach to the Muslim kin, neighbors, and curious onlookers some key values of Christianity, some key texts, and something about the nature of Christian community. Because public preaching to evangelize is not permitted, but naming ceremonies cannot be forbidden, these ceremonies have become one of the most important ways in which the Christian community reaches beyond the walls of the church.

"A large captive audience is exposed to nothing less than a full gospel message taking up to an hour. This is a culturally acceptable way in a country that does not allow open proclamation in other circumstances."²⁶ Contemporary naming ceremonies provide an opportunity for a zealous evangelical Christian man to stage in a quite lengthy and public manner his Christian status. The evening before the biki he might play Christian music that circulates on cassette tapes (and occasionally on the radio) through amplifiers at his house, and he might choose to play one of the sermons that circulate on cassette through the same system as a kind of warm-up for the event. Thus the circulation of Christian music and sermons in cassette form finds a moment of broadcasting that is simultaneously familial and public.

Christian men who take evangelism seriously put a great deal of thought into how they can seize upon their wives' successful production of a child to stage an audibly impressive event, spending hours choosing music and segments of sermons. The father may put up lights and assemble chairs in front of his compound to attract young men to chat and listen late into the night. The following day the actual bikin suna will occur, attracting a large and visible crowd. Chairs and mats will be made available in abundance to accommodate the crowd, which will include neighbors, friends, and kin who are not Christian. Once again an amplification system may be deployed to expand the range of the event beyond the immediate onlookers, so that it can be heard beyond the walls of neighboring compounds. Thus women in seclusion may also hear the celebration. The walls of the compound will be very permeable after the ceremony, so that women of all backgrounds may enter the compound, visit the mother and give a small gift, and admire the baby.

As Birgit Meyer has argued in the context of Pentecostalism, the use of loudspeakers, which has become such a prominent feature of religious competition in Africa today, is not simply to reach the congregation inside a church (or a mosque) but is also a way "to communicate one's presence to the world outside. The fact that 'being heard' means 'being there' indicates how Pentecostalism seeks to capture public space not only through images but also through sound."²⁷ Evangelical Christians in Maradi similarly stake a claim to public presence through this kind of audible celebration, in this case not in the context of a church but strikingly in the home of a church member in the midst of a neighborhood that may be largely Muslim.

Focusing on the name itself in the sermon provides precisely the kind of bridge evangelists tend to seize upon between Christianity and Islam. All the Old Testament names will be familiar to Muslims, although the Qur'anic forms of those names are often slightly different than the forms used in the Christian community. Similarly the stories attached to those names may differ in subtle ways. Many New Testament names are also well known, but little may be known about the nature of the community that values those names. Thus the naming ceremony offers an unusually rich occasion to articulate the differences and commonalities between Christianity and Islam while emphatically "naming" a child as a member of the Christian milieu.

Christian weddings also have a significant performative dimension, although the practice of holding such weddings in a church reduces the likelihood that a Muslim audience can be drawn. Like a bikin suna, there may be events leading up to the wedding outside the home of the bride or groom in which music is played over loudspeakers and lights are put up to attract young people to visit and chat in the evening. The wedding ceremonies I have seen were deliberately held outside in the church courtyard to accommodate the crowd rather than inside the church building. Many Muslims did in fact attend without actually having to enter the church.

While a Muslim wedding in Maradi does not entail the public appearance of the bride and groom together at the actual religious ceremony, it is an event that involves the groom and the male kin of the bride and groom. Sometimes the bride and groom are not even in the same village or country at the time of the formal ceremony. For Christians, the couple itself is at the center of the ceremony. Their parents may or may not even be present—in the earliest weddings of converts it was often a missionary who more or less stood in as parent. When Christians describe the difference between their weddings and a Muslim ceremony, they comment that a Christian ceremony is one in which there are questions. By this they mean that for Muslims the public consent of both bride and groom are not necessary, and indeed given the youth of the bride in many cases (Muslim girls may marry as young as thirteen, and in exceptional cases even younger), it would be difficult to stage "consent" in any convincing manner. Some of the traditional ceremonies, now falling into decline, would even require the bride to attempt to run away (in play?) until the groom gives her and her girlfriends small gifts. For Christians, it is this public response to the questions, Do you take this man? Do you take this woman? that is absolutely distinctive. It highlights women's choice in marriage and the sense that Christian marriage entails the creation of a couple, and that couple in marrying enter as full adults into a broad community—their marriage is not a marriage simply between two families. The public pairing is related to the emphasis on monogamy, a choice of the one partner for life patterned after God's creation of Eve to be Adam's helpmeet. There will be no other members of this marriage. One can easily understand why, when Christian men decide to violate their Christian monogamy, they cannot do so through a Christian marriage.

Once the naming or wedding ceremony is over, the occasion for broadcasting is not yet complete. Bulletins listing such events will be read in evangelical churches throughout the country. Furthermore, Christians invest scarce funds to have information about names, naming ceremonies, and weddings relayed over the radio through the independent radio station. To someone unfamiliar with the social terrain of Niger, the lengthy announcements of family events over the radio is tedious and a bit mystifying. But through such radio announcements, individuals once again make public their success in creating Christian households and in reproducing. They show their willingness to dedicate a child to the Christian community and to be publicly known as part of the Christian community. Christians elsewhere in Niger thereby gain news of their friends and family. At the same time, Muslims are made conscious of the presence of Christians, of the vitality of their community, and of the tenacity with which they lay claim to their women and children. The airwaves carry other interesting news with implications for the perception of community and population, such as name changes of individuals who convert and movements of functionaries from one post to another in the country.

MUCH OF the literature on religion and the media emphasizes too forcefully the use of media in contests with the state.[28] It seems to me that the consideration of reproductive politics suggests that media (broadly construed to include public performance that both deploys mass media and that can itself be disseminated in mass form) are significant not so much against the state but in the context of the state. Perceptions of population size are important in part because the rhetoric of democracy implies a quantification of power—populations are counted and then they vote, and resources and influence will be distributed accordingly. It is important for Christians as well as Muslims that they *count*. The fact that in Niger such systematic census taking is honored more in the breach than the observance does not seem to diminish the sense that numbers count. In fact, in the absence of "real" numbers, these techniques of community formation and broadcasting may take on even more importance as a means of staking a claim to the public sphere in Niger. At the same time, Muslim and Christian populations today encounter a media context that is saturated with messages emanating from international and national institutions that promote, whether openly or not, population *reduction*. This broader media context is therefore quite complex—communities struggle to be seen and to count in a state that seems determined to deploy statistics and population counting largely in the service of population reduction.

As the secular orientation of the state of Niger is increasingly under fire, however, it seems clear to me that the state, too, needs Christians to count. A visible, audible, credible Christian presence in Niger makes it more possible for the state to argue against a narrow equation of "Nigérien citizen" with "Muslim voter."[29] The evangelical Christian presence provides a counterpublic that is not so much counter to the state as counter to a notion of the public as narrowly Muslim, or of Christians as inevitably Catholic, or of non-Muslims as inevitably pagan. Hence despite the many tensions that permitting a lively public sphere has created, the Nigérien state has fitfully supported the emergence of a variety of radio stations and newspapers through which the kind of population "broadcasting" I have described above occurs. While freedom of the press is regularly under siege, the ostensibly secular state nevertheless seems to recognize that the elimination of a diverse public culture would not be in its interest.

Moreover, because this subtle announcement of who is and who is not Christian does not on the face of it appear to be political, argumentative, or offensive, its very quotidian nature has meant that it has been largely ignored by an occasionally censorious state, by Muslim protesters more inflamed by Pentecostal sermons, and by scholars (including myself) more drawn to spectacular moments of confrontation. In a way, the brilliance of the bikin suna, and of the affiliated media it draws on and employs, is that they cannot readily be critiqued. In conjunction with broader popular performative modes, media can be used in ways that are innocent of preaching or polemic but that nevertheless are part of the self-constitution and *pronouncement of community*. This self-proclamation is at the same time a declaration of autochthony, for by deploying the familiar vehicle of the bikin suna, Christians mark themselves as participating in the familiar texture of local life, as being indigenous—not Western or alien. Indeed, it is this very "Hausa" texture to the bikin suna among Christians in Maradi that occasionally prompts criticism by other Christians differently situated nationally and ethnically.

Thus the use of the media is very much something that must be read and understood in the context of national competition, just as competition over population occurs in a national register. Nevertheless, the modes of making public are bound up in locality—in ethnic style and vernacular culture. The bikin suna becomes the vehicle par excellence of simultaneously engaging with and rendering Christianity distinct from Muslim Hausa culture. We need to embed our discussions of the media in much broader practices and performances. The question of how populations make themselves visible and audible—and therefore countable—is likely to guide us toward questions that are less immediately spectacular but that begin to help us account for subtle phenomena such as those noted by Appadurai and Johnson-Hanks around the politics of reproduction. Considering new media (such as radio, television, and cassette sermons) in isolation from older performative modes (such as the bikin suna) renders those media perhaps more exotic than they should be and at the same time occludes the subtle linkages between the registers of the body, the family, and the community on the one hand, and the state and international institutions on the other.

What is at issue here is not so much identity as the very constitution of a body of adherents, some of whom are far too young to have an identity. The Christian community does not exist in advance and then deploy the media. One might just as readily argue that individuals create a Christian public by using the media (broadly construed) to call a community into being.[30] The media in the context of religious competition are simultaneously the site of expression of identity or community and a means of constituting that community, of staking a claim. Those struggles can have implications for the shape and style of family formation, for the definition of gender roles, and for ongoing generational tensions.

The tendency in the study of religion and media to focus on divinity and the demonic to the exclusion of the mundane and profane has meant that it inevitably emphasizes particular charismatic figures at the expense of broader populations and communities. We often know much more about preachers (or Muslim leaders) than we do about members of the churches (or mosques) they lead. There has been surprisingly little work done on how media serve in unspectacular ways to convey news and information about individuals, families, churches, and so on, with implications for demarcating and protecting those communities. It is through this kind of subtle signaling, broadcasting, and rendering oneself audible or visible, I would suggest, that minority communities telegraph their presence to the majorities that surround them, making claims to being distinctive, autochthonous, and transnational all at once. While all parties to Niger's unruly public culture have the potential to telegraph similar messages, Christians appear to be particularly adept at this stitching of local performance with new media to make themselves count. This politics of numbers occurs as Muslim communities experience themselves as being under siege by international donors intent on reducing their numbers. It is hardly surprising, therefore, that when Muslims and Christians clash, perceptions about women's sexual behavior, anxieties about fertility, and mistrust of the state and international agents seem all to come to a head.

Notes

1. Jennifer Johnson-Hanks, "On the Politics and Practice of Muslim Fertility: Comparative Evidence from West Africa," *Medical Anthropology Quarterly* 20, no. 1 (2006): 21.

2. Ibid., 14.

3. Ibid.

4. Arjun Appadurai, *Fear of Small Numbers: An Essay in the Geography of Anger* (Durham, NC: Duke University Press, 2006).

5. Barbara M. Cooper, "Anatomy of a Riot: The Social Imaginary, Single Women, and Religious Violence in Niger," *Canadian Journal of African Studies* 37, nos. 2–3 (2003): 467–512.

6. Appadurai, *Fear*, 43.

7. Eliza Griswold, "God's Country," *Atlantic Monthly*, March 2008, www.theatlantic.com/doc/200803/nigeria.

8. Cooper, "Anatomy"; Barbara M. Cooper, "Population and Piety: Demographic Imperatives and Sudan Interior Mission Interventions in the Sahel, 1930–1960," paper presented at fiftieth anniversary meeting, African Studies Association, New York, October 18, 2007.

9. SIM now stands for "serving in mission." See http://www.sim.org.

10. Barbara M. Cooper, *Evangelical Christians in the Muslim Sahel* (Bloomington: Indiana University Press, 2006); Cooper, "Population."

11. See also Nancy Rose Hunt, "'Le bébé en brousse': European Women, African Birth Spacing, and Colonial Intervention in Breast Feeding in the Belgian Congo," in *Tensions of Empire: Colonial Cultures in a Bourgeois World*, ed. Frederick Cooper and Ann Laura Stoler (Berkeley: University of California Press, 1997), 287–321; Hunt, *A Colonial Lexicon of Birth Ritual, Medicalization, and Mobility in the Congo* (Durham, NC: Duke University Press, 2003).

12. Barbara M. Cooper, "La rhétorique de la 'mauvaise mère,'" in *Niger 2005: Une catastrophe si naturelle*, ed. Xavier Crombé and Jean-Hervé Jézéquel (Paris: Karthala, 2007), 199–226.

13. Pastor Cherif Yacouba, interview by author, Maradi, October 24, 2000.

14. Marcia Wright, *Strategies of Slaves and Women: Life-Stories from East/Central Africa* (New York: Lilian Barber, 1993).

15. Dorothy Hodgson, *The Church of Women: Gendered Encounters between Maasai and Missionaries* (Bloomington: Indiana University Press, 2005).

16. Tsibiri church records (hereafter cited as TCR), "List of Professing Christians 1933," 1933–58, SR-2, box 188 (Fort Mill, SC: SIM International Archive).

17. TCR, "Letter from D. V. and D. M. Osborne to 'Dear Friend,'" May 1930.

18. TCR, "Le procès-verbal," elders' meeting, October 2, 1945.

19. TCR, "Le procès-verbal," elders' meeting, February 5, 1946.

20. TCR, "Le procès-verbal," elders' meeting, March 5, 1946.

21. TCR, "Le procès-verbal," elders' meeting, June 4, 1946.

22. TCR, Resumes 1930, 45 SR 2/A, 188.

23. TCR, "Letter from Marie Schroeder to 'Dear Prayer Partner, June 1944,'" SR 2/A, 188.

24. TCR, "L'ordre du jour," elders' meeting, October 2, 1945.

25. TCR, "Le procès-verbal," elders' meeting, October 2, 1945.

26. PDRM\Isch (Projet de Développement Rurale de Maradi), "Report on the Spiritual Impact of the Maradi Integrated Development Project" (1989): 3.

27. Birgit Meyer, "Impossible Representations: Pentecostalism, Vision, and Video Technology in Ghana," in *Religion, Media, and the Public Sphere*, ed. Meyer and Annelies Moors (Bloomington: Indiana University Press, 2006), 296; see also Meyer, chap. 7 of this volume.

28. Dale Eickelman and Jon W. Anderson, eds., *New Media in the Muslim World: The Emerging Public Sphere* (Bloomington: Indiana University Press, 1999).

29. Dorothea E. Schulz, "Morality, Community, Publicness: Shifting Terms of Public Debate in Mali," in Meyer and Moors, *Religion, Media*, 134; cf. Charles Hirschkind, *The Ethical Soundscape: Cassette Sermons and Islamic Counterpublics* (New York: Columbia University Press, 2006).

30. For similar observations, see Birgit Meyer and Annelies Moors, introduction to Meyer and Moors, *Religion, Media*, 1–25.

FIVE

Public Debates about Luo Widow Inheritance
Christianity, Tradition, and AIDS in Western Kenya

RUTH PRINCE

> Nyanza Luos could face extinction in six years due to AIDS, two leaders said yesterday.... A one-day seminar opened by [the] Provincial Commissioner ... was told that wife inheritance and certain traditional norms were critical factors contributing to the high AIDS toll among the Luo population.
>
> —"Luos Facing Extinction," *Daily Nation* (Nairobi)

> What is the value of this program on Luo custom? We are taking our people backward; we stop their development and keep them from knowing God and the ways of today!
>
> —listener to the radio program *Chike Luo*

SINCE THE 1990s Luo culture, in the form of the levirate, or so-called widow inheritance, has become the focus of heated public debate in western Kenya and beyond in relation to the HIV/AIDS pandemic.[1] Reports in the East African media, such as the article quoted above from the *Daily Nation*, as well as scientific articles, link widow inheritance to a high HIV prevalence among the Luo population in western Kenya, while NGOs, church groups, international organizations, and government officials organize campaigns to combat widow inheritance. Media reports and international conferences on AIDS, the Web sites of

NGOs such as Human Rights Watch, and Christian newsletters feed the global circulation of this knowledge. Framed in terms of risk and individual rights, they create a powerful discourse linking Luo widow inheritance to infection, patriarchy, and the oppression of women.

These attacks on Luo culture are countered by a vocal defense of "Luo tradition" and widow inheritance, known in the Dholuo language as *tero mon* (to take a woman or wife), or simply *tero*, as the center of Luo identity, cultural continuity, and the restoration of sociomoral order in what is regarded as the present era of confusion. While HIV/AIDS has become known as a Luo illness, widow inheritance has, for some, become a focus of negotiations about what it means to be a Luo in a world in which the Luo, together with other Africans, find themselves at the margin. Refuting the association of the practice with infection and death, widow inheritance here becomes a key to the resuscitation of growth. Some Luo claim in a traditionalist idiom that the rejection of widow inheritance by Westernized, urban, or born-again Luo, and the infringement of so-called Luo traditions by widows who refuse inheritance, are both a symptom of the decay of moral values and moral community, and a cause of what people describe as "the death of today" (*tho tinende*), as people disregard the traditional rules that hold kinship groups together. Calls abound therefore for a stricter adherence to tero. Placed at the center of regeneration or growth, tero becomes a condition of both ethnic identity and family and community survival. In the village of Uhero, where I have conducted fieldwork since 1997, such debates about widow inheritance and tradition have been common in everyday conversations, while tensions have often surfaced around widows and tero, particularly around funerals. Public debates about widow inheritance in relation to tradition, Christianity, and more recently, AIDS, also dominate Dholuo-language Internet sites, radio programs, newspapers, and magazines; while numerous Dholuo-language publications promote Luo tradition.

Observers and activists who oppose widow inheritance tend to assume an absence of public debate about Luo tradition among Luo people and present their struggle as that of ahistorical tradition meeting modern public health and development campaigns—of educating the Luo community to evaluate and give up its "age-old" traditions. However, Luo people have been occupied during much of the past century in debating about themselves—about the value and content of Luo culture, of identity, personhood, moral community, progress, and the sociomoral order. Christianity has played a role in these public debates, because Christianity and colonialism introduced the binary opposition between Christianity and tradition and thus shaped the moral language and categories of the debates, and also because the majority of Luo are Christian and such debates have been to a large extent about the relation between Christian and Luo identity.[2] Although those who attack widow inheritance tend to assert that it is un-Christian or even anti-Christian (and antimodern), many of those who defend it are Christian and, moreover, draw on the language of Christianity. Hence the debate is more about how to be Christian, and about the relationship between Luo and Christian identity, than about whether or not to be Christian.

Historical debates among Luo people about widow inheritance and other practices that make up Luo tradition have played a critical role in Luo imaginations of themselves and the so-called Luo Nation.[3] They have thus shaped the emergence of a Dholuo-speaking public—if we define the public, following Michael Warner, by the circulation of discourse[4]—in the sense that a public debates about itself and exists by virtue of being addressed. Following these debates underlines that this public culture is highly politicized, as it is a space in which, over the past century, issues of moral conduct and moral community have come under critical scrutiny.

Tero Past and Present

The levirate, the continuation of a creative marital union after the death of a husband by one of his classificatory brothers, has been described as a characteristic of Nilotic societies.[5] According to the oldest published account of Luo customs,[6] in the early twentieth century tero was a matter of belonging to a place and group. In this patrilineal, virilocal society, the man who would take a deceased husband's place (*jater*, one who takes [the widow]) ensured the widow's continued attachment to her husband's group, and her children's belonging to this group and its place. If a woman was widowed while of child-bearing age, she could continue to have children in her dead husband's name and they could make claims to patrilineal land.

The choice of the man took time. A year or so after bereavement, the family met and the widow (*chi liel*, wife of the grave) chose a jater from her husband's patriliny. The couple's first intercourse was referred to as *ng'ado* (cutting) the liminal mourning period of *chola*.[7] The widow's hair was shaved, and amid celebrations she was given a new skirt made of animal skins, marking her renewed status as a wife. A ritual meal was shared by jater, widow, and children. The widow continued to stay in her husband's home and to feed her family from her gardens; her jater participated in building her a new house and in ritual, but he was apparently not obliged to support the widow economically and did not normally live with her, as he usually was a married man living in his own family compound.[8] Tero ensured that widows' procreative capacities remained within her husband's lineage, while providing security for the widow and her children.[9]

Until the early 1980s, tero was mainly practiced within the agnatic group,[10] but since then it has changed substantially. First, in many cases the act of sexual intercourse has become central to the rituals of tero, which are in some cases even reduced to it. The focus on sexual cleansing is reflected in the emphasis placed on the "traditional rules" (*chike*) surrounding tero rather than on the responsibilities of the levirate. On losing her husband, a widow is said to enter a state of chola, in which she cannot continue daily life. Her movements are restricted; she cannot eat with her children, and she poses a danger to others, particularly those who are also in a vulnerable, transitional state (such as new mothers and newborns). Her incapacity to act extends to her adult children, who are blocked in their future pathways (for example, sons should not build their own houses). This state of chola, also referred to as *chilo* (dirt), is lifted only when the widow is sexually united with another man who cuts the chola. Alone, she is dangerously incomplete; after sexual intercourse she can reenter normal everyday life. After cleansing the widow, the jater is supposed to build a new house for her, as she cannot stay in the house that her dead husband built, but this practice receives less emphasis than that of sexual cleansing. Although earlier sources on Luo customs mention the widow's chola,[11] it appears that over the course of the twentieth century the traditional rules or prohibitions that surround the widow have become more stringent and rigorously applied and explicitly focused on the sexual act rather than the broader rituals that involve the wider kin group. While in the past a widow could apparently wait for a year or more before she found a jater, at present she is often under pressure by her in-laws to get sexually cleansed weeks or even days after the death of her husband. If she refuses tero, she is often accused of blocking the growth of her children and bringing misfortune and sickness to her family.

Second, in recent years it has become more common for a "professional" inheritor or jater to sexually cleanse the widow, and he is usually paid for it, as the widow's male agnates are reluctant to risk HIV infection. The jater is also supposed to build the widow a new house, but people complain that itinerant *jotero* often leave before completing this work. In this case, tero is performed like a job, paid for and consummated on the spot—leading many Luo to argue that tero has become a business (*ohala*). Moreover, the sexual cleansing ritual has come to substitute for the responsibilities of the levirate, allowing the widow's affines to argue that they have no further obligations toward her.

Third, in a situation of increasing land scarcity and poverty, tero has also become a means through which a widow's in-laws attempt to gain control over her husband's land and property. Over the last decade there have been numerous reports—filed by Kenyan and foreign researchers, journalists, NGOs, and churches—about Luo widows, and sometimes their children, being forced off their husband's land and their property confiscated by in-laws. During my fieldwork there were several conflicts between widows and their in-laws about land and property, even in cases when the widow went through sexual cleansing, and many mothers were taking in their widowed daughters who had been forced to leave the husband's home.

From the limited evidence at our disposal, it would seem that these shifts in the practices of tero occurred in the past two decades and are related to distinct, but connected, historical developments: impoverishment and land scarcity, and AIDS. Due to the breakdown of Kenya's formal economy and the associated loss of the wage-earning opportunities that for long have sustained household income in rural Nyanza Province, people increasingly rely on their assets, especially land, to pay for school fees, bridewealth, building, medicines, and funerals.[12] Together with the transfer of land into individual and alienable private property,[13] and compounded by mounting demographic pressure, land has become scarce.[14] Struggles to possess land have ensued among families and within lineages, in which men usually are the dominant actors.[15] Men's control over land (and women), bolstered by colonial designations of them as household heads and the importance of patrilineality in customary law, was enhanced by postcolonial tenure reform and commoditization of land.[16] With land titles and the associated practice of personal property devolution, a man's death implies competition for his property. While gendered relations with land have always been intertwined with marital ties, the concept of individual land ownership means that men can use the law to deny women access to land.¹⁷ Taking the widow now often means taking her title deeds.

The HIV pandemic has further changed tero, most obviously because HIV/AIDS, by killing mainly younger people, has produced a problematic new category of persons—young widows, who have only given birth to few, if any, children; have briefly or never resided in their rural marital homes; and cannot count on much affection, care, or material support from their in-laws when their husband dies. Moreover, young widows are increasingly seen to be spreaders of disease and death, attributed variously to HIV infection or the "traditional" illness *chira*, brought about by breaking the rules of tradition. Their bodies are considered to be polluted and dangerous, threats to the lineage rather than vessels of growth.¹⁸ Questions of ownership become pressing in this situation of strained economic resources, and the young widows' vulnerable position allows such questions to be put forward more boldly.

In sum, various concerns about women's sexuality, marriage, and kinship, together with fears of infection and misfortune, and struggles over land and property, have contributed to an increasingly rigorous and inflexible notion of tradition concerning widows and tero. Rather than protecting women's and their children's belonging to the land, the manipulation of tradition allows the severing of ties between widows, lineage, and land, as the widow's brothers-in-law refuse to take on the long-term responsibilities of tero, while claiming control of their dead brother's land.

A fourth shift in the practices of tero is the refusal of some widows to go through tero, to be sexually cleansed or to be inherited by an in-law. This phenomenon has a long history in western Kenya, which is intertwined with that of Christianity. Mission churches opposed widow inheritance as a form of polygamy, and refusal to follow tero continues to be associated with membership in these churches—in particular with being saved or born again within the Anglican revivalist movement that took hold in western Kenya in the 1940s—as well as with Pentecostal churches. Saved or born-again Christians refuse tero because they consider it heathen and backward. The degree to which saved widows have been able to refuse tero depends, however, to a large extent on their in-laws' support or, if that is lacking, on their economic independence and thus ability to make their own choices. Opposition to tero and other Luo traditions within the Anglican Church and the revivalist movement, together with the perceived independence of saved and urban women, contributed to the traditionalist backlash and the consolidation of traditional rules around tero as well as other practices.

Fighting Widow Inheritance: Tradition, Patriarchy, and Infection

From the early 1990s onward widow inheritance emerged as a prominent issue of public debate, in the context of both the HIV/AIDS pandemic and struggles for women's rights and gender equality in Kenya. The high rates of infection in western Kenya began to capture much public attention both nationally and internationally and to be linked with the Luo tradition of widow inheritance. An epidemiological study argued that widow inheritance encouraged the spread of HIV;[19] scientific papers reported that there were many young widows, that many widows were HIV positive, and that many widows were inherited by being sexually cleansed.[20] A body of research by Kenyan and foreign social scientists emerged, which focused on AIDS, culture, widow inheritance, and the demography and epidemiology of widows in Kenya and elsewhere.[21] While there is no scientific evidence of the role of tero in HIV transmission,[22] the culturalist explanation of the Luo HIV pandemic gained wide acceptance in Kenya and beyond.[23]

These issues have been intensely reported in the East African and world media. An early article on the subject in the *Daily Nation*, quoted at the beginning of this chapter, reported that "wife inheritance and certain traditional norms were critical factors contributing to the high AIDS toll among the Luo population" and that "Nyanza Luos could face extinction in six years due to AIDS."[24] More recently, there has been a steady stream of articles on the association between widow inheritance, culture, and HIV/AIDS. The articles report that widows' affines are not only forcing them to be inherited but are appropriating their land, property, and other assets.

Luo women's vulnerability, through the institution of widow inheritance, to HIV/AIDS, landlessness, and poverty has been taken up by national and international advocacy groups, NGOs, churches, and Christian mission groups[25] that for diverse motives seek to "empower" widows to reject tradition, resist male domination and sexual oppression, make choices and exercise rights, and take control of their lives. Thus, local and international NGOs create and support widows' groups in Nyanza, and human rights groups seek to address widows' property rights and the discrimination against women in customary law, as well as promoting a rights-based response to the HIV pandemic.[26] Evangelical groups such as Springs Ministries, started in Kisumu by a Luo widow funded by Christian groups in North America, have encouraged the formation of widows' groups around shared identities of being born again, organized "widows' workshops," and supported widows' refusal of tero through providing training and microcredit.[27] And members of the Luo Council of Elders—a body that in recent years has risen to prominence as an authority in matters pertaining to Luo culture (see below)—are invited by USAID and other donor agencies to workshops on this pertinent problem.[28]

Churches have added a diversity of voices to these debates about widow inheritance, culture, gender relations, and infection. Some, such as Legio Maria, an independent offshoot of the Catholic Church, continue to support tero, while the growing numbers of Pentecostal and evangelical churches in Kenya actively oppose it. After a century of opposition, the Anglican and Catholic Churches have been involved in more subtle negotiations about reshaping tero. For example, the Catholic Church serving Uhero and nearby villages attempts to take over the role of the jater, including the building and blessing of a new house by the priest, and the sharing of a ritual meal by the widow and her church group members in the new house. Within the Anglican Church of Kenya, some clergymen suggest that a widow's sexual needs should be acknowledged and propose to allow widows to remarry in church, but not before establishing the HIV/AIDS status of their late husbands in order to discourage wife inheritance.

These alliances between Christians, human rights activists, feminists, and scientists in the struggle against widow inheritance and for women's rights have emerged in the context of increasing donor support for civil society and of a proliferation of NGOs working on issues of gender inequality, law, and human rights. After the government's violent crackdown on pro-democracy protesters in 1990, major donors such as the United States made aid conditional on political and legal reform and poured money into supporting civil society against the state.[29] This shift, together with the emergence of western Kenya as an epicenter of the HIV/AIDS pandemic in East Africa, and of the AIDS industry around it, has opened up a space for discussion and promotion of human rights and women's rights—through workshops, seminars, politicians' speeches, policy documents, and development and HIV/AIDS projects. The rights-bearing individual subject—and associated discourses of women's empowerment, gender equality, choice, and freedom—is here promoted as both the means of fighting the HIV pandemic and the basis for the proper development of Kenyan society so as to reduce poverty and improve the quality of life.

"The problem of widow inheritance among the Luo" thus presents a mélange of interrelating arguments, circulated among diverse actors and audiences across different scales, linking local controversies to global institutions and ideologies and connecting scientists to church members, feminists to new and old conservatives. While there are moves to seek compromises, the bulk of church, NGO, government, and media discourse about widow inheritance is negative. Like earlier Christian struggles against widow inheritance, and broader colonial opposition to African culture, it proposes a radical opposition, which in contemporary moral language pits modernity and science (and, for some, Christianity) together with freedom, equality, universal rights, and health against tradition, superstition, patriarchy, oppression, and infection. Rather than recognizing the multiplicity of relations that can take shape around it, tero is here interpreted only within the framework of gender antagonism and regressive tradition. The experience of dispossessed widows shows that tero as practiced today can indeed serve the domination and control of women by men, but it should be clear that this is only one aspect of a complex situation. Focusing on culture misses the point when trying to address widows' plight—empowerment and choice are premised on economic possibilities and not cultural scripts.

Moreover, while much of this discussion about widow inheritance, tradition, and infection seems to assume that Luo tradition is only now meeting history, in the guise of the HIV/AIDS pandemic and attempts to combat it, Luo people have in fact been engaging in a critical conversation about Luo tradition since long before the pandemic. From the early decades of the twentieth century, issues concerning identity that have often focused on women's behavior, gender relations, and proper conduct have come under public scrutiny and have been publicly debated.

Christianity, Luo Tradition, and Widow Inheritance

Since the early decades of the twentieth century, Christian opposition to Luo culture, together with the perceived loss of traditional morality associated with labor migration and urban life, have fed into a debate among ordinary Luo migrants as well as among intellectuals and the educated elite about the value of Luo culture and so-called traditional morality. Such debates have themselves taken shape among concerns about marriage, kinship, ethnic identity, and the construction of the Luo nation.[30] The Luo Union, which emerged during the 1930s among Luo urban migrants and which grew to boast thousands of members across East Africa, was an organization that explicitly promoted itself as a defender of Luo identity and culture, using the slogan *Riwuok e teko* (unity is strength).[31] It took an active role in policing the moral boundaries of being Luo. During the 1950s, for example, urban members began rounding up single Luo women living in Nairobi and Kisumu and sending them back to rural Nyanza.[32] This project of Luo "moral ethnicity"[33] was supported by the founding of the Kisumu printing press and by Dholuo-language publications such as the magazine *Ramogi*, which circulated widely. Meanwhile Luo intellectuals were constructing the history of the Luo nation[34] and writing nostalgic ethnographies of the society and culture they grew up in, which they feared was being forgotten or rejected.[35]

While traditionalists often opposed the polarity between Christianity and modernity on the one hand, and Luo tradition and Luo identity on the other—arguing that one can be both Christian and Luo—it is notable that such polarities still shaped the terms of the debate.[36] As Webb Keane shows in the case of Indonesia,[37] engaging in debates with Christians forces even those who argue against them to position themselves within binary patterns, which differ from previous modes of debate in the introduction of a new spatiotemporal framework (before-then, self-other, us-them). Tradition was thus fashioned in the face of Christianity.[38]

In 1987 the conflict that gripped one of Kenya's leading elite families over where and how to bury the Luo lawyer S. M. Otieno brought arguments about tradition, identity, and patriarchy versus Christianity, modernity and women's rights onto the national stage.[39] Otieno's Gĩkũyũ widow, Wambui, argued that theirs had been a Christian, modern marriage, that Otieno did not follow traditions, and that, as his wife, she had the right under Kenyan law to bury him in Nairobi. However, it was the argument brought forth by Otieno's brother and other clan members— that Otieno should be buried according to Luo custom and tradition in his rural homeland, and that customary law rather than the a person's lifestyle should govern the decision—that was eventually upheld. David Cohen and E. S. Atieno Odhiambo suggest that the decision in favor of the clan was more acceptable to "the core of power constituted in Kenya by the office of the President, in the person of Daniel Arap Moi and in the interests and resources of a male, polygamous and patriarchal African national bourgeoisie"[40] than a decision in favor of Wambui's argument for women's individual rights. This was in the political context during the 1980s of strict control over individual expression and over the media, and in a public culture of patriarchy.[41] In the late 1980s churches provided the few voices of opposition to Moi's regime, but Wambui's arguments about Christian and modern identity and women's rights, and her identification with activist churches—in the midst of the law case, she announced that she had become born again—did not succeed against the powerful patriarchal and authoritarian interests of the state.

We can understand these concerns about moral ethnicity, the sociomoral order, and Luo identity in part as a response to moral panics concerning the increasing independence of women and their challenges to the patriarchal gendered, generational, and kinship order supported by the colonial and postcolonial state. While in the 1940s and 1950s literate Luo, mainly male, were writing passionate articles in *Ramogi* about Luo moral values and female challenges to them, by the 1960s Luo migrants in Nairobi were tightening controls over their compatriots' behavior through their elaboration of "Luo rules" that, if broken, would lead to the illness chira.[42] By the turn of the twenty-first century, these rules had become extremely elaborate and extensive,[43] to the extent that they pervaded and invaded almost every aspect of daily life.[44]

"Tero Is Our Culture"

Debates about traditional order and cultural practices were prominent in the village where I conducted fieldwork. People were concerned that the rejection of tradition by, for example, saved, or born-again, Christians and the urban elite was undermining family relations and shared sociomoral order, but also that the use of unrelated, professional inheritors was turning tero into a business and displacing it from its proper locus in the home and the patrilineal group. Such debates also took place on the radio, on the Internet, in local newspapers, and in many pamphlets and booklets published in Kisumu and in Nairobi.[45] Many of these traditionalist productions argued that everyday life and kinship relations should be governed by an increasingly codified and absolute body of rules. Thus Raringo's booklet *The Traditional Rules of the Old Man in His Home* lists 330 rules and promises a second volume.[46] This "return" to an authentic traditional sociomoral order promises to recenter Luo moral community in marriage, kinship, and the rural home.

As discussed above, this defense of Luo tradition is not new. Since the 1990s, however, the movement has gained momentum. For some, the HIV/AIDS pandemic lent further weight to arguments against "Western" and in favor of "traditional" values, as people argued that "the death of today" was an expression of the loss of traditional morality. Rejecting the association made between culture and infection—and the wider global discourse about "African AIDS" and "African sexual culture"—traditionalists argued for solutions rooted in "African morality."[47] Traditionalism has been radicalized by the HIV/AIDS pandemic—as arguments about ethnic identity and cultural continuity are now also about ethnic survival—and perhaps also by the increasingly audible discourses on women's rights. Positioned in a dichotomous debate, Luo traditionalism gives the impression of a radical conflict between one and the other and sometimes proposes radical solutions. However, traditionalism continues an ongoing dialogue with and about Christianity, about the relation between Luo and Christian identity, about virtue and moral community, about how to orientate oneself to the past and to the future.

Widow inheritance—linked to sex and infection, sickness and death, and historically to the struggle between tradition and modernity, continuity, and rupture—lies at the center of traditionalist concerns. While economic interests may motivate the pursuit of tero by some widows' in-laws, tero is also highly symbolic of Luo culture. It is therefore not surprising that for some it appears as the "most solemn ritual," around which to collect one's thoughts about the past, present, and future. One of the most striking exponents of these issues is Professor G. E. M. Ogutu, a leading Kenyan academic involved in the Luo Council of Elders, a body that was set up in 1990 as a reborn Luo Union and currently numbers over a hundred members.[48] While the council is often presented in the media as a conservative cultural force, much of Ogutu's work has debated the relations between Luo identity, Christianity, and development. In a small book on "past, present and future Luo thought and practice," Ogutu asks, "Are the traditional Luo beliefs and practices repugnant? Do they retard economic development? . . . Can one be a Christian, educated, wealthy, et cetera, and still remain a Luo in thought and practice?"[49] The book continues the public debate about these issues in the wake of the S. M. Otieno trial mentioned above, the HIV/AIDS pandemic, and continuing opposition among the mainline and Pentecostal churches to Luo tradition and particularly to widow inheritance. Ogutu deplores how contemporary Luo have left their norms of identity [and] violated the covert rules that are intended to govern individual behaviour. The consequence is that the Luo cannot escape being attacked and killed by *chira*, [arising from, e.g.] a widow who has not gone through *tero/golo chola* (widow cleansing and leviratic union) visiting her children in their houses, particularly in towns. . . . Inconsiderate variation of tradition, because one was educated or rich, has led to the loss of many precious lives in Luo society. . . . The worst hit are *Jonanga* (the affluent families or urban salariat) which deny that the rural base could be endowed with a sense of morality, law and order, and who quip that they are too civilised and modern to be guided by archaic Luo norms and values. (13–14)

While the national and international media represent Luo (and, by implication, African) culture as problematic, indeed destructive, Ogutu proposes a firm cultural identity as a solution to Africans' present epidemiological, economic, and epistemological predicament. Underlining his argument's political ambitions, he dedicates his work to "the Luo youth in Diaspora who are being called upon to find and water your roots" (xi). While demanding a place for Luo culture in the contemporary world, and a firm commitment of Luo people to ethnic identity, Ogutu does not advocate parochialism—"We cannot afford to stay outside the modern world" (19)—nor unthinking reproduction of customary practice: "Culture is never static, but responds positively to the forces of change and continuity." "My hope," he writes, "is that the book will stimulate the reader to reflect on what needs to be changed and how?" (24).

Yet Ogutu's position on continuity and change is ambiguous and shifting. In relation to widow inheritance, he agues, "Widow cleansing has turned out to be the most abused and scoffed at ritual and yet it was the most elaborate and solemn ritual among the Luo." He acknowledges that while the practice must be maintained, this may require changes: "Given that the majority of Luo people have converted to Christianity, our church elders should liaise with the traditional elders to determine how to inculturate widow cleansing practices by, for example, formulating special widow/widower cleansing prayer/masses." He even suggests that that "identity-imprinting cultural rites [such as tero] should be put into proper perspective," including, potentially, the replacement of sexual with symbolic intercourse (12). And yet he remains highly ambivalent about possible changes and cautions readers, "Here there is no salvation, no wealth, no education, no foreign or non-Luo origin, no westernisation. Marriage had been sealed by bridewealth and ritually consummated on the nuptial night; and now, a husband is lost, wife and children are left behind, ritual cleansing is the answer. Any unorthodox alternative *ok kony* (will not do)" (25). And he concludes his argument unambiguously in favor of restoration: "We cannot abandon our rituals and survive. They are the *Ngusu mag Piny* (nerve center of our very being as a people)" (26).

The ambiguity in Ogutu's writings should be placed in the context of the broader political project of which they are part. Ogutu's shifting position on tero, calling for both limited adaptation and strict adherence, is reflected in his various engagements with different parties in the ongoing debates about culture, identity, AIDS, and human rights. As a leading figure in the Luo Council of Elders (LCE), he promotes Luo culture and its continuity, yet he has also acted as a cultural adviser on reports produced by Human Rights Watch and USAID on widow inheritance and women's property rights in Kenya.[50] The LCE has taken part in workshops debating widow inheritance, HIV/AIDS, and the question of cultural change with AIDS educators, church leaders, widows' groups, and women's rights activists, and politicians.

Luo politicians have also entered the debates about widow inheritance, as they attempt to position themselves variously as national politicians beyond ethnic politics and as spokesmen for the Luo. For a politician, however, such interventions entail a highly charged situation. This became evident in the heated debate that emerged over the suggestion by the then opposition leader Raila Odinga, during a workshop on AIDS in 1999 attended by Ogutu and other members of the LCE, that the Luo practice of widow inheritance was contributing to the spread of HIV in the Luo populations and that it should be reviewed and even scrapped. Reported in the *Daily Nation*, Odinga's comments enraged Justice Kwach, the lawyer for the clan in the S. M. Otieno case, who told Odinga that he had no authority to discuss Luo culture. Several Luo politicians from rival parties joined in, accusing Odinga of embarrassing the Luo by soliciting funds from donors to hold seminars on culture and AIDS in Nyanza, "as if only Luos were suffering from the disease."[51] They argued that that culture was not responsible for the upsurge in AIDS cases and told Odinga to use the funds donated to the Jaramogi Oginga Odinga Foundation "to fight poverty instead of holding seminars on Luo culture."[52] Odinga denied the accusation that he was encouraging the rejection of cultural practices—"I never discussed these issues," he told a political rally in Kisumu. He challenged Kwach's credentials as an authority on Luo cultural matters and asked Ogutu to write to Kwach to explain what had been discussed.[53]

Questions of the place of Luo tradition in modern Kenya and its relation to progress, development, as well as Christian identities were taken up by the audiences and elders of the radio program *Chike Luo* (Luo Traditions), which discussed Luo culture with a Dholuo-speaking audience and was broadcast on the KBC (Kenya Broadcasting Commission, the state-owned radio station) in 2001. Listeners could write to the program with questions about Luo tradition, which were answered by a panel of "Luo elders" (residents of both rural Nyanza and Nairobi city, and including a councillor and a policeman). During one broadcast the following question, sent in by a young man, was debated: "What is the value of this program on Luo custom? We are taking our people backward; we stop their development and keep them from knowing God and the ways of today!" In his response, an elder argued that tradition was not opposed to Christianity, that "God gave us our culture as well as the Bible," and that the "death of today" was due in large part to the fact that Luo people had forgotten their heritage and left the traditional rules governing kinship and community.

Questions of who the gatekeepers of tradition were, and how far a supposedly traditional practice could be bent to accommodate contemporary life and the HIV/AIDS pandemic, also occupied the program. During one broadcast, an elderly woman asked whether she could twist the rules of tero by building a new house for her widowed daughter-in-law, instead of having the latter taken by a jater and risking HIV infection: "I don't want tero in my home as the world is bad with disease." The radio elders, disinclined to "break the Luo rules," adjudicated against this: "AIDS does not enter into this. Even if she has rings of [herpes zoster, or shingles] around her waist, a jater must take her and she must complete the rules of her husband. This is clear Dholuo." Yet in the following week's broadcast, a different elder reluctantly contemplated innovation. The daughter-in-law of a saved widow, who had "followed chike" in a new way, by spending a night in her church instead of in a house with a jater, asked the program elders if she too could do this when her own husband died. In this way, she argued, she would be following the rules laid out by the preceding generation in her marital home, maintaining the generational sequence and order that the Luo rules demand. "This is difficult!" the elders exclaimed, faced with her very Luo argument, and the advice remained ambiguous: "It means that if your husband dies, you will have to follow what your mother-in-law did and go to sleep in the church. In that way, you follow her wisdom. But is that good? Really?"

The women who posed these questions were trying to cope with the dilemmas of following the Luo rules in the era of AIDS. Their proposals to follow tero but avoid sexual intercourse were mainly rejected by the male radio elders—perhaps because these solutions were not dependent on men. While male traditionalists stress the importance of wives (and widows) for cultural and social continuity, they cannot easily accept that women may take control of chike and threaten the male prerogative to define the rules. Such debates about the rules underline again how they are tied to struggles about power and authority between men and women. However, it would be wrong to reduce the debate to women's progressive struggle for freedom against men's reactionary clinging to patriarchal hierarchy. Women as well as men are searching for a "return" to some form of stability and orientation in troubled times and may be drawing on tradition to do so.

This brings us to questions of power and authority in the debates about widow inheritance, culture, identity, and infection. Who speaks and whose voices are heard? What relation does this circulation of discourse about widow inheritance in the media, on the radio, in print publications, and in development or HIV/AIDS projects have to the issue of tero in people's lives?

Within the traditionalist discourse, male voices dominate. Luo men have, since the early decades of the twentieth century, made use of the press and other media to promote discussion of Luo culture and to create the idea of a Luo nation, while extending its visibility, legitimacy, and authority. Much of traditionalism positions itself against women's independence from men—as expressed in their refusal to follow tero—and against the individualist rights-based discourses of HIV/AIDS and development projects. Traditionalism, and its defense of patriarchal power, has at times been backed up by state power, most noticeably by President Moi during the S. M. Otieno trial discussed above, but also in the fact that neither Kenyan constitutional law nor customary law recognizes the rights of married women to their husband's property.[54] However, more recently, government officials, senior civil servants, as well as Luo politicians have incited controversy among their Luo constituents, by throwing their weight behind the fight against widow inheritance, through endorsing the eradication or modification of widow inheritance on public health grounds.

Traditionalism is also backed up, in everyday life, among ordinary villagers by the circulation of talk about "Luo rules" and their application to the minutiae of daily life as well as events such as funerals and tero. Here, women as well as men, young as well as old, participate in discussions about the Luo rules and how to follow them properly. Moving from the media to everyday life, we thus see a more differentiated sociology of traditionalism. In the current era of what many see as moral decay, many are searching for some moral stability through a "return" to tradition. It is significant that while global and national discourses against widow inheritance promote a language of rights, widows who refuse tero draw instead on the historically deeper and perhaps more resonant language of Christianity. The extent to which opposition to widow inheritance will outlast the projects promoting it remains to be seen, and probably resides with Christian churches. Invoking saved, or born-again, Christian identities appears to provide more legitimacy than the discourse of rights when opposing Luo traditionalism.

IN THIS chapter, I have used debates about widow inheritance to prize open a historically constituted public culture in western Kenya that has been occupied with issues of Luo identity, Christianity, moral personhood, moral community, and progress. Contemporary arguments linking Luo widow inheritance and HIV infection put forward by the assemblage of public health, AIDS, development, and human rights discourses, together with certain churches, have historical precedents in mission Christianity as well as in colonial conflations of African culture and African sexuality with disease.[55] Creating an Other—the traditional, the primitive, the backward—was crucial to the Christian and colonial civilizing mission.[56] Like earlier Christian discourses on African sexual culture, current attacks on widow inheritance also make the intimate sphere of sex and sexuality visible, a subject of public scrutiny. Deploying the contemporary language of individual risk, autonomy, responsibility, and rights, these attacks thus continue the project, began by mission Christianity, and continued more recently by HIV/AIDS campaigns, of making sexuality into a moral object, one that is crucial to the making of the modern individual subject.[57]

It is this conflation of culture, sexuality, and disease, together with the language of individualism, that traditionalists have responded to both during the last century and at present. Arguing that the pursuit of self-interested individualism was a threat to the sociomoral Luo order, traditionalists pursued a project of constructing the Luo nation, a moral community of shared values and codes of conduct. Proper gender relations, and in particular the scrutiny of women's conduct, were crucial to this moral community based on kinship, generational, and gendered hierarchy. The current revival of traditionalism can be understood as a response to the perceived threat posed by the growing dominance of discourses on women's rights and gender equality, promoted by HIV/AIDS and public health projects, and backed up by donors, NGOs, churches, and sometimes by politicians and government officials.

Widow inheritance has been an important, even central, issue around which the politics of self and other, and contested notions of moral personhood and political community, have formed and been debated. It coalesces conflicts about gender relations, kinship, personhood, and the sociomoral order that are at the heart of alternative constructions of moral community and progress. Christianity has played a crucial role in these debates and in shaping various identity politics as it shaped the language through which people continue to debate and engage moral issues. Christianity has also provided a language through which women, in particular, are able to contest male elders' codification of Luo rules in ways that give the elders pause for thought.

Notes

1. Dholuo-speaking people make up the third-largest ethnic population in Kenya. While there are large Dholuo-speaking migrant populations in other areas of Kenya, the Luo "homeland" is Nyanza Province, in western Kenya, which includes the city of Kisumu, the third-largest town in Kenya.

2. Ruth Prince, "Salvation and Tradition: Configurations of Faith in a Time of Death," *Journal of Religion in Africa* 37, no.1 (2007): 84–115; Wenzel Geissler and Ruth Prince, *The Land Is Dying: Contingency, Creativity and Conflict in Western Kenya* (New York: Berghahn, 2009).

3. A. B. C. Ocholla-Ayayo, *Traditional Ideology and Ethics among the Southern Luo* (Uppsala: Scandinavian Institute of African Studies, 1976); David W. Cohen and E. S. A. Odhiambo, *Siaya: The Historical Anthropology of an African Landscape* (London: James Currey, 1989); see also Matthew Carotenuto, "Riwuok e teko: Cultivating Identity in Colonial and Postcolonial Kenya," *Africa Today* 53, no. 2 (2006): 53–73.

4. Michael Warner, *Publics and Counterpublics* (New York: Zone, 2002); see also Jürgen Habermas, *The Structural Transformation of the Public Sphere: An Inquiry into a Category of Bourgeois Society* (Cambridge, MA: MIT Press, 1989); Craig Calhoun, ed., *Habermas and the Public Sphere* (Cambridge, MA: MIT Press, 1992).

5. E. E. Evans-Pritchard, *The Nuer: A Description of the Modes of Livelihood and Political Institutions of a Nilotic People* (Oxford: Oxford University Press, 1940); Evans-Pritchard, "Luo Tribes and Clans," *Rhodes-Livingstone Journal* 7 (1949): 24–40; Evans-Pritchard, "Marriage Customs of the Luo of Kenya," in *The Position of Women in Primitive Societies and Other Essays in Social Anthropology*, ed. Evans-Pritchard (London: Faber and Faber, 1965), 228–44.

6. Paul Mboya, *Luo kitigi gi timbegi* (A Handbook of Luo Customs) (Kisumu: Anyange Press, 1938), chap. 12.

7. Elderly Luo say that *chola* refers to the banana leaf string the widow wore after the interment. See also Mboya, *Luo*, 116. A similar word is used among some Bantu-speaking groups in East Africa.

8. Evans-Pritchard, "Marriage Customs"; Gordon M. Wilson, *Luo Customary Law and Marriage Laws Customs* (Nairobi: Government Printers, 1968).

9. Margaret Hay, "Women as Owners, Occupants, and Managers of Property in Colonial Western Kenya," in *African Women and the Law: Historical Perspectives*, ed. Hay and Marcia Wright (Boston: African Studies Center, Boston University, 1982), 120.

10. Betty Potash, "Wives of the Graves: Widows in a Rural Luo Community," in *Widows in African Societies: Choices and Constraints*, ed. Potash (Stanford: Stanford University Press, 1986), 44–65.

11. For example, Mboya, *Luo*.

12. Elizabeth Francis, "Migration and Changing Divisions of Labour: Gender Relations and Economic Change in Koguta, Western Kenya," *Africa* 65, no. 2 (1995): 197–215.

13. R. J. M. Swynnerton, *A Plan to Intensify the Development of African Agriculture in Kenya* (Nairobi: HM Stationery Office, 1955).

14. S. Coldham, "The Effect of Registration of Title upon Customary Land Rights in Kenya," *Journal of African Law* 22, no. 2 (1978): 100–101.

15. Achola O. Pala, "Daughters of the Lakes and Rivers: Colonization and the Land Rights of Luo Women," in *Women and Colonization: Anthropological Perspectives*, ed. Mona Etienne and Eleanor Leacock (New York: Praeger, 1980), 186–213. See also Parker Shipton, "The Kenyan Land Tenure Reform: Misunderstandings in the Public Creation of Private Property," in *Land and Society in Contemporary Africa*, ed. R. E. Downs and S. P. Reyna (Hanover, NH: University Press of New England, 1988); Shipton, "Debts and Trespasses: Land, Mortgages, and the Ancestors in Western Kenya," *Africa* 62, no. 3 (1992): 357–88; Shipton, "Land and Culture in Tropical Africa: Soil, Symbols, and the Metaphysics of the Mundane," *Annual Review of Anthropology* 23, no. 1 (1994): 347–77.

16. A. O. Pala, "Changes in Economy and Ideology: A Study of the Joluo of Kenya (with Special Reference to Women)" (PhD diss., Harvard University, 1977); Hay, "Women as Owners." Cf. Martin Chanock, *Law, Custom and Social Order: The Colonial Experience in Malawi and Zambia* (Cambridge: Cambridge University Press, 1985).

17. Pala, "Daughters"; Francis, "Migration"; Margarethe Silberschmidt, *"Women Forget That Men Are the Masters": Gender Antagonism and Socio-economic Change in Kisii District, Kenya* (Uppsala: Nordiska Afrikainstitutet, 1999). When Potash conducted her study of Luo widows (1973–76), land registration had just commenced in Nyanza Province. Hence, although people experienced land shortages in some areas, widows' rights still seemed secure. However, Potash quotes the director of social services of Nyanza Province complaining (in a 1984 newspaper report) that older widows were forced off their late husband's land and mentions a woman's organization that built a dormitory for homeless widows in Kisumu. Potash, "Wives," 35.

18. Several factors have undermined women's affinal relations: the decline in and delay of bridewealth; the increasingly common pattern of young women having children with

different men before getting married; and women's independent economic activities, making them less reliant on marriage. The economic and emotional burden of AIDS has put further strains on marriage and affinal relations.

19. T. M. Okeyo and A. K. Allen, "Influence of Widow Inheritance on the Epidemiology of AIDS in Africa," *African Journal of Medical Practice* 1, no. 1 (1994): 20–25.

20. Nancy Luke, "Widows and 'Professional Inheritors': Understanding AIDS Risk Perceptions in Kenya," paper presented at the annual meetings of the Population Association of America, May 8–11, 2002, Atlanta.

21. L. A. Adeokun and R. M. Nalwadda, "Serial Marriages and AIDS in Masaka District," *Health Transition Review* 7 (suppl.) (1997): 49–66; Jacob Adetunji and Jacob Oni, "Rising Proportions of Young Widows and the AIDS Epidemic in Africa," paper presented at the annual meeting of the American Sociological Association, August 6–10, 1999, Chicago; Isaac Luginaah, David Elkins, Eleanor Maticka-Tyndale, Tamara Landry, and Mercy Mathui, "Challenges of a Pandemic: HIV/AIDS-Related Problems Affecting Kenyan Widows," *Social Science and Medicine* 60, no. 6 (2005): 1219–28; Nancy Luke, "The Cultural Significance of Widowhood," paper presented at the virtual conference on African Households, Population Studies Centre, University of Pennsylvania, 2001; J. R. S. Malungo, "Sexual Cleansing (Kusalazya) and Levirate Marriage (Kunjilila mung'anda) in the Era of AIDS: Changes in Perceptions and Practices in Zambia," *Social Science and Medicine* 53 (2001): 371–82; James Ntozi, "Widowhood, Remarriage and Migration during the HIV/AIDS Epidemic in Uganda," *Health Transition Review* 7 (suppl.) (1997): 125–44.

22. K. Agot, B. O. Agot, W. O. Agingu, J. O. Ndinya-Achola, and E. A. Bukusi, "Sexual Behaviour and HIV Prevalence in Inherited and Un-inherited Widows in Bondo District, Kenya: Baseline Results," U.S. National Institutes of Health, NLM Gateway, http://gateway.nlm.nih.gov/MeetingAbstracts/102282591.html.

23. For example, IRIN (Integrated Regional and Information Networks: Africa) 28.3.2003; D. Nyong'o and O. Ongalo, "From Despair to Hope: Women's Right to Own and Inherit Property," http//www.policyproject.com/pubs/countryreports/KEN_InheritanceRights.pdf. Nyong'o and Ongalo claim, "In no other community in Kenya is the twin problem of societal and cultural practices—which discriminate against women and thereby translate into widespread of [sic] HIV/AIDS—more stark than within Luo Nyanza." All websites cited here were accessible during research for this chapter but may no longer be so.

24. *Daily Nation*, October 14, 1994.

25. Kenyan groups include the Education Centre for Women in Democracy (Siaya), the Federation of Women Lawyers in Kenya, the JaRamogi Oginga Odinga Foundation, and the Kenya AIDS Intervention Prevention Project Group. The international groups active in this controversy include Amistad, the Association for Women's Rights in Development, Concern, Family Health International, Human Rights Watch, MS-Kenya (Danish Association for International Cooperation), and Plan International. Religious groups include the Catholic Register, Giovani Impegno Missionario, Springs Ministry, and the Association of Adventist Women. See also V. N. Kimani, "Human Sexuality: Meaning and Purpose in Selected Communities in Contemporary Kenya," *Ecumenical Review (WCC)* 56, no. 4 (2004): 404–21.

26. Human Rights Watch, "AIDS: Success in Fight Threatened by Rights Abuses: Conference Must Promote Rights-Based Approach to HIV Pandemic," July 17, 2006, http://hrw.org/english/docs/2006/07/17/canada13744.htm; see also Human Rights Watch, "Double Standards: Women's Property Rights Violations in Kenya," March 3,

2003, http://www.hrw.org/reports/2003/kenya0303/; Association for Women's Rights in Development, "HIV/AIDS and Land Ownership Rights," http://www.awid.org/go.php?stid=1629.

27. http://www.springsministriestrust.net; see also "Widows Conference, Organised by Springs Ministries, Kisumu, Kenya, December 2004," *Newsletter of the Ecumenical HIV/AIDS Initiative in Africa* 7 (March 2005): 4–6, http://www.wcc-coe.org/wcc/what/mission/ehaia7-e.pdf.

28. The United States President's Emergency Plan for AIDS Relief (PEPFAR), "Kenya: Education Leads Tribal Elders to Support Women's Inheritance Rights," February 2006, http://www.pepfar.gov/pepfar/press/84657.htm.

29. W. Maina, "Kenya: The State, Donors and the Politics of Democratization," in *Civil Society and the Aid Industry*, ed. Alison Van Rooy (London: Earthscan, 1998).

30. David W. Cohen and E. S. Atieno Odhiambo, *Siaya: The Historical Anthropology of an African Landscape* (Nairobi: East African Publishing House, 1967); see also David W. Cohen and E. S. Atieno Odhiambo, "Ayany, Malo and Ogot—Historians in Search of a Luo Nation," *Cahiers d'études africaines* 27, nos. 105–6 (1987): 269–86.

35. Mboya, *Luo*; A. B. C. Ocholla-Ayayo, *The Luo Culture* (Wiesbaden: Steiner, 1980); Ochalla-Ayayo, *Traditional Ideology*.

36. Prince, "Salvation."

37. Webb Keane, "Materialism, Missionaries, and Modern Subjects in Colonial Indonesia," in *Conversion to Modernities: The Globalization of Christianity*, ed. Peter van der Veer (New York: Routledge, 1996), 159–60.

38. See also J. D. Y. Peel, *Religious Encounter and the Making of the Yoruba* (Bloomington: Indiana University Press, 2000).

39. See David W. Cohen and E. S. Atieno Odhiambo, *Burying SM: The Politics of Knowledge and the Sociology of Power in Africa* (London: James Currey, 1992).

40. Ibid., 78.

41. A. Haugerud, *The Culture of Politics in Modern Kenya* (Cambridge: Cambridge University Press, 1993); Lynn Thomas, *Politics of the Womb: Women, Reproduction, and the State in Kenya* (Berkeley: University of California Press, 2003).

42. Parkin, *Cultural Definition*; see also Toshiharu Abe, "The Concepts of Chira and Dhoch among the Luo of Kenya: Transition, Deviation and Misfortune," in *Themes in Socio-Cultural Ideas and Behaviour among the Six Ethnic Groups of Kenya*, ed. Nobuhiro Nagashima (Tokyo: Hitotsubashi University, 1981), 127–39.

43. For example, Raringo, *Chike jaduong e dalane* (The Rules of the Old Man in His Home) (Nairobi: Three Printers and Stationers, 2001).

44. A striking parallel with the proliferation of Luo rules is the elaboration, among the Melanesian Kwaio, of menstrual taboos. Rather than being age-old traditions, these taboos arose in the 1940s, at a time when Christianity opened up new avenues for women's independence, and David Akin argues that they reconstituted disciplinary control by men over women. By the 1990s, these taboos had grown so stringent and onerous that violations became almost inevitable, and the costs of paying compensation for breaking them impoverished whole communities. See Akin, "Concealment, Confession, and Innovation in Kwaio Women's Taboos," *American Ethnologist* 30, no. 3 (2003): 381–400.

45. Among others, Malo, *Jaluo*; Raringo, *Chike jaduong*; Ogot, *Southern Luo*.

46. Raringo, *Chike jaduong*.

47. See Bethwell A. Ogot, *Politics and the AIDS Epidemic in Kenya, 1983–2003* (Kisumu: Anyange Press, 2004).

48. Carotenuto, "Riwuok."

49. G. E. M. Ogutu, *Ker Jaramogi Is Dead, Who Shall Lead My People? Reflections on Past, Present, and Future Luo Thought and Practice* (Kisumu: Palwa Research Publications, 1995), 13. This text is written in English and interspersed with Dholuo terms, which the author translates himself. Subsequent references appear in parentheses in text.

50. D. Nyong'o and O. Ongalo, "From Despair to Hope: Women's Right to Own and Inherit Property," http://www.policyproject.com/pubs/countryreports/KEN_InheritanceRights.pdf.

51. *Daily Nation*, May 25, 1999.

52. Ibid.

53. *Daily Nation*, May 24, 1999.

54. Eugene Cotran, "Marriage, Divorce and Succession Laws in Kenya: Is Integration or Unification Possible?" *Journal of African Law* 40, no. 2 (1996): 194–204; Kibwana Kibwana and Lawrence Mute, eds., *Law and the Quest for Gender Equality in Kenya* (Nairobi: Claripress, 2000). The new constitution that was put up for referendum in 2005 did encode improved women's property rights, but it was rejected by the electorate because it also encoded a massive increase in presidential powers.

55. Megan Vaughan, *Curing Their Ills: Colonial Power and African Illness* (Cambridge: Polity Press, 1991).

56. Jean Comaroff, "The Diseased Heart of Africa: Medicine, Colonialism, and the Black Body," in *Knowledge, Power, and Practice: The Anthropology of Medicine and Everyday Life*, ed. Shirley Lindenbaum and Margaret Lock (Berkeley: University of California Press, 1993): 305–27.

57. See Wenzel Geissler and Ruth Prince, "Life Seen: Touch and Vision in the Making of Sex in Western Kenya," *Journal of Eastern African Studies* 1, no. 1 (2007): 123–49.

SIX

"Arise, Oh Ye Daughters of Faith"
Women, Pentecostalism, and Public Culture in Kenya

DAMARIS PARSITAU

A STRIKING feature of Pentecostalism in Kenya is the proliferation of ordained female church leaders, many of whom are founders, presidents, bishops, evangelists, healers, or prophetesses in these churches. Moreover, women who are single, divorced, or widowed have assumed leadership roles in both religious and seemingly secular circles. While I discuss here Jesus Is Alive Ministries, Faith Evangelistic Ministries (also known as the International Church of the Four-Square Gospel), and the Single Ladies Interdenominational Fellowship, many more examples could be given.[1] In these churches and ministries, women have assumed leadership positions to a degree that has not been replicated in Kenyan public life more broadly. It is therefore important to understand the processes that led to these significant developments in the Pentecostal and charismatic movements in Kenya in order to draw lessons for women's participation in public life. It is also important to understand the tensions and conflicts that arise in the context of a patriarchal public culture within which the female leadership of religious groups has not been a common institution.

Jesus Is Alive Ministries International (JIAM) was founded by Bishop Margaret Wanjiru in 1993, Faith Evangelistic Ministries (FEM) was founded by Evangelist Teresia Wairimu in 1989, and Single Ladies Interdenominational Fellowship (SLIF) was founded by Rev. Elizabeth Wahome in 2004. It is in these three ministries that Kenyan female leaders have been able to record their most remarkable achievements, crossing gendered boundaries and proving leadership as founders, overseers, prophetesses, healers, bishops, and politicians. These ministries have extensive services and programs that are specifically designed for women, especially those considered to be vulnerable, such as single and poor women. The three female leaders have also served as effective role models to other women in Kenya. Some of the leaders of the smaller ministries mentioned above have been directly or indirectly mentored and inspired by the lives of these founders.

Before these new ministries had emerged, other less well-known female leaders began working on the Kenyan Christian scene in the 1970s. For example, Philomena Mwaura has documented how evangelist Margaret Wangare started preaching, healing, prophesying, and planting churches in the early 1970s. Her ministry involved faith healing, preaching, and holding revival meetings, contributing to the growth of Pentecostal Christianity in Kenya in the 1970s. Irrespective of their size and prominence, these female-led ministries and churches have been critical to the growth, expansion, and renewal of Pentecostal and charismatic Christianity in Kenya.[2] They display and maintain a set of features that highlights women's prominence in spiritual contexts that has had a direct influence on their participation in public life more generally. However, women's engagement with religious patriarchy is a complex issue whose particular dynamics and effects must be understood within specific sociohistorical contexts.[3] In this regard, it is surprising how little academic attention has been devoted to the crucial roles these women play in public life and their impact on women's empowerment in Kenya. A false division may obtain in much of the literature on Pentecostalism in Africa insofar as it emphasizes the gifts of the spirit at the expense of Pentecostals' engagement with public life.

Women and Pentecostalism

Several recent studies from Africa and beyond have highlighted the challenges and successes of female participation in Christian churches.[4] Brigid Sackey's examination of changing gender relations in Ghanaian African-instituted churches and Pentecostal and charismatic groups, for example, brings out some of the salient comparative themes.[5] She shows how women have managed to make a breakthrough in the religious sphere in spite of problems created by gender hierarchies. She also demonstrates "how women are gaining strong social popularity and pervasive influence in Ghana and West Africa generally through their role as church founders, religious leaders, healers, mothers, social workers, politicians, custodians, and partners in development."[6] She also emphasizes the ways in which women are reclaiming leadership. She uses the word *reclaim* to indicate that women are not new to leadership in some West African societies. Among the several examples she cites is Grace Tani, who founded the Church of the Twelve Apostles, the first Ghanaian spiritual church, in 1914.

Mwaura stresses the positive impact of African-instituted churches and Pentecostal Christianity on women in Kenya.[7] Her key observation, echoed in many of the studies mentioned above, is that women are crucial to the founding, expansion, and sustenance of churches. Pentecostals stand out in this respect, because they have been particularly adept at using female talent. They have enabled women to serve in a variety of religious roles as teachers, ministers, evangelists, and missionaries. David Maxwell contends that in southern as well as Central Africa, Pentecostalism has given women legitimate reasons to challenge patriarchal authority.[8] Assessing the impact of Pentecostal Christianity on women, Charlotte Spinks argues that it offers women an alternative community, a particularly significant feature in unstable states dominated by churches that subscribe to patriarchal messages.[9] According to Spinks, the opportunity for everyone to access gifts of the spirit in Pentecostalism provides a source of human dignity and spiritual purpose in the face of often degrading circumstances and potent forms of activity and leadership denied in other spheres of life. Spinks argues that women identify easily with Pentecostal-charismatic movements, because their rejection of the sociocultural status quo at certain stages of their institutional development appeals to those aspiring to escape from marginalization in patriarchal societies. Moreover, the prosperity gospel teachings support and legitimize ambitious young women who seek to break away from traditional bonds in order to achieve economic, social, and political independence. Marie Griffith's account of Women's Aglow Fellowship International reaches a similar conclusion.[10] By focusing on the charismatic fellowship's emphasis on prayer, she presents a compelling interpretation of the cultural work involved in creating and sustaining an organization that embraces values such as nurturance, empowerment, and self-esteem.

However, while the scholars mentioned above have recognized the empowering potential of Pentecostal Christianity, none of them deals directly with the influence of these churches and ministries on women's participation in public life in Africa. Although some in Kenya still debate women's roles in public life, many Pentecostal and charismatic churches and ministries have provided an enlarged space for women to contest it. Each of the women in the case studies I present here has contested Kenyan public culture in a different way.

Bishop Margaret Wanjiru of Jesus Is Alive Ministries

Wanjiru started her ministry as a street preacher in the early 1990s. She is a single mother of three and the first woman to be ordained a Pentecostal bishop in Kenya. Before becoming a televangelist and the founder of the JIAM, she was saved at a crusade and thereafter began preaching on the streets of Nairobi with a group of South African Christians. In 1998 she moved to her strategically placed premises along Haile Selassie Avenue within the central business district in Nairobi and began her televised show, *The Glory Is Here,* the same year. The church can accommodate thousands of people and conducts at least three services on Sundays and a host of others on weekdays. The JIAM grew into a megachurch with diasporic communities and offices in Uganda, the United Kingdom, the United States, and South Africa. At present her ministry boasts some twenty thousand members locally and internationally. In 1997 she was ordained a minister and became a reverend, and in 2002, Bishop Arthur Gitonga of the Redeemed Gospel Church ordained her a bishop.

Besides being a televangelist, Wanjiru is also a shrewd businesswoman and is said to have helped empower many women in her church spiritually, economically, and socially. And while she is an inspiration to thousands of women, her ministry is not a women's ministry but a church that has followers across gender, ethnic, and age divides. She runs a branch of the Good Samaritan Project, a Bible school, *Faith Digest* magazine, a cafeteria, Glory Development Fund, and a fleet of buses. In 2007, Wanjiru was selected by *True Love,* a leading women's magazine in East Africa, as one of the fifty most influential women in East Africa for spearheading spiritual empowerment of thousands of women and people and for being the first ordained female Pentecostal bishop in Kenya.

Life has not always been a smooth ride for Wanjiru. She dropped out of school after becoming pregnant when she was seventeen, found jobs cleaning toilets in factories, and tried witchcraft to escape abject poverty. She confessed that she got so deeply involved in witchcraft that she graduated from black magic to white magic, whereupon she grew wealthy.[11] However, her association with witchcraft was short-lived and unstable. She claims that God saved her from witchcraft, and her life was totally transformed through an act of salvation. She often draws on Revelation 6:7–8 in her teachings about the ways in which the devil seeks to rule people through witchcraft.[12]

From 2003 onward Wanjiru began to spread her influence beyond the ministry and its related business ventures. A culmination of this expansion was her candidacy in the parliamentary elections of 2007. Announcing her decision to run for election to thousands of jubilant church members along Haile Selassie Avenue, she said that God had given her a prophesy through a visiting American preacher, Prophetess Brenda Todd. Todd had told Wanjiru that although she had been prodded by God from time to time to join politics, the appointed time had come and she could not disobey God any more.[13] The announcement was met with loud applause and shouts of hallelujah from the crowd. Wanjiru justified her entry into politics by likening herself to Esther in the Bible, who rescued her people from destruction. In a sermon on Christmas Eve 2007, she explained, "The Bible says that when a nation was about to be destroyed because of the wickedness of Haman, Esther was already in place and prepared for the task of redeeming the situation. When God says yes, no man can say no."

Todd likened Wanjiru to King David, who was chosen by God and anointed by Samuel, as explained in 1 Samuel 8:4–9. After the anointing ceremony, Wanjiru asked the crowd to vote for her, saying, "When the righteous are in authority," as Proverbs 29:2 puts it, "the people rejoice." In fact, Wanjiru's entry into politics had already started with opposition against a draft constitution proposed by the government in 2006. It was at this time that Wanjiru and many other Pentecostals mobilized Kenyans to vote against the proposed draft during a national referendum.

One of the provisions of the proposed constitution that irked Pentecostals in particular was to allow Muslims to have kadhi courts, known elsewhere as shari'a courts. They are intended to decide on private issues of marriage, divorce, and inheritance as they affect Muslims. Pentecostals argued that the provision seemed to elevate Islam which is a minority religion in Kenya. A broader constellation of Christians advocated a secular constitution that would treat all religions equally. They argued that Kenya was overwhelmingly Christian and that if any religion should be favored, it should be Christianity. Other contentious issues in the draft were clauses that touched on social and ethical issues such as abortion and same-sex unions. Together with the kadhi issue, these liberal proposals made Wanjiru to lead Pentecostal and Evangelical church members in mobilizing opposition against the proposed constitutional draft. Asked why she opposed the draft, she said, in an interview with me in 2006, that it was because of the arrogance of the government: "We have tried our best to negotiate with all parties ever since 2002. We have put our demands on the table, that the constitution should be made neutral when it comes to religious matters, but for some strange reasons the government is still insisting on including the kadhi courts in the constitution. Time has come for us to show the government that we have a constituency that cannot just be ignored. They have ignored our pleas, now it is time to tell our people to ignore them."[14]

In November 2006, Wanjiru announced that she would stand for Parliament in Nairobi's Starehe Constituency, the key constituency that houses her church, Parliament, and central government offices. Campaigning against the then sports minister Maina Kamanda, she featured on an Orange Democratic Movement ticket and was successfully elected as a member of Parliament for the constituency. After the protracted negotiations between her sponsoring party and the party of President Mwai Kibaki, Wanjiru was made the assistant minister for housing and shelter.

It is possible to gain an insight into the difficulties Wanjiru faced during the campaign by considering the dispute that erupted between her and the man who claimed to be the father of her children. The decision to contest the elections coincided with Wanjiru's announcement that she would marry her South African fiancé, Rev. Samuel Matjeke. No sooner had she finished the announcement and called for a church celebration than the man claiming paternity appeared, asserting that he was still married to her according to Gĩkũyũ traditional marriage rites and that they had lived together as husband and wife between 1978 and 1983. He also insisted that he had paid three thousand Kenyan shillings as bridewealth in 1978. During an event that unfolded like a soap opera, phone-ins, editorials, letters to the editor, cartoons, and newspaper columns debated the nature of African traditional marriage and the place of bridewealth in contemporary Kenya. The editorials in the *Daily Nation* in particular did not mince words in condemning Wanjiru, thereby asserting the patriarchal public culture within which she pursued her ambitions.[15]

Wanjiru, for her part, had little time for the man or the hostile press and interpreted the incident as the work of her political opponents. She admitted that the claims coming after she had singlehandedly raised her children made her feel like "slapping someone." "I will not tolerate nonsense from anybody," she added.[16] The issue assumed a new dimension when a group calling itself Maendeleo ya Wanaume (Association for the Welfare of Men),[17] sponsored the man to seek a court injunction to stop the bishop's wedding, asked for paternity tests, and demanded his conjugal rights. Wanjiru's sons gave a press conference denouncing their alleged father, arguing that they did know him and were not interested in knowing him now. However, a court order stopped the wedding.[18]

Wanjiru's case shows how prominent female Pentecostals, while grappling with tradition and patriarchy, are not immune to controversy and paradox in their own lives. While fighting patriarchy and promoting the rights of women, she also condemns homosexuality and lesbianism and exhibits intolerance toward other faiths, including Islam. Her condemnation of abortion, adultery, and premarital sex can be out of tune with the women she purports to lead. Moreover, while she highlights and celebrates her achievements as a single woman, she also wants to get married so that she can become a respectful member of Parliament. As Wanjiru's success demonstrates, Pentecostal women who engage with the national public culture may experience a tension that can be as creative as it is potentially destructive of their ambitions.

Evangelist Teresia Wairimu of Faith Evangelistic Ministries

FEM, one of Nairobi's best known Christian ministries, was started in 1989 by Wairimu together with a group of seventeen women, most of whom were single. A mother of three, Wairimu says that God called her to evangelism in 1985. In the 1990s she became the first female preacher to hold regular revival crusades at Uhuru Park in Nairobi. FEM has consolidated its position among Kenyan Pentecostal and charismatic churches and ministries through its monthly crusades. Each month, the ministry also holds seminars, luncheons, and conferences for women in major towns such as Nairobi, Nakuru, Mombasa, and Eldoret. These meetings focus on women's spiritual, economic, and social empowerment. Wairimu owns *Ebenezer* magazine, an annual publication that highlights the activities of her ministry. She also runs ministries for young people and a mercy ministry for those living in slums such as Korogocho in Nairobi. She proudly claims to have preached in over twenty countries. Her European ministry office is in London, and she has a FEM chapter in the United States called Teresia Wairimu Evangelistic Ministry, based in Dallas.[19]

Wairimu thus shares important characteristics with Margaret Wanjiru, such as a pronounced entrepreneurial attitude to her calling, a strong urban bias in her operations, and an unapologetic commitment to raising her children without a husband. The two charismatic leaders also fought the same cause in 2005–2006, when Kenyans debated the new draft constitution. Wairimu supported Wanjiru's conservative messages about the corrosive effects of same-sex unions and of abortions, while both women were also alarmed by the draft constitution's apparent elevation of Islam. Through prayer and fasting, Wairimu engaged her followers in a spiritual war against the devil, which she saw as a force trying to destroy Kenya. However, although Wairimu played her part in mobilizing Pentecostal and charismatic opposition against the draft constitution, her approach to conventional politics has been more critical than Wanjiru's. Speaking out against the sins of corruption and tribalism, Wairimu has preferred a prophetic voice to party-political rhetoric. She has warned that "when politicians plot to devour the sheep, preachers have a God-given responsibility to protect the sheep." During a sermon at Uhuru Park in 2005, she went on to declare, "The Church must be the voice in Kenya. If you don't want to hear what the Church is saying, move your citizenship elsewhere, because Kenya will be a God-fearing nation. Our nation is set apart for Jesus Christ. Kenya is a springboard for revival."[20]

Among the epithets Wairimu has adopted are Prophetess to the Nation and Watchman to the Country. Referring to Ezekiel 33:1–9, she insists that "God has called us to be watchmen, we are to watch over our city, we must watch over our nation. And for this reason I prophesy to Kenya every day. Kenya, you are great and you shall do great things for Jehovah." Addressing her words more directly to politicians, she observes that "God has not called these politicians to be watchmen. They don't have the mandate. That is why they scream and shout, even when they are tearing the nation apart."[21] Apart from being a prophetess and watchman, Wairimu is also a renowned healer. Thousands of testimonies have been delivered at her crusades about her charismatic gifts of healing and deliverance. But unlike Wanjiru, Wairimu loathes controversy and cuts the image of a dignified woman.

"Arise, Oh Ye Daughters of Faith"

Rev. Elizabeth Wahome of Single Ladies Interdenominational Fellowship

Although both Wanjiru's and Wairimu's ministries strive to improve their followers' welfare through spiritual healing and material charity, SLIF is perhaps the clearest example of how committed these new female-led ministries can be to the idea of welfare and empowerment. It is dedicated to uplifting the lives of single women in Kenya by empowering them spiritually, socially, and economically, and by so doing, it addresses critical issues around inadequate healthcare, poverty, low self-esteem, loneliness, and marginalization. Elizabeth Wahome is its founder and head, though she herself has been happily married for many years. She founded this interdenominational ministry in June 2004 as a prayer and support group, and it has grown to become a large organization and a vibrant church. After realizing that most Christian churches did not address their needs, Wahome claims that she received a vision from God to start SLIF to give lonely single women fellowship. After holding weekly fellowships and listening to these women, she talked to her husband and friends about her vision and raised some money to assist needy women to start small businesses. The ministry headquarters is based in Zimmerman, Nairobi, and had a membership of about 250 women by 2005. In 2006 membership grew to about 1,200 women, and according to SLIF's own projections, it will have tripled from that by the end of 2008. The ministry has branches in Tanzania and Uganda, with plans to start other branches in Botswana, Malawi, Zimbabwe, the Seychelles, and Australia. Membership in this organization is restricted to single women, but married women and their spouses can join as partners and mentors.

Four categories of single women are identified by SLIF: separated and divorced women, single mothers, spinsters, and widows. For each category biblical references are found, and they are accorded their distinctive roles within the ministry. Separated and divorced women are represented by Hagar, the handmaiden of Sarah, Abraham's wife (see Genesis 21:13–14). Abraham sent Hagar away, together with her son, Ishmael, into the wilderness, where they suffered from hunger and thirst, and she felt the pain of seeing her son faced with imminent death. In her pain and despair, she cried to God, who is said to have heard her cry and answered. Wahome draws many parallels between

Hagar's story and that of many separated and divorced women who are left with sole responsibility for raising their children.

The second category is that of single mothers, women who have not been married but have children as a result of what Wahome describes as "carelessness and sin." In Kenya such women are often despised and stigmatized as husband snatchers and home wreckers. Most single women are shunned, even in churches, as women of loose morals who prey on married men to feed and educate their children. This category has been inspired by the newness of Christ, as mentioned in 2 Corinthians 2:1. Spinsters, the third category, are referred to in Matthew 1:21–23. These are women who have been patiently waiting and searching for a husband to marry them. This was the situation of Wahome herself before she got married, at the age of thirty-nine. When she finally found a widower and married, she was no longer able to have children. She has, however, revealed that she has a grown daughter whom she raised singlehandedly after the man who impregnated her denied responsibility. This may have contributed to her passionate ministry toward the single women as she can relate to their challenges. She draws parallels between this group and the Virgin Mary, who remained chaste until an angel appeared to her that she would become pregnant. This group is encouraged to stay expectant, pregnant with hope and faith, until a suitable brother (as lay men are referred to in Pentecostal circles) shows up like the angel. Wahome exhorts women in this category to preoccupy themselves with serving God while waiting for a husband.

The last group is that of widows as represented in Luke 2:36–38. According to Wahome, widows have a special place in the heart of God, the defender of the oppressed. She quotes Psalm 68, where God is said to be a husband to widows and a father to their children. All the five categories of single women are encouraged to rise above victimhood and value themselves as children of God. At home and in the church, the women are encouraged to work as the bride of Christ, active in evangelism and ministry.[22] They are encouraged to realize that they are not alone because Jesus is their husband, provider, councillor, and helper. Images of biblical women such as Hagar, Deborah, Ruth, Mary, Elizabeth, and Magdalene abound in this ministry. They are declared to be women of excellence and models to be followed. Single women's apparent weakness is turned into a powerful, prophetic recovery of both church and community.

SLIF's motto reads, "To all who mourn in Israel, he will give a crown of beauty for ashes, a joyous blessing instead of mourning, festive praise instead of despair. In their righteousness, they will be like great oaks that the lord has planted for his own glory" (Isaiah 61:3). Of the women I interviewed several pointed out that participation had enhanced their self-esteem and confidence; others insisted that SLIF had totally transformed their lives. One woman shared her testimony:

> I got saved last month in a SLIF plenary meeting and as you can see I am cuter today. In fact I feel beautiful inside and out. I was working in a bar as a prostitute, but not anymore. When I got saved, Mum [Wahome] got me a job. I worked as a maid, and God gave me a favor with my employer because I did my job well. If it was cleaning the house, I did it with an anointing. I got talking with my employer, and I told her that I have a daughter to feed and raise singlehandedly. She doubled my salary. Besides, I started making woollen cloths for babies, which I exhibit at the SLIF annual exhibition, and now I have a lot of orders. I have seen God, and I will serve Him faithfully.[23]

As this woman indicates, during various meetings, women are invited to share their experiences, and they are prayed for and given encouragement. Every participant is urged to engage in social and economic pursuits with Christian ethics and with a determination to be open to God's prospering grace. In conferences and seminars, successful single women are invited to speak to their fellow members. For example, in one meeting the chief guest was Lucia Kiwala, a high-ranking functionary with the United Nations who encouraged single women to rise above victimhood and to value themselves. SLIF has also developed various programs such as Sister's Keepers Ministry, which encourages women to watch over each other. These are usually networks of prayer support groups in which women listen to each others' problems and pray together. The ministry also has weekly meetings such as Bible study, committee meetings, and prayer groups, all of which lend women space to talk about problems and challenges. SLIF has recently started to train women in information technology, tailoring, and nutrition. About sixty women receive training in these skills annually.

SLIF's annual exhibitions are held at the ministry's headquarters to display and sell the wares that have been produced by women who have been given training or funding to start small-scale businesses.[24] In an effort to assist women living in Nairobi's poorest areas, SLIF has also opened a bureau that advertises jobs and encourages employers to hire one of their "honest born-again . . . secretaries, accountants, housekeepers, and baby sitters."[25]

Pentecostal and charismatic Christianity, as Linda Woodhead has argued, may offer women a safe space for the articulation of desires, frustrations, and experiences in wider, more public settings—not only in churches, but in small groups and parachurch organizations.[26] Secondary institutions, such as prayer groups, offer a forum for healing not only by God, but through the love and support of one's sisters in Christ. SLIF meetings are dominated by women's concerns, concerns that they would find difficult to express if men were present. During the time for testimonies, women spend a great deal of time talking about their challenges, abusive boyfriends, bills to be paid, food and clothing for their children, and so forth. They testify in public about the changes they have realized, the benefits of salvation, and what SLIF has done for them. Pragmatic reasons fuse into spiritual ones, and vice versa, as women join Pentecostal and charismatic groups in an effort to improve their lives and their social status.

Wahome has been described as a crusader for vulnerable women. She has been recognized and honored for selfless service to scores of women from broken homes or marriages. Recently, the Latin University of Theology, based in California, conferred on her an honorary degree in theology to commemorate more than forty years of fighting the stereotypes and prejudices so common in African patriarchal cultures. In its commendation, the university cited her personal struggle to overcome cultural inhibitions and her selfless service to scores of women from broken homes or marriages whose shattered dreams have been restored by her efforts.[27]

PENTECOSTALISM OFFERS its adherents access to the Holy Spirit, and many Kenyans feel empowered by that promise. It is, after all, spiritual gifts and not gender that qualify individuals to be delivered and valued. The priesthood of all has legitimized women's aspirations for top leadership in the church. The trust in empowerment brought about by the Holy Spirit speaking directly through each individual, who then interprets the Bible directly, also has significantly empowered female leaders. The uniqueness of the Pentecostal experience and the theological importance of a calling account for the multiplicity of female roles in Pentecostal and charismatic organizations and movements. The major shift in ideology from mainline Christianity to Pentecostalism has heralded a new phase that has significantly affected the status of women, not least single women. And while the role of women in church ministry and leadership remains a contentious issue within Pentecostalism, women have made progress in challenging patriarchy in the church and in public culture. The experience of the second birth can lead to a revaluing of the self in relation to God and others that undermines patriarchal public culture. It is this experience that has set Pentecostals apart from many of the other evangelicals in Kenya.

Contradiction and paradox abound, however, in the three cases discussed in this chapter. The democratizing ethos of Pentecostalism coexists with hierarchical leadership based on charisma. The identification of unmarried women as a constituency is compatible with holding marriage as a value. A critique of the hatred and parochialism promoted by politicians does not stop intolerance toward homosexuality and Islam. Yet perhaps coherence would be too much to expect of Pentecostalism, because it is not a policy-making institution. Pentecostalism is not a panacea to solve Africa's ills, but it can nevertheless offer insights into how Africans negotiate those ills, not least when politicians and foreign donors' policies fail them.[28] The cases presented here show how Pentecostals are able to move from victimhood to an active engagement with their circumstances, from reliance on national and local politicians to the cultivation of transnational connections. The highly public involvement of women in these processes is itself remarkable in a country like Kenya, sparking off developments whose full consequences are yet to be seen.

Notes

1. Examples include Faith Harvest International Ministries, founded by Evangelist Zipporah Kimani; Deborah Arise Africa, Rev. Nancy Gitau; Zion Prayer Mountain and Kenya House of Prayer, Evangelist Alice Mugure; Charismata Ministries, Evangelist Mama Mwai; Ladies Homecare Fellowship, Rev. Judith Mbugua; Jubilee Christian Centre, Rev. Cathy Kiuna; Rivers of Joy Christian Church, Rev. Esther Maingi.

2. Philomena N. Mwaura, "Gender and Power in African Christianity: African Instituted Churches and Pentecostal Churches," in *African Christianity: An African Story*, ed. Ogbu Kalu (Pretoria: University of Pretoria, 2005), 430.

2. By highlighting the ways in which women have contested patriarchal public culture, I seek to qualify the rather dismal perspective on Pentecostalism offered in Paul Gifford, *African Christianities and Public Life: A View from Kenya* (London: Hurst, 2009).

3. H. Kelly Chong, "Negotiating Patriarchy: South Korean Evangelical Women and the Politics of Gender," *Gender and Society* 20 (2005): 697

4. B. O. Bateye, "Female Leaders of New Generation Churches as Change Agents in Yorubaland" (PhD diss., Obafemi Awolowo University, Ile-Ife, 2001); Chong, "Negotiating Patriarchy"; Deidre Helen Crumbley, "Impurity and Power: Women in Aladura Churches," *Africa* 62, no. 4 (1992): 505–22; Cornelia Butler Flora, "Pentecostal Women in Colombia: Religious Change and the Status of Working-Class Women," *Journal of Interamerican Studies and World Affairs* 17, no. 4 (1975): 411–25; R. Marie Griffith, *God's Daughters: Evangelical Women and the Power of Submission* (Berkeley: University of California Press, 1997); Marja Hinfelaar, *Respectable and Responsible Women: Methodist and Roman Catholic Women's Organizations in Harare, Zimbabwe (1919–1985)* (Zoetermeer, Netherlands: Boekencentrum, 2001); Dorothy L. Hodgson, *The Church of Women: Gendered Encounters between Maasai and Missionaries* (Bloomington: Indiana University Press, 2005); Cynthia Hoehler-Fatton, *Women of Fire and Spirit: History, Faith, and Gender in Roho Religion in Western Kenya* (Oxford: Oxford University Press, 1996); Isabel Mukonyora, *Wandering a Gendered Wilderness: Suffering and Healing in an African Initiated Church* (New York: Peter Lang, 2007); Philomena N. Mwaura, "'A Burning Stick Plucked Out of the Fire': The Story of Rev. Margaret Wanjiru of JIAM," in *Her-Stories: Hidden Histories of Women of Faith in Africa*, ed. Isabel A. Phiri, D. B. Govinden, and Sarojini Nadar (Pietermaritzburg: Cluster Publications, 2002): 202–24; Mercy Amba Oduyoye, *Daughters of Anowa: African Women and Patriarchy* (Maryknoll, NY: Orbis, 1995); Oyeronke Olajubu, *Women in the Yoruba Religious Sphere* (Albany: State University of New York Press, 2003); Isabel A. Phiri, *Women, Presbyterianism and Patriarchy: Religious Experience of Chewa Women in Central Malawi* (Blantyre: Christian Literature Association in Malawi, 1997); Brigid M. Sackey, *New Directions in Gender and Religion: The Changing Status of Women in African Independent Churches* (Lanham, MD: Rowman and Littlefield, 2006); Charlotte Spinks, "Panacea or Painkiller? The Impact of Pentecostal Christianity on Women in Africa," in *Annual Journal of Women for Women International* 1, no. 1 (2003): 21–24.

5. Sackey, *New Directions*.

6. Ibid., 6.

7. Mwaura, "Gender and Power," 442.

8. David Maxwell, *African Gifts of the Spirit: Pentecostalism and the Rise of a Zimbabwean Transnational Religious Movement* (Oxford: James Currey, 2006), 12; see also David Martin, *Pentecostalism: The World Their Parish* (Oxford: Blackwell, 2002), 98–99.

9. Spinks, "Panacea."

10. Griffith, *God's Daughters*.

11. See the details of Wanjiru's life story in Mwaura, "Burning Stick."

12. The press coverage of Wanjiru's alleged involvement in witchcraft includes articles in *Daily Nation*, January 14, 17, 19, 2007; *Miracle Magazine*, December 2002.

13. Bishop Wanjiru's sermon on Christmas Eve 2007. This message is also posted on her church's Web site, http://www.jiam.org. All Web sites cited here were accessible during research for this chapter but may no longer be so.

14. Margaret Wanjiru, interview by author, Nairobi, August 23, 2006. She gave the same explanation in a television interview with Swale Mdoe, June 29, 2007.

15. *Daily Nation*, January 16, 19, 2007. The editorials were full of condemnation for the bishop for denying the alleged husband and for insulting him publicly.

16. *Kenya Times*, January 15, 2007.

17. The association derived its name from the state-sponsored women's organization Maendeleo ya Wanawake.

18. Wanjiru's experiences with witchcraft also came to haunt her after she had announced her political ambitions. Rumors circulated through text messages and on the

"Arise, Oh Ye Daughters of Faith"

Internet that she had taken Raila Odinga, the leader of the Orange Democratic Movement, to South Africa to consult powerful witches. In *Miracle Magazine*, December 2002, Wanjiru delves into her past involvement with witchcraft in a sermon entitled "Three Levels of Witchcraft."

19. This information is based on Wairimu's story as compiled and told by Francis Manana, professor of Evangelism and Missions at the Pan-Africa Christian College. See http://www.dacb.org/stories/kenya/wairimu_teresia.html.

20. Wairimu reproduced her sermon "We Must Watch Over Our Nation" in *Revival Springs*, no. 113 (2005): 8–10. The sermon is based on Ezekiel 33:1–9.

21. This prophesy was announced in one of her evangelistic crusades in Nairobi in October 2005. The prophesy is also found in *Revival Springs*, no. 113 (2005): 8–10.

22. See also Griffith, *God's Daughters*.

23. Roseline Akinyi, interview by author, Nairobi, September 12, 2006.

24. For further details, see Stephen Mburu, "Interview with Sabina Muchunu: My Long Walk to Financial Freedom," *Sunday Nation*, August 24, 2008.

25. See *Single Ladies' Moments* 2 (March–May 2005).

26. Linda Woodhead, ed., *Religions in the Modern World: Traditions and Transformations* (New York: Routledge, 2002), 332.

27. Juma Kwayera, "A Crusader to Uplift the Lowly," *Sunday Standard*, December 14, 2008.

28. See Harri Englund, "Pentecostalism beyond Belief: Trust and Democracy in a Malawian Township," *Africa* 77, no. 4 (2007): 477–99.

PART THREE

A Plurality of Pentecostal Publics

SEVEN

Going and Making Public
Pentecostalism as Public Religion in Ghana

BIRGIT MEYER

RELIGION IN the public sphere and public religion have recently become much-debated issues and research foci in the study of religion, identity, and politics in Africa. There are good empirical reasons to evoke these and related terms so as to further our understanding of the place and role of religion in society, as I have also experienced in my own research in Ghana over the past twenty years. Between 1988 and 1992, over several stints of fieldwork, I conducted research on the African appropriations of Christianity and the appeal of Pentecostalism.[1] During that period, the country was governed by the Provisional National Defense Council (PNDC) of J. J. Rawlings, who had come to power through a coup and wielded full control over the media in the context of a one-party system. Remarkably, while limiting Christian churches' appearance in the media, the first Rawlings government (1979–92) assigned radio time to the neotraditional Afrikania movement that criticized "brainwashing" by Christian conversion and propagated African traditional religion as a respectable and authentic alternative. Afrikania echoed the PNDC's cultural policy of *sankofa*,[2] which strove to leave behind Christian ideologies in favor of an African identity grounded in indigenous cultural heritage. From the mid-1980s onward, churches—especially Pentecostal ones—became extremely popular. Notwithstanding their increasing appeal, which was at least partly due to people's growing disappointment with the government's inability to deliver "development" and "progress," they played a minor public role.

However, returning to Ghana in 1996 for a new research project on popular culture (in particular, popular video movies), I noted much to my amazement that the public sphere had undergone a big transformation. Under the pressure of the World Bank and the International Monetary Fund, the PNDC had instigated a democratic constitution, implying the gradual liberalization and commercialization of media such as film, radio, television, and newspapers.[3] The new radio and television stations were to be formally secular, yet at the same time operated on a commercial basis. Many Pentecostal churches immediately seized the new opportunities to buy airtime and became a markedly public force.[4] While the appeal of Christianity was not new as such, I was struck by its public omnipresence, as well as the fierce public attacks leveled against local religious traditions and Afrikania. Flooding the public sphere, Pentecostal images and sounds devoted to "spiritual warfare" were impossible to be ignored in southern Ghana.[5] This had immediate implications for politics. As, under the aegis of democracy, politicians now had to compete for votes, many of them started to use Pentecostal churches as stages for a ritual cleansing from past sins and for the performance of a cleansed, born-again identity. During the campaign for the elections in December 2008, the mobilization of Pentecostalism by politicians was unprecedented in its intensity, with the presidential candidate (and then the elected president) John Atta Mills openly supporting this brand of Christianity, and seeking spiritual support from the Pentecostal Nigerian preacher T. B. Joshua.

Puzzled by these new developments, along with many scholars witnessing similar processes throughout Africa and elsewhere, I developed a keen interest in the manifestation of religion in the public sphere in general, and in the rise of the latest variant of Pentecostalism—with its flamboyant pastors, skillful use of media, emphasis on the prosperity gospel, and mobilization of a mass following—in particular. While religion's regained public vitality is widely recognized today, scholars are only beginning to address the theoretical issues raised by its public reemergence in our time.

Before sketching the stakes in current debates about religion in the public sphere, it needs to be noted that the term *public* itself is far from clear. *Public* can refer to matters that concern a community as a whole, being open to all persons and hence generally known. Following from this, *a* public is a group for which what is qualified as public is accessible. While, taken in this broad sense, *public* is a term that pertains to matters and groups characterized by openness and accessibility; it is at the same time a normative, specific concept that is grounded in post-Enlightenment modern Western societies. For Jürgen Habermas,[6] as many interlocutors and critics have noted, the rise of the public sphere marked the emergence of a new sphere for critical and rational debate that was independent from either the state or the market. In the German original, the term *Öffentlichkeit* is used for both the public sphere, understood as the sociospatial arena of debate, and the public, understood as the body constituted by participating in this arena.

The coexistence of a broad understanding of *public* in terms of openness and accessibility and a more narrow, historically specific understanding is quite confusing, as it mixes neutral and normative uses of the term. The normative understanding of publics and the public sphere often informs debates about and scholarly work on the nature of the public sphere. This comes to the fore markedly in recent, at times heated, discussions about the public manifestation of religion, in particular Islam, in northern European societies. Taken as a prime model of secularization,[7] in this region religion had been confined to the private sphere. There existed a "secularist truce," a secularist contract that guaranteed religious freedom on the one hand, yet banished religion from the public sphere on the other. However, with the rise of culturally and religiously plural societies, the secularist truce seems to be eroding. Secular and religious positions are at loggerheads, and that raises major questions about the nature of the public sphere as secular and religion as private by definition. While from a normative perspective that regards religion as a private matter, public religion is an anomaly, from an empirical perspective it is a reality. Its existence challenges the secularization thesis that posits an intrinsic relation between modernity, the rise of the public sphere, and the retreat of religion into the private sphere.

Quite a number of authors—including Habermas himself[8]—have argued that the exclusion of religion from our definition of the public sphere is challenged by obvious developments in Western societies that do witness—albeit to varying degrees—what José Casanova has called the "de-privatization of religion."[9] In his seminal book *A Secular Age*, Charles Taylor points out that religion in modern societies is subject to transformation, rather than simply vanishing or returning after a period of repression.[10] In other words—and here Taylor's perspective resonates with Talal Asad's position outlined in *Formations of the Secular*—secularization changes modern religion instead of abolishing it.[11] While it may be premature to circumscribe the current age as postsecular, it is high time to adopt a postsecularist approach that seeks to grasp what religion means in our time beyond the secularization narrative, the point being to understand how the relations between the religious and the secular, religions and the state, the public and the private, shift over time.[12] In doing so, it is important to be aware of the ideological and normative dimension enshrined in the use of the term *public* and to be alert to the politics of its use, rather than to unreflexively reproduce it in scholarly analysis.

From an Africanist perspective, recent scholarly work on the role and appeal of religion in the twenty-first century still appears Eurocentric. Even though the critique of the secularization thesis has raised scholars' awareness of the problematic confluence of theoretical and normative assumptions about the proper place of religion, it is still the case that such normative assumptions inform views of Africa as lacking institutions that promote democracy and civility and thus as lagging behind the ideal of the modern public sphere. It is one of the concerns of this volume to challenge such views with grounded historical and ethnographic explorations of how movements within Christianity actually become a public force and matters of public concern in Africa. The point here is to move out of the normative framework in which much thinking about the public sphere and publics still takes place and to adopt a broader understanding of public as common, open and accessible, as outlined above.[13] Taking some distance will allow for a better understanding of the normative stakes of actual debates about the nature of the public sphere and public religion. We need to achieve a fruitful synergy between detailed empirical investigations and critical reflection on theoretical and normative concepts around public religion so as to advance a truly global understanding of religion in our time.

I find it useful to take a practical approach that investigates actual strategies and acts through which public religion materializes. It makes sense to distinguish between *going public*, assuming a public appearance through which a religion is visible and audible to others, and *making public*, the public expression of matters that hitherto were not open and accessible. Moving between the levels of historical and ethnographic work and theoretical reflection, in this chapter I highlight some important issues and raise questions for our understanding of public religion, in particular Christianity, in Africa.[14] Although my main point of reference is the rise and popularity of Pentecostalism in Ghana, this chapter does not offer a case study per se.

I shall stress the need (1) to contextualize the rise of Pentecostalism as a public religion by taking into account historical legacies and current particularities that shape Ghana's public sphere, (2) to approach the public sphere from a praxis-oriented, rather than normative, perspective that explores how religious publics actually come into being through shared images, texts, sounds, and styles of binding, and (3) to consider limitations that follow from Pentecostalism's strong public appearance. My overall concern is to contribute to developing a broader research agenda on public religion, and the role of Christianity in African public culture, that links up with debates about religion in the public sphere, yet all the same takes into account the specificity of African lifeworlds.

Historical Legacies

The salient public presence of Pentecostalism across Africa currently receives much scholarly attention. However, it would be a mistake to regard the public manifestation of Pentecostalism—often regarded as public religion par excellence—as an entirely new phenomenon, as if earlier on religion in Africa would have been confined to the private sphere. The rise of Pentecostal-charismatic churches as a public force in the aftermath of "democratization" must be situated in a longer trajectory, paying particular attention to the transforming relationship between state and religion from precolonial to colonial and postcolonial times. While the modern notion of public (as opposed to private) cannot be applied to precolonial African societies in a meaningful manner, it is certainly the case that calling upon indigenous gods and spirits was part and parcel of (chieftaincy) politics, espousing an open and accessible (and thus public in the broad sense) as well as a hidden or secret dimension. With regard to the colonial period, it would be a mistake to assume that colonial administrations and missions, though introducing religion as a modern category into African societies,[15] actually placed religion in the private sphere. Certainly within the policy of indirect rule, but also in the cooperation between colonial administration and missions in the field of education, religion was a strong public factor.[16] Instead of taking the public sphere as a normative model that brings about a distinction between public and private spheres and locates religion in the latter, we need more detailed historical research on the meaning of *public* and the shifting place of religion—or better, religions—in African societies in the aftermath of colonization and independence. In this way it will be possible to understand the legacies of the past in Pentecostal ways of going public in our time.

The contemporary Ghanaian state still faces the colonial legacy of the distinction between Christianity and traditional religion. It entailed not only the reconfiguration of indigenous worship practices as a less advanced kind of religion but also the significantly different valuation of Christianity and traditional religion with regard to their capacity to instill modern personhood and civic virtues. With the rise of Christianity as the religion of civilization and modernity—one that claims to open people's eyes—traditional religion was increasingly pushed out of the public sphere. Of course, this by no means put an end to local spirits and modes of worship, but it implied their relocation in a framework of backwardness and secrecy—a hidden and thus all the more powerful base to fall back on in times of hardship.[17] The relocation yielded a complicated hierarchical relation between Christianity, which became public and respectable, and traditional religion as increasingly barred from view, yet recognized as all the more powerful. Based on this relational framework, it became the project of Christian churches to cast light on what was shrouded in the secrecy of traditional worship. This drive toward exposure—a kind of making public—underpins contemporary Pentecostal preachers' struggle to unmask the "powers of darkness" that are found to be at the heart of traditional religion. Thus, for Pentecostals the very act of making public is enshrined in a longstanding Christian mode of revelation that seeks to *unmask* what lies *hidden* behind the surface of appearances.[18] Making public is thus not a neutral act but inscribed in a Christian logic of outreach and revelation.

What Is New?

There is a remarkable tension between Pentecostal modes of gaining public presence by going public and statements about secular democracy. In Ghana associations such as the National Media Commission and the Commission on Human Rights and Administrative Justice seek to insert civic virtues that befit the new democratic constitution into news reporting and media programming. In its report on broadcasting standards, the National Media Commission states that the content of religious programs "shall be prepared with due regard and respect for the beliefs and sensibilities of all religions." All the same, many Christian-Pentecostal programs on television and radio launch fierce attacks against traditional religion, and to some extent Islam. Even though television and radio stations are formally secular, much airtime is sold to Pentecostal churches that use the media according to their own logic, often employing spectacular modes of bringing across their message. In the wake of the 2008 elections, journalists critiqued the remarkable preparedness of politicians to rely on spiritual forces, as this "weakens rationalization and reality of the development issues, so much so that even elites ... who are expected to radiate higher reasoning to illuminate the development path, are under the heavy sway of the prophets, Voodoo priests, Malams, juju-marabout mediums, witchdoctors, Shamans and other spiritualists to the injury of Ghana's larger progress."[19] Clearly, in the Ghanaian setting the emphasis on civic virtues embedded in secular democracy, on the one hand, and the spectacular public presence of (especially Pentecostal) religion, on the other, are at loggerheads.[20]

In Ghana, as in many other African countries, the adoption of a democratic constitution *and* the concomitant liberalization and commercialization of mass media transformed the public sphere. This new public sphere not only involves citizens by granting them the right to elect and critically debate the government, it is also shaped by neoliberal capitalism and the forces of the market, which are eagerly seized by Pentecostal media ministries. No longer fully dominated by the state, Pentecostals got unprecedented possibilities for public manifestation, using commercial structures for the spread of the gospel. The simultaneous turn to democracy and commercial media allowed for the manifestation of Pentecostalism as a public religion.[21] At stake is the emergence of a striking hybrid form that blurs Habermas's classical ideal public sphere—with the salon and coffeehouse as the habitat of the responsible citizen—*and* what he described as a degeneration of this ideal model into a commercialized culture industry that addresses people as consumers. In other words, in Ghana, as in many other African countries, the public sphere is a new, open setting for critical debate *as well as* a stage for spectacle (especially miracles) and display of religious identity. This hybridity, and the ensuing ambivalence and contestation, should be at the center of our research on religion in the current public sphere in Africa. While the public sphere hardly conforms in practice to normative positions grounded in secular democracy, it is all the more important to study such positions in action, as they are mobilized against religious encroachment.

Not only is the actual public sphere more messy than one might assume on the basis of a normative and Eurocentric position that associates it with civic values and secular democracy, public religion itself also has distinctive features. Common views of Christianity are challenged by the ways in which Pentecostal-charismatic churches appear in public and propel a distinct imagination of the world by making skillful use of the mass media. In a marked distinction to Max Weber's analysis of sixteenth- and seventeenth-century Calvinists and Puritans in *The Protestant Ethic*[22]—all too often evoked in addressing the consonance between the spread of Pentecostalism and neoliberal capitalism[23]—for Pentecostals the world is not a compromising setting from which to shy away. Instead, the world requires action and transformation, although this is full of difficulties and dangers. In this sense, Pentecostal cosmology is strongly oriented toward world making. Consumer items, as the prosperity gospel also stipulates, are an inalienable part of it. Commodities and gifts are far from bad per se, because their positive or negative nature entirely depends on the spirit that is supposed to be behind them. In principle, anything can be imbued with the Holy Spirit, and thus be a blessing in a born-again's life. This is what accounts for the close connection between the spread of capitalism, consumerism, and the appeal of the prosperity gospel. Pentecostalism embeds neoliberal economics.

Instead of using a normative lens to state how far the current African public sphere is (or is not) removed from Habermas's classical model, critical questions need to be asked. What is the relation between the constitution of new arenas for critical debate, entailing the cultivation and expression of new civic virtues, and the embracing of market structures by key public players? How do religious movements, in particular Pentecostal-charismatic churches, mediate between both? How do being a citizen, a Christian, and a consumer come together—or rub against each other—in the public display of a born-again identity? Which notion of citizenship underpins the concomitant promotion of development and engagement in faith-based organizations? How can we get beyond the Protestant ethic as the guiding template in assessing, or even judging, how Pentecostalism thrives in the interface of democratization and the market?

Religious Publics—From Abstraction to Embodiment

Over the past few years there has been a shift in understanding from the public sphere as disembodied—as a zone of rational debate and communicative interaction grounded in concepts—to a recognition of shared sentiments and tastes, based on appeals made to senses and emotions. This move has yielded more attention to the public sphere as a concrete arena or stage for appearance, as the saying that certain groups are "going public" also implies.[24] The public sphere is in principle accessible to all citizens, and yet it is filled with signs and markers of separate (religious) identities. In Ghana's capital, Accra, Pentecostal-charismatic churches excel in asserting their presence by spreading images, texts, and sounds throughout the public space of the city. Indeed, a Pentecostal church service not only addresses the church members and visitors who are present but also a broader audience outside that should hear and be touched by the message.[25] Powerful sound amplification systems are enveloped in a broader project of spreading the gospel by reaching the ears of even unbelievers, suggesting a remarkable alignment between media technologies and religion. In this volume, Barbara Cooper (chapter 4) also addresses the importance of using airwaves for the making of religious countercommunities—an observation that resonates with Charles Hirschkind's work on sound and listening in creating an alternative public that is geared to expressing and achieving Islamic piety.[26] The act of expressing religious identity through sound waves is prone to raise conflicts. In Accra, year after year there have been fierce conflicts between Pentecostals and the traditional Ga, who require Christians to respect the taboo of noisemaking before the annual Homowo festival.[27] In such a conflict, sound is called upon in a broader struggle over the staging of identities, in which making "noise" or keeping "silent" become key issues of conflict. These issues are almost impossible to resolve for a formally secular state that has in the past been heavily involved with African heritage politics (sankofaism), yet increasingly realizes the need to acknowledge the power of Pentecostal constituencies.

With the rise of public religions, the public sphere has increasingly been recognized as forming a site for the expression of styles of identity and politics of belonging, in which the staging of particular (religious) identities, and modes of inclusion and exclusion, are hotly contested concerns.[28] Looking at how the public sphere operates in practice, it appears as a site of negotiation and struggle, in which different publics claim presence and power, making themselves visible and audible to others through specific aesthetic styles. The point is to explore actual processes and power structures in which publics are formed, so as to find out why and how certain publics become more present and powerful than others, generating tensions between dominant and counterpublics.

With regard to the Ghanaian setting, for instance, it is clear that Pentecostal pastors have been quite successful not only in conquering public space through images, texts, and sounds. They also contribute to mobilizing a particular, new religious public that espouses a born-again personal identity and more and more successfully recasts the Ghanaian nation as a site of a spiritual battle between God and Satan. This attempt to envelop public culture with Christianity, by making skillful use of modern mass media, may well be described as a Pentecostalization of the public sphere. It occurs through a particular style of mobilization that is centered around new iconic figures of success and seeks to involve people by generating commitment. While some attention is being paid already to the various styles through which male pastors address and seek to bind their audiences,[29] it is high time, as Damaris Parsitau points out (chapter 6 of this volume), to also turn to female pastors who act as alternative figures of success, thereby questioning gender stereotypes and allowing for women's identification with public figures.

One intriguing aspect of current Pentecostal modes of public appearance is that personal, intimate, or secret matters move center stage, becoming prime matters to be made public. Far from being a merely personal affair, conversion implies that people are on the move and articulate their new identity to the outside world. Indeed, as James Pritchett puts it (chapter 1 of this volume), conversion signals the construction of, and membership in, a new public. The interconnection between public and personal is also relevant to understanding recent modes of exposing matters that would so far not have been found suitable for public consumption. In becoming a public force, Pentecostalism turns the personal into a matter of public concern.[30] Over the past years, in Ghana as in many other countries, many new radio programs have emerged, run by Christian (and often Pentecostal) hosts, that evolve around intimate and sexual matters.[31] What hitherto remained concealed from public exposure and was assigned to the sphere of the intimate or secret (such as involvement with witchcraft, evil spirits, and so on) have become public issues—as scandals and public confessions of the love life of "fallen pastors," their secret affiliations with occult forces, and the corrupting craze for wealth amply show. Independent cultural entrepreneurs also participate in this logic of uncovering, as with the Ghanaian and Nigerian popular video industry, which at least to some extent thrives on Christian modes of making public.[32] Implying the transgression of older boundaries between public and personal, and the casting of intimate and secret matters as public themes, Pentecostal and other modes of going and making public require more attention in future research.

Going and Making Public

Pentecostal Media and a New Shared Style

Throughout Africa, the public sphere has become the site for the staging of new religious identities that stand in a more or less complicated relation to the state and to each other. Much has been written about the failure of postcolonial authoritarian African states to offer their citizens convincing national identities that command their commitment at the expense of ethnic or religious identities. This is the setting in which we need to situate the rise of new religious imagined communities that thrive through the accessibility and use of media and new technological infrastructures. Benedict Anderson has stressed the power of shared imaginations—materializing through language, symbols, and images, and communicated through media—to induce and affirm a sense of belonging.[33] In his perspective, "communities," or publics, revolve around mediated imaginations that are able to transcend the (spatial) distance between members by generating a feeling of togetherness.

Studying the eager adoption of new—or better, newly accessible—media by Pentecostal-charismatic churches, scholars have pointed out that it makes sense to regard media not as foreign but intrinsic to religion. Once religion is understood as linking the realms of humans and spirits—as a practice of mediation—it makes no longer sense to posit a sharp distinction between religion and media.[34] Adopting a view of religion as mediating between humans and spirits raises intriguing new questions about the media use of public religions such as Pentecostal-charismatic churches. Investigating Pentecostal media use from this perspective, one notices a salient adoption of new media technologies into church services and Christian outreach. In the process, media are often naturalized and taken for granted or hailed as especially suitable technologies to convey a sense of divine presence. The point is that media are fully incorporated in religious communication among practitioners, and between them and God. Media such as the microphone, radio, television, films, or books are sanctified as suitable harbingers of divine power, without which it could not be transmitted. Thus, Pentecostals adopt and incorporate new technologies by authorizing them as vehicles of the Holy Spirit and thus as indispensable in the project of outreach.[35] At stake here is a confluence of media technologies and the spiritual realm that is to be reached through media—in this sense, God is located in the medium. The drive to use mass media in the religious project of spreading the gospel makes Pentecostalism a religion that swamps the public sphere with its texts, images, and sounds.

Indeed, as religious imagined communities depend on accessible infrastructures through which information circulates and is being shared, we need to take into account the concrete processes through which such communities come into being. Importantly, being part of a particular imagined community is not only a matter of the mind but of common structures of experience that mobilize commitment through a shared style.[36] Paying attention to style opens up a broader field of inquiry that alerts us to the importance of public appearance and modes of doing things without assigning them to mere outward and hence secondary matters. Inducing as well as expressing strong shared moods through a religious aesthetics, a religious style makes people feel at home. In a world of constant change, style offers some continuity and stability. Style is defined by a relationship between appearance, recognition, and identification. Expressing a distinct identity that is recognized by both those who associate with a style and who do not do so, style belongs to the public domain.

Thriving on repetition and serialization, style induces a mode of participation through the techniques of mimesis and emulation that yields a particular habitus. As Michel Maffesoli has argued, sharing images generates not only strong feelings of togetherness and speaks to, as well as mirrors, particular moods and sentiments, but it also forms people into a particular, common appearance.[37] Religious style, then, constitutes a particular kind of religious subjects who conceive of themselves and the divine in a particular way, employ particular mediation practices to access the realm of spirits, and constitute themselves through particular techniques of the self, modes of consumption, and practices of sharing united in the image of God.

Attention to style allows us as researchers to take seriously the actual appearance of religion—in the built environment, in mass-mediated audiovisual images, and in the bodies of religious practitioners—without reducing appearance to a mere outward expression. Taking into account the actual emphasis placed on appearance by religious people is a suitable point of entry into the approach to religion from a material, sensory angle. Significantly, it is commonly acknowledged that appearance is a prime concern for those participating in Pentecostal churches. A person's appearance—the type of clothes, the car, the house—is seen as the indication of an interior spiritual state. Since, in accordance with the prosperity gospel, wealth is regarded as a sign of blessing from the Lord, much emphasis is placed on what might be viewed as "mere outward things" from a more orthodox Christian perspective. Of course, not all people attracted to these churches are healthy and rich, but the guiding idea is that participation may work in favor of this aim, by calling the Holy Spirit into the materiality of being. Participation works very much by sharing certain patterns of consumption and ways of doing and sensing things together, even if by sheer mimicry. In this way, people feel like somebody, although they may find it very difficult to bring their lives fully in line with the blessed state of the idealized born-again. In other words, as religious identities and communities materialize through style, style is of central importance in public religion and the public sphere.

The Cost of Public Appearance

Last but not least it needs to be pointed out that the emergence of new public spheres, and new possibilities of being in public and becoming a public, does not imply that all religions become public in the same manner. To turn to Ghana once again, there is a host of Pentecostal-charismatic megachurches that make sophisticated use of new media. With their language grounded in both the Bible and business, and their commercial, money-oriented outlook and theology, Pentecostal churches appear as successful mergers of church and business corporation, a point that is also often raised against these churches. Thus far, mainstream churches and Islamic groups, let alone traditional cults, have been somewhat reluctant to follow the Pentecostal example. It is not only a question of availability of funds but also a question of outlook. Though for different reasons, these religious groups were less prone to use the mass media so as to broadcast their messages to an anonymous mass audience.

Marleen de Witte has compared differences in attitudes toward media and mass mediation between representatives of the neotraditional Afrikania movement, on the one hand, and the International Central Gospel Church, run by Mensa Otabil, on the other.[38] Afrikania is heavily indebted to the state project of sankofaism that was central to state cultural policy in the period up to 1992. Dissatisfied with the current erosion of sankofaism and the perceived failure on the part of the state to bind citizens into this heritage project, Afrikania strives to strengthen traditional culture and religion. In the present public sphere, however,

Afrikania is not very successful. Not only does Afrikania lack the funds to produce effective televised services, it also finds itself always already positioned as Christianity's Other, and thus equated with stereotypical views of traditional religion as the repository of the powers of darkness. It is virtually impossible to counter the Pentecostal symbolic violence vis-à-vis traditional religion by broadcasting alternative images. The main problem here is that the traditional priests associated with Afrikania are not eager to be visualized in front of television cameras.[39] We encounter here a "public performance of secrecy"[40] that asserts that African power owes its efficacy to being hidden from view. Hence Afrikania—all attempts to modernize and adapt to contemporary religious forms notwithstanding—occupies a quite marginal position in the public sphere. In analyzing a decisively public religion such as Pentecostalism, we need to place it in a broader religious field and assess how differences in access to media, as well as conventions of representation and appearance intrinsic to particular religious traditions influence the degree to, and the mode in which, religions actually go public.

In distinction to traditional cults, Pentecostal churches fully engage in what I call a public performance of revelation, striving to assert the reality of spiritual power through compelling mass-mediated images. What we encounter here is not a conservative, reverse move out of the system of mass media and information networks, as suggested by Manuel Castells.[41] In his view, the adoption of modern mass media technologies into religion is supposed to ultimately destroy religion's legitimacy and its claims to point a way out of the system. I disagree with his claim that in this process "societies are finally and truly disenchanted because all wonders are on-line and can be combined into self-constructed image worlds."[42] On the contrary, this type of church prides itself in being able to guide people right into such networks and to offer powerful symbols around which a community of born-again practitioners is being concentrated. This process, however, is inherently unstable, as church leaders lack the power to ultimately control the frequency and intensity with which audiences participate in the actual church or live up to the Christian moral standards. Opting for a mass organization and spreading out into the public sphere may easily come at the cost of what is lamented as watering down. This is not only a criticism made by historic churches against Pentecostal-charismatic megachurches, but also by now an often heard lamentation in Pentecostal circles themselves. Such worries express concerns about the ultimate impossibility of concentrating a Christian mass audience into the organizational form of a church, a point also made by Ilana van Wyk (chapter 9 of this volume).

Congregating around the iconized image of the pastor, spectators form part of a new kind of community that is quite different from the congregational model that still organizes social relations among practitioners and church leaders in historic churches. The new kind of community excels by the marked contrast between the utmost control that the church leadership wields over the carefully designed images of the pastor-star and his ideal congregation, and its actual lack of control over the mass audience that attends services or watches the televised program. While editing can eliminate inappropriate forms of behavior and thus produce a perfect image, it is far more difficult to extend such forms of inclusion and exclusion to the world of the spectators. Binding them through a shared style requires much work and is potentially unstable.

OUR UNDERSTANDING of Pentecostalism as a public religion requires that we take seriously its material, tangible dimension. Ultimately, this calls for a revision of a still common view of religion as situated in opposition to matter, as if materiality and religion could belong to two entirely different spheres. In fact, we need not only to rethink the public sphere, taking leave of idealist, elitist, Eurocentric and all-too-abstract notions, but also to develop fresh approaches to religion in general, and Pentecostalism in particular. Rethinking the public sphere in our time requires rethinking religion, and vice versa.

Notes

1. Birgit Meyer, *Translating the Devil: Religion and Modernity among the Ewe in Ghana* (Edinburgh: Edinburgh University Press, 1999).

2. *Sankofa* (depicting a bird looking back, meaning "go back and take it") is an Akan symbol that stands for the Ghanaian state project of cultural heritage.

3. Birgit Meyer, "Money, Power and Morality: Popular Ghanaian Cinema in the Fourth Republic," *Ghana Studies* 4 (2001): 65–84; Meyer, "'Praise the Lord': Popular Cinema and Pentecostalite Style in Ghana's New Public Sphere," *American Ethnologist* 31, no. 1 (2004): 92–110.

4. See, for example, J. Kwabena Asamoah-Gyadu, *African Charismatics: Current Developments within Independent Indigenous Pentecostalism in Ghana* (Leiden: Brill, 2005); Paul Gifford, *Ghana's New Christianity: Pentecostalism in a Globalising African Economy* (London: Hurst, 2004).

5. A report published by the U.S. State Department states, "According to the 2000 government census, approximately 69 percent of the country's population is Christian, 16 percent is Muslim, and 9 percent adheres to traditional indigenous religions or other

religions. The Muslim community has protested these figures, asserting that the Muslim population is closer to 30 percent." U.S. State Department, "Ghana: Religious Freedom Report," 2002, http://atheism.about.com/library/irf/irf03/blirf_ghana.htm. Within Christianity, Pentecostalism is a major force. Not only do Pentecostal-charismatic churches grow (both in numbers and the number of members), its emphasis on the Holy Spirit and fighting demons is also appealing to mainstream Anglicanism, Presbyterianism, Catholicism, and Pentecostalism. See also Gifford, *Ghana's New Christianity*.

6. Jürgen Habermas, *The Structural Transformation of the Public Sphere: An Inquiry into a Category of Bourgeois Society* (Cambridge, MA: MIT Press, 1989).

7. Peter Berger, ed., *The Desecularization of the World: Resurgent Religion and World Politics* (Grand Rapids: Eerdmans, 1999).

8. Jürgen Habermas, "On the Relation Between the Secular Liberal State and Religion," in *The Frankfurt School on Religion: Key Writings by the Major Thinkers*, ed. Eduardo Mendieta (New York: Routledge, 2005): 327–38.

9. José Casanova, *Public Religions in the Modern World* (Chicago: University of Chicago Press, 1994).

10. Charles Taylor, *A Secular Age* (Cambridge, MA: Harvard University Press, 2007).

11. Talal Asad, *Formations of the Secular: Christianity, Islam, Modernity* (Stanford: Stanford University Press, 2003).

12. See also Hent de Vries, ed., *Religion: Beyond a Concept* (New York: Fordham University Press, 2008).

13. See also Karin Barber, *The Anthropology of Texts, Persons and Publics: Oral and Written Culture in Africa and Beyond* (Cambridge: Cambridge University Press, 2007), 137.

14. These issues have emerged from the research program Modern Mass Media, Religion and the Imagination of Communities, which I directed between 2000 and 2006 and which encompassed nine research projects on religion and the public sphere in West Africa, South Asia, Brazil, and the Caribbean. The key proposition of the initial program proposal was that the relationship between the postcolonial nation-state, media, and religion has been significantly reconfigured since the mid-1990s and has entailed the emergence of a new public sphere characterized by the blurring of neat, modernist distinctions between public and private, religion and politics, debate and entertainment. The main concern of the program, as formulated in the original proposal, was to chart the emergence of such new arenas in concrete locations on the basis of thorough empirical investigations and, at the same time, to question and rethink the rather normative Western concepts that are usually employed as analytical tools. Seeking to appreciate cultural particularities and yet to yield generalizable analyses, the program proposal made a plea for detailed historical and ethnographic exploration in the framework of a comparative perspective. For more information, see Modern Mass Media, Religion and the Imagination of Communities, Research Centre Religion and Society/Amsterdam School for Social Science Research, University of Amsterdam, http://www.pscw.uva.nl/media-religion.

15. David Chidester, *Savage Systems: Colonialism and Comparative Religion in Southern Africa* (Charlottesville: University Press of Virginia, 1996).

16. Karen Fields, *Revival and Rebellion in Colonial Central Africa* (Princeton: Princeton University Press, 1985).

17. Meyer, *Translating the Devil*.

18. Birgit Meyer, "Religious Revelation, Secrecy, and the Limits of Visual Representation," *Anthropological Theory* 6, no. 4 (2006): 431–53.

19. Kofi Akosah-Sarpong in *Ghana News*, September 4, 2008.

20. Marleen de Witte, "Business of the Spirit: Ghanaian Broadcast Media and the Commercial Exploitation of Pentecostalism," paper presented at the European Council of African Studies Conference, Leipzig, 2009.

21. Birgit Meyer, "Pentecostal and Neo-liberal Capitalism: Faith, Prosperity and Vision in African Pentecostal-Charismatic Churches," *Journal for the Study of Religion* 20, no. 2 (2007): 5–28.

22. Max Weber, *The Protestant Ethic and the Spirit of Capitalism* (New York: Charles Scribner's Sons, 1920).

23. For example, Peter Berger, "Max Weber Is Alive and Well, and Living in Guatemala: The Protestant Ethic Today," http://www.economyandsociety.org/events/Berger_paper.pdf; Sandy Johnston, *Under the Radar: Pentecostalism in South Africa and Its Potential Social and Economic Role* (Johannesburg: Centre for Development and Enterprise, 2008).

24. Birgit Meyer, "From Imagined Communities to Aesthetic Formations: Religious Mediations, Sensational Forms, and Styles of Binding," in *Aesthetic Formations: Media, Religion, and the Senses*, ed. Meyer (New York: Palgrave Macmillan, 2009).

25. Marleen de Witte, "Spirit Media: Charismatics, Traditionalists, and Mediation Practices in Ghana" (PhD diss., University of Amsterdam, 2008).

26. Charles Hirschkind, *The Ethical Soundscape: Cassette Sermons and Islamic Counterpublics* (New York: Columbia University Press, 2006).

27. Rijk van Dijk, "Contesting Silence: The Ban on Drumming and the Musical Politics of Pentecostalism in Ghana," *Ghana Studies* 4 (2001): 31–64.

28. Peter Geschiere, *The Perils of Belonging: Autochthony, Citizenship, and Exclusion in Africa and Europe* (Chicago: University of Chicago Press, 2009).

29. De Witte, "Spirit Media."

30. The making public of private matters is a broader development. Politics in the West appears to be a field in which ever more is exposed about the private life of politicians. What is so interesting about the Ghanaian setting is the fact that it is not so much secular forces but Pentecostals who engage in casting private and secret matters into public concerns.

31. For example, Tilo Grätz, "Religious Radio Broadcasting in Benin," paper presented at the European Council of African Studies Conference, Leipzig, 2009.

32. Meyer, "Religious Revelation."

33. Benedict Anderson, *Imagined Communities: Reflections on the Origin and Spread of Nationalism* (London: Verso, 1991).

34. Hent de Vries, "In Media Res: Global Religion, Public Spheres, and the Task of Contemporary Comparative Religious Studies," in *Religion and Media*, ed. Vries and Samuel Weber (Stanford: Stanford University Press, 2001), 4–42. See also Harri Englund, "Witchcraft and the Limits of Mass Mediation in Malawi," *Journal of the Royal Anthropological Institute* 13, no. 2 (2007): 295–311; Jeremy Stolow, "Religion and/as Media," *Theory, Culture and Society* 22, no. 4 (2005): 119–45; Meyer, "Imagined Communities."

35. Marleen de Witte, "Altar Media's *Living Word*: Televised Christianity in Ghana," *Journal of Religion in Africa* 33, no. 2 (2003): 172–202; De Witte, "Spirit Media."

36. Meyer, "'Praise the Lord'"; Birgit Meyer, "Religious Sensations: Why Media, Aesthetics, and Power Matter in the Study of Contemporary Religion," in *Religion: Beyond a Concept*, ed. Hent de Vries (New York: Fordham University Press, 2008), 704–23.

37. Michel Maffesoli, *The Contemplation of the World: Figures of Community Style* (Minneapolis: University of Minnesota Press, 1996).

38. Marleen de Witte, "The Spectacular and the Spirits: Charismatics and Neo-traditionalists on Ghanaian Television," *Material Religion* 1, no. 3 (2005): 314–35; De Witte, "Spirit Media."

39. A recent intriguing exception is Kwaku Bonsam, a self-declared native priest and former Christian, who has since 2008 sought public appearance and the limelight of television to expose the hypocrisy of Pentecostal pastors.

40. Mattijs van de Port, "Priests and Stars: Candomblé, Celebrity Postscripts, Discourses, and the Authentication of Religious Authority in Bahia's Public Sphere," *Postscripts: The Journal of Sacred Texts and Contemporary Worlds* 1, nos. 2–3 (2005): 301–24.

41. Manuel Castells, *The Rise of the Network Society* (Oxford: Blackwell, 1996).

42. Ibid., 406.

EIGHT

From Spiritual Warfare to Spiritual Kinship
Islamophobia and Evangelical Radio in Malawi

HARRI ENGLUND

FOLLOWING THE hotly contested presidential and parliamentary elections of 1999, mosques and churches became the targets of arson attacks in some parts of Malawi. During the campaign, leading politicians rarely highlighted religious differences between the incumbent, Bakili Muluzi, a Muslim, and his main rival, Gwanda Chakuamba, a Christian.[1] Yet, as is discussed in this chapter, for specific historical reasons, popular mistrust of Muslims loomed large during and after the elections. When Muluzi was declared the winner, some Christians allegedly burned mosques in the Northern Region, where the majority of Muslims were migrants from the Central and Southern Regions. In Chinsapo, a township in Malawi's capital, Lilongwe, in the Central Region, where I have conducted ethnographic research, it was churches that were torched. No more than two churches in a township of some thirty thousand residents had this fate, apparently randomly chosen at night. One of them was the Faith for Healing Life Church, a Pentecostal church established by a migrant from Blantyre, Malawi's commercial capital, in the Southern Region.[2] A building made of thatch and soil, it burned like a bonfire before any of its members had arrived on the scene. Although members and nonmembers alike were convinced that Muslim youths in the same township were responsible, church members ruled out retaliation in kind. Time and again, church elders and lay members asserted that they would retaliate only through prayer. Fervent prayers took place in church members' homes and on the site of their torched church, weapons of a warfare that was waged in the name of the Holy Spirit.

Pentecostal and charismatic Christians, in Chinsapo Township and elsewhere, often single out Islam as their key spiritual adversary, closely associating its diabolical nature with Satanism and witchcraft.[3] Yet if the bellicose rhetoric of spiritual warfare is examined in its specific historical and ethnographic context, a fresh perspective on the vexing issue of religious polarization can be gained. The members of the Faith for Healing Life Church refrained from physical violence, and there is no evidence to suggest that the attacks on mosques in the Northern Region were carried out by Pentecostal Christians. In this regard, the well-motivated concern among the so-called civil-society organizations in Malawi about religious and political intolerance could benefit from an appreciation of how some spiritual orientations can actually defuse the specter of violence. Human rights organizations, for example, have issued statements and convened meetings to condemn so-called fundamentalism, whether of Muslim or Christian complexion, and to assert the place of religion in the private sphere of citizens' lives. One event in 2006 had as its guest of honor Justin Malewezi, Malawi's former vice president, widely respected for his moderate views. "Now and then we notice fundamentalist views on radio and preachings seeping into religious discourse and practice," Malewezi observed. "Such language may pave the way for an outburst of violence, and this would be so destructive and alien to the peaceful Malawi we know."[4]

Interesting in Malewezi's statement is not only his concern over language use but also his understanding of the role radio plays in Malawi. As the only mass medium in the country, radio has been central to both political and religious developments.[5] Malewezi did not specify whether he considered fundamentalism a problem for both Christians and Muslims, but it would seem that Muslims, whatever their political advantage during Muluzi's regime, are rather less well represented on the airwaves. Of the twenty-one broadcasting stations that the Malawi Communications Regulatory Authority (MACRA) had licensed by 2006, only one, Radio Islam, focused on Muslims, while six stations had a broadly Pentecostal or evangelical profile.[6] Yet just as there is no gainsaying close analysis of what spiritual warfare entails in the rhetoric and practice of township Pentecostals, so too are the procedures of evangelical radio stations in Malawi rather more complex than what labeling them as fundamentalist would seem to suggest. In 2006, for example,

Transworld Radio, a Malawian-run evangelical station, discovered that its broadcasts were affected by interference from Radio Islam.[7] Upon receiving a complaint from Transworld Radio, MACRA ordered Radio Islam to suspend its broadcasts until the problem of overlapping transmission signals was solved. Although Radio Islam professed its innocence, rumors were rife that the incident was merely another step in the rivalry between Muslims and Christians. The born-again officials of Transworld Radio did not, however, seek to escalate the apparent conflict. The issue was reported by the secular mainstream media, whereas Transworld Radio not only followed the appropriate procedures by filing a complaint with MACRA, but also organized prayer meetings among its staff to expedite a swift resolution of the problem. Rather than inciting its listeners to confront Muslims in person, the station engaged in spiritual warfare.

Spiritual warfare, in other words, merits the kind of attention that dismissals of religious intolerance or fundamentalism cannot provide.[8] This chapter examines spiritual warfare from the perspective of the two domains mentioned above: township Pentecostalism and Transworld Radio.[9] The focus is on Transworld Radio's weekly program of testimonies delivered in the Chichewa language by its listeners, but the themes and allusions that these depictions of spiritual warfare carry are best analyzed within the ethnographic and linguistic appreciation I have acquired through fieldwork in Chinsapo since 1996.[10] The station draws the testimonies it broadcasts from an audience that largely corresponds to the born-again population in Chinsapo: impoverished, relatively poorly educated, and only partly urbanized in a predominantly rural country.[11] This perspective on spiritual warfare and radio broadcasting indicates some of the intellectual resources for thinking about claim making that expands the scope of human relationships despite all the public interventions to narrow it down, from politicians' ethnoregionalism to the individualism of Malawi's dominant human rights discourse.[12] What are the prospects for democratic membership in a country characterized by ethnic and religious diversity amid entrenched economic inequalities? To look for answers only within a seemingly secular public culture, or to ignore or condemn spiritual arguments when they do engage public affairs, is to lose out on alternative intellectual resources. A nuanced look at spiritual warfare, for example, can uncover a sense in which Pentecostals' vigilance against enemies within as much as without provides a basis for the expansion of trust and public responsibility.

It should be clear that at issue is not a blueprint to solve democracy's problems in Malawi or elsewhere. The objective is to explore the rights and obligations of membership that this analysis throws into relief.

Islamophobia, Poverty, and Pentecostalism

At some 12 percent of the national population, Muslims form a significant minority in Malawi. Conversion to Islam commenced in the mid-nineteenth century along the shores of Lake Malawi.[13] Many non-Muslim Malawians use the Chichewa words for Muslims (*asilamu*) and Yao (*aChawa*) interchangeably, although not all people who identify themselves as Yao are Muslims (or vice versa). A merchant class dominated by entrepreneurs of South Asian extraction also contributes to Islam's visibility in Malawi's urban centers. On Fridays, merchants close their shops for part of the day in order to attend mosques, pursued by beggars who are aware of the day's religious significance. Although popular resentment against these entrepreneurs—their profiteering, exploitative labor relations, and segregated lifestyle—had simmered for a long time in Malawi, as in other countries in the region, its public expression found few outlets before the democratic transition in the early 1990s. An important aspect of the new public discourse was a heightened sense of Muslims' religious particularity, suspicions of Satanism often fuelling popular reflections on Asian entrepreneurs' wealth.[14] A Muslim's ascension to state presidency in the 1994 elections sharpened the public focus on religion and ethnicity. Bakili Muluzi, who led the country for two terms until 2004, never cultivated the image of a pious Muslim, but his fraternization with local and foreign Muslim entrepreneurs brought resources to the patronage that increasingly characterized his regime. Although he owed his victory to the popularity of the United Democratic Front (UDF) in the populous Southern Region, his Yao identity reinforced popular associations between Islam, exploitation, and the Yao. For many non-Muslim Malawians, the UDF's emphasis on trading rather than agriculture and manufacture seemed to confirm a particular ethnicized and Islamic economic policy that only a few would benefit from.[15]

In spite of the new constitutional freedoms that it heralded, the democratic transition did not improve the economic fortunes of Malawi's impoverished majority.[16] The poverty incidence by head count rose from 60 percent in 1992 to 65 percent in 2000, endemic food insecurity deepened, a famine devastated many parts of the country in 2001–2002, and Malawi ranked as the third worst country in the world in terms of income inequality in 2001.[17] In places such as Chinsapo Township, religion was by no means the only domain within which the poor debated Malawi's inequalities and governance. Yet Muluzi's Muslim identity served to polarize township dwellers' views on his rule. When it was announced in 1999 that he had won a second term in office, the chairman of a township mosque climbed to the roof of his house and shouted that the Yao had won and that Islam would rule in Malawi. A successful landlord, he went on to declare that if any of his tenants had voted for some other party than the UDF, they should leave his houses immediately. Such public acts of agitation, and the arson attacks mentioned above, were rare, and public discourse in Chinsapo was sustained by rumor and gossip rather than by physical violence.[18]

A particularly persistent rumor concerned the imminent Islamization of Malawi, associated with the state visit by the Libyan leader Muʻammar Gadhafi and with the funds and business partnerships Muluzi was seen to secure in Saudi Arabia and elsewhere in the Middle East. One aspect of the alleged Islamization was to replace every church in the country with a mosque, while Gadhafi would buy the entire country in order to build oil rigs in Lake Malawi and export its riches. Township dwellers also held views on the Lebanese newcomers who had joined entrepreneurs of South Asian extraction as owners of restaurants and shops and as operators of various services in urban centers. One Pentecostal pastor, for example, told his audience at a social gathering that the Lebanese were evil people (*anthu oipa*), who ruined the economy wherever they went. They conducted business, he said, with fake money, took their wealth away from the country where it was produced, and instead imported guns and thieves.

Muluzi was defeated in his thinly veiled ambition to continue in office for an unconstitutional third term, and Bingu wa Mutharika was elected state president in 2004. Although apparently handpicked by Muluzi, Mutharika soon distanced himself from the UDF and established a new political party, the Democratic Progressive Party. For many impoverished Malawians, such as Chinsapo residents, Mutharika's forthright approach to his predecessor's economic mismanagement and his determination to improve Malawi's food security came as a breath of fresh air after the depths of cynicism associated with Muluzi's regime. An experienced international civil servant and a Roman Catholic, Mutharika could display a very different image than Muluzi. However, although the new regime played down religious differences, it could not avoid the polarization between Christians and Muslims that had become one aspect of the new Malawi. Muluzi had imposed Cassim Chilumpha, a Muslim, as his successor's vice president, and the relationship between Mutharika and Chilumpha became increasingly sour after the 2004 elections, culminating in Chilumpha's house arrest and court case. He was widely seen to be loyal to Muluzi, whose leadership in the UDF remained uncontested. From time to time the media would report on expressions of discontent by various organizations within the Muslim Association of Malawi (MAM). One public statement in 2005, for example, criticized Mutharika for "discrimination and oppression," citing public appointments and Chilumpha's "harassment" as evidence of a bias against Muslims.[19] Another statement complained that the MAM had been deprived of its role in distributing relief maize that Chilumpha had solicited from Muslim organizations in South Africa.[20] Muslim youths have also occasionally threatened to stage protests against what they have called "the discriminatory style of leadership of President Mutharika."[21]

Mutharika's administration consistently denounced these statements as ill-informed and politically motivated, pointing out that it had promoted Muslims to public office. At any rate, these arguments have kept the Muslim issue alive in Malawi's public culture, and discussions about Islam by no means waned in Chinsapo Township after the 2004 elections. However, it would be an exaggeration to say that a Pentecostalization of public culture has taken place in Malawi.[22] One public face of Islam in Malawi has long been its business community of South Asian extraction, widely resented and rarely encountered in any other capacity than as profiteering shopkeepers and exploitative employers. A Muslim's ascension to the presidency owed little to religious allegiances but eventually accentuated popular suspicions of Islam. Unbridled impoverishment and hunger only tarnished further the public image of the Muslim minority, whatever Muluzi's own unprincipled preferences for allies and the poverty of many Malawian Muslims themselves. It was in this context that Pentecostal Christians in Chinsapo and elsewhere found public resonance for their views on Muslims' evil ways and Satanism. Although other Christians, particularly Catholics, could still be singled out for condemnation, the Pentecostal preoccupation was increasingly with Islam. Its association with exploitation and immorality entailed a compelling complex of meanings and experiences within which to expound on demons, witches, and the devil. Osama bin Laden's name became known in the township after 2001, but it was striking how little the public discourse contributed to the vilification of Muslims as terrorists. To the extent that Pentecostals and others summoned up terror, it was terror of a spiritual kind, its effects evident in the everyday situations of poverty, misfortune, and disease.

The historical and economic context suggests that Islamophobia did not result from Pentecostalism. By the same token, Pentecostal and Muslim leaders have increasingly been locked in disputes that actually make their interventions resemble each other. Both Pentecostals and Muslims organize so-called crusades in public areas such as marketplaces and bus depots. Muslim crusades mimic Pentecostal practices by combining fiery preaching with singing and dancing.[23] Their preaching often seems to spend more time on the Bible than the Qur'an, focusing on the alleged contradictions in biblical teaching, such as its views on circumcision and the consumption of alcohol. Another public medium for the Christian-Muslim conflict has been letters that are usually circulated by Pentecostals. Signed by the devil, their contents evoke themes in *The Screwtape Letters*, the novel by C. S. Lewis.[24] Yet they resonate with contemporary Malawian concerns about the many ways in which the devil attempts to sow confusion (*chisokonezo*) among Christians. The devil typically advises demons to direct Christians' thoughts away from the Bible or the sermon they are listening to, to make them fall asleep when they are supposed to study the Bible, to disobey pastors, and so on.[25] These letters have attracted the attention of the mass media in Malawi, with some journalists asking why Christians, particularly Pentecostals, are singled out for the devil's machinations. Muslim leaders have responded by pointing out Pentecostals' near-obsession with the devil. It has enabled them to conclude that many Pentecostals are former or current Satanists themselves, their knowledge of the demonic world rather too sophisticated to be possible without personal involvement in it. Pentecostals often find it easy to counter these comments by asserting that because Muslims and Satanists are one, the devil has no reason to mention Muslims in the letters.

In 2007 an incident involving a different kind of letter, apparently originating from Muslims, showed the thin line that can separate the two spiritual adversaries. The letter, promptly disowned by the MAM, appeared to be signed by eight Muslim organizations in the Northern Region.[26] It contained a warning against the current "demonic regime" and swore Muslims' preparedness to wage physical warfare against "Kaffirs." "Muslims are people who love death more than life," the letter was reported to assert. Unlike with most other letters in circulation in Malawi, the author of this letter was arrested by the police, identified as a man resident in Mzuzu town, a former Muslim who had joined a Pentecostal church. The thin line separating some Muslims and Pentecostals is also evident in the suspicions of Satanism leveled against fellow Pentecostals. A well-known founder of a Pentecostal church in Lilongwe, for example, became embroiled in a scandal in 2003, when human body parts were rumored to have been stored in his refrigerator. The beleaguered pastor protested his innocence on the public radio, but the incident was merely a high-profile example of how the spiritual warfare against demons is waged as much within as without Pentecostal congregations.

Yet at the level of their public discourse, few Pentecostals in Chinsapo are prepared to see anything else than a yawning gap separating them from Muslims. They refer to Muslims as lost people (*anthu otayika*), selfish (*odzikuza*) in their business dealings, and adulterous (*achimasomaso*) in their appetite for polygamy. Muslim shopkeepers of South Asian extraction are said to prey on the children of their employees. One pastor in Chinsapo, for example, told me that the wife of one such employee had come to seek prayers from him against the satanic schemes that the husband had been taught by his Muslim master. Human sacrifice is a common theme in this public discourse, its topics often launched by Pentecostals but eagerly sustained by township dwellers regardless of their denomination. A long-standing rumor maintains that Muslims gather in mosques during the day but meet clandestinely in a particular building in Lilongwe's low-density Area 3 at night. This building, constructed for the Freemasons during the colonial era, is said to shelter Muslim-Satanists who indulge in drinking human blood and comparing the body parts of the people they have killed. In 2005 the high frequency of fatal road accidents received an explanation in the rumor that Satanists' world congress was going to take place in the country later that year. Large amounts of human blood were required to quench the delegates' thirst.

Alongside these contentious claims exists, however, a more subtle discourse on the common ground between Muslims and Christians, expressed by ordinary adherents during everyday encounters. I have heard Muslims in Chinsapo explaining to their Christian neighbors historical and theological affinities between the two world religions, beginning with the doctrine of monotheism. Gule Wamkulu (also known as Nyau), a male secret society associated with the Chewa, who are the autochthonous inhabitants of Lilongwe, stands as a contrast to both Islam and Christianity, not least because of persistent attempts by migrants in Chinsapo, often led by Muslims, to eliminate it.[27] Muslims say that because their worship appears to revolve around many characters rather than one God, the initiates in this secret society curse God (*amalumbira pa Mulungu*). The parallels with Pentecostalism are also clear in Muslims' emphasis on the power of prayer, which is said to make the use of charms and medicines (*mankhwala*) redundant. Whether it is protection against witchcraft or support for success in business, prayer alone can have the desired outcome. By subscribing to Pentecostals' discourse on the diabolical nature of "black medicine" (*mankhwala achikuda*) and the healers who provide it, Muslims challenge the public discourse on their involvement in Satanism and witchcraft.

Discursive challenges and counterchallenges never afford perfect descriptions of what actually takes place in the everyday lives of Muslims and Pentecostals, both of whom are susceptible to using black medicine despite their public injunctions against it. Both also refer to this predicament as backsliding (*kubwerera*). Yet the most significant reason for the frequent blurring of discursive distinctions is the impossibility of insulating oneself from contact and cooperation with people who do not share one's religious identity. Not only are Muslims, along with witches and Satanists, enthusiastically welcomed in Pentecostal churches because their second birth in the Holy Spirit is seen to prove the strength of Pentecostal prayer, but many Pentecostals in Chinsapo also encounter Muslims on a daily basis as they make their living as vendors, security guards, and casual laborers. Few Pentecostals miss the opportunity to engage Muslims in a discussion on spiritual matters, but many also realize that desirable transformations presuppose peaceful coexistence in everyday life. As a result, township dwellers lead rather more ambiguous lives than what their polarized discourses, and occasional outbursts of intolerance, would seem to suggest. Without even blinking, a Pentecostal pastor, for example, proceeded during his conversation with me from the topic of Muslims' Satanism to a story of how a friendship between himself, a Chewa, and a Yao Muslim had involved good-humored tutoring on one another's languages and customs (*miyambo*). Another example is the business of a young Pentecostal, whose location for selling secondhand clothes in the city was, before the crackdown on street vending in 2005, next to a Muslim's spot for similar business. The neighbors would often look after each other's merchandise when one of them was away, a pattern of ad hoc cooperation that was common across religious and ethnic divides in Lilongwe.

Spiritual Warfare on the Airwaves

Under the circumstances described above, spiritual warfare does more than fuel a public discourse that is only partially translated into practice. Spiritual warfare informs a way of engaging with the world and contains within its bellicose discourse a potential for the expansion of spiritual kinship.[28] Broadcasters at Transworld Radio's Lilongwe office are clear that the experience of the second birth in the Holy Spirit often reinforces a person's struggle with demons and witches rather than diminishing the concern with them. These broadcasters dismiss the suggestion that their programs actually incite such concerns and fears, pointing out, as many born-again Christians do, that the new condition enables people to engage demons in earnest.[29] However, just as Islamophobia has to be understood in the context of specific historical and economic processes, so too does spiritual warfare assume specific forms and consequences in the lives of Transworld's listeners in Malawi. Far from being left to answer to God as a lone believer, the born-again on Transworld Radio in Malawi narrates a whole range of relationships within which the struggle is fought and the salvation realized.

The testimonies (*maumboni*) delivered on the weekly program *Ndamasulidwa* share their narrative form with testimonies heard in churches and crusades. The broadcasters and their born-again public make, however, a distinction between the radio and churches as media for publicizing the good news of baptism in the Holy Spirit. Both settings of testimony serve not only to strengthen born-again Christians' own commitment but also to convince others of the necessity of their condition. The specific import of testimonies broadcast on the radio lies in their capacity to reach people who do not attend Pentecostal churches. These testimonies amplify the impact of crusades carried out in public spaces by expanding the scope for winning new brothers and sisters in Christ. Their mediation of spiritual warfare is, in other words, essential to the expansion of spiritual kinship.

The name *Ndamasulidwa* is derived from the verb *kumasula* (to set free, release). Its literal translation, "I was released," summons up the unchaining of the subject from the confines of his or her previous life. The passive voice is significant because it draws attention to the limits of the subject's own choices. God works, as is seen below, through human relationships that constitute and, during the second birth, reconstitute the subject. The program's emphasis on personal transformation is, however, often unclear to those listeners who come to the station's studios in Lilongwe and Blantyre.[30] The editors of the program have to explain time and again that they do not seek accounts about God's miracles as such but testimonies on the many ways in which God saves people from their misfortunes and misdemeanors. Thanking God (*kuthokoza Mulungu*), in other words, has to emerge from the contrast between the old life and the new. The experience of becoming born again does not have to be recent, and some testimonies are delivered by listeners who have been pastors for several years. The editors of *Ndamasulidwa* deny that the program is used by pastors to publicize their own work. Before their testimonies are recorded, the guests on the program are explicitly warned against mentioning the names of the churches with which they are, or have been, associated, although the names of the persons who played a significant role in their transformation can be stated. The topic of Islam poses particular problems for the editors. While they share the Islamophobia of their born-again public, the editors reject testimonies that demonize Islam, if only because of the complaints they would receive from Muslim organizations and the media regulator. When Islam does figure in broadcasts, the producers deploy subtler methods of demonstrating the necessity to leave it behind. Editorial discretion is also made necessary by the program's fifteen-minute slot. Most guests have far more to say than what can be broadcast, and while some testimonies are complex enough to warrant broadcast in two fifteen-minute segments, the editors often cut the material down to what they consider to be the essence of God's work in a particular case.

The editors' own born-again sensibilities are crucial to their editorial input. No one at Transworld Radio expressed doubt over the veracity of the testimonies they broadcast, however fantastic their details might seem to outsiders. Verification is, however, an issue for the producers, who tend to treat every new testimony with some initial skepticism. The reason is the false motives that may draw people to the studios, some seeking instant fame, others driven by hatred of other religions or by a desire to take revenge on their enemies. In such cases, the editors have no qualms about rejecting the testimony even if its narrator claims to be a born-again Christian. More complicated are the situations in which the editors find the narrated events plausible but regard the narrator as a lapsed Christian. He or she may have experienced what the testimony says, but something in the person's current demeanor tells the producers that he or she is a backslider. Such impressions may also result in rejecting the testimony, whatever its other merits are. The editors rarely have the opportunity to investigate their guests' background and rely therefore on their own sensibilities as born-again Christians. As such, the knowledge that is presented and evaluated is intensely personal for both the editors and their guests, and what is personal is always a function of the specific relationships that constitute persons. Some testimonies are disqualified not because the editors consider their details fantastic but because the editors, brothers and sisters in Christ, sense that the persons recounting them are subject to radically different sorts of relationships.

The radical difference between those who are born again and those who are not is often indicated by the work of the devil. Many testimonies involve descriptions of the narrator's subjection to demonic forces and witches, all understood to fall within the devil's orbit. The producers of *Ndamasulidwa* admit that they sometimes find certain aspects of testimonies frightening (*zochititsa mantha*), but they consider it their public duty to broadcast even those details that revolve around the devil's work in this world. Just as *Ndamasulidwa* shows its listeners the many ways in which God saves, so too does it teach (*kuphunzitsa*) them about the virtually infinite deceptions and horrors that besiege those who fall under the devil's reign. The program invariably ends with the presenter encouraging (*kulimbikitsa*) the listeners to take heed of the testimony in order to realize the power of God. Those who are not yet born again are often addressed directly in the presenter's final words. A typical question is, What are you waiting for? (*mukudikira chiyani?*), followed by assurances about the unique redemptive capacities of Jesus Christ. The presenter also uses idioms familiar from churches and crusades in Malawi to drive home the point that the time to mend our lives is now (*nthawi yokonza miyoyo yathu ndi ino*). She asks whether, when Jesus returns, the listener wants to be found at a beer party or, in an allusion to witchcraft, flying (*kuuluka*) at night. The program ends with the uplifting beats of Malawian gospel music, sung in Chichewa.

The Demons Within and Without

One of the recurrent themes in the program is that salvation is for everyone (*kupulumutsidwa ndi kwa aliyense*). Its editors are keen to emphasize the diversity of not only the testimonies but also the kinds of persons who give them. Religious, ethnic, generational, and gender differences are all accommodated insofar as people with diverse backgrounds bear testimony to the same promise of salvation. In practice, however, men's testimonies outnumber those of women by two to one, in spite of women's strong presence in Pentecostal churches, and most testimonies describe transformations among Christians. The idea of diversity is cherished because the apparent unpredictability of who gives a testimony is thought to prove the universal need for salvation. The reassuring, even ecstatic, descriptions of finding security in Jesus (*chitetezo mwa Yesu*) are often combined with descriptions of ongoing spiritual warfare. Richard Bika,[31] a young man reporting on his sexual exploits before finding Jesus, for example, admitted, "Satan still follows me" (*Satana amandilondolabe*), enticing him to adopt his old habits of womanizing and beer drinking. He declared, however, that he fights a war (*ndimamenya nkhondo*) and is now able to defeat (*kugonjetsa*) Satan. When asked by the journalist who recorded his testimony whether he had been unaware of sexually transmitted diseases when he had indulged in promiscuity,[32] Bika stated that he had known about them but lacked, in his English phrase, *self-control* because he did not have Jesus (*ndinalibe Yesu*).[33] Another witness to the power of Jesus, Flolensi Chiruzi, a middle-aged woman, described how she had never been explained what receiving Jesus entailed in spite of her dutiful attendance at a Christian church. "I did not have Jesus Christ's peace" (*mtendere wa Yesu Khrisitu ndinalibe*), she said, but when she had been introduced to born-again Christianity through a fellowship meeting, her friends in her church started to call her names, claiming that Pentecostalism was a satanic or demonic religion (*chipembedzo cha Satana kapena ziwanda*). Her church leader was equally disapproving and called born-again Christians mad (*amisala*). "The war continues" (*nkhondo idakalipo*), Chiruzi concluded and reported that those who had joined with her the born-again fellowship had really changed (*anasinthadi*) and understood (*amazindikira*) the power of Jesus.

Christian identity, in other words, is no guarantee of salvation. By highlighting hypocrisy and ignorance among Christians, *Ndamasulidwa* encourages exploration of inadequacies as much within as without. The program does not mention the previous Christian denominations of its guests, but the editors have confirmed to me that in the vast majority of cases the guests have moved to worship in Pentecostal and charismatic churches, despite the room for charismatic fellowship that has been created in some Anglican, Catholic, and Presbyterian congregations in Malawi. As such, the only spiritual orientations that the program does denounce by name, in addition to the ubiquitous references to witchcraft, tend to be Islam and the Gule Wamkulu secret society. Although the editors often censor their guests' diatribes against these orientations, they are mentioned when the guest is their former adherent. A former Muslim can speak with authority about the deplorable nature of Islam while lending credence to the dictum that salvation is indeed for everyone.

One testimony by a former Muslim,[34] broadcast in two parts, described the guest's upbringing in a Muslim family and his subsequent life as a wasted youth (*mnyamata wotayika*). The habits of promiscuity and beer drinking, so often reported on *Ndamasulidwa*, acquired a special effect when the guest described the response he had received from his Muslim elders. Complaining about the troubles his misbehavior was causing in his marriage, the guest had been told that there are many women. Why not just take another woman and marry her? (*Akazi ndi ambiri. Osangotenga mkazi wina ndi kumukwatira basi?*). The testimony continued by pointing out that this sort of advice was unacceptable, particularly coming as it did from someone who claimed to follow a religion (*chipembedzo*). The guest stated that when there is trouble in the family, a spiritual guide should offer counseling that brings the spouses together to discuss issues. It was not, however, his disillusion with spiritual guidance in Islam that eventually made him a born-again Christian. When all was well, he said, he would not think of the Savior (*Ambuye*) and indulged in bad habits. The change took place gradually as he was compelled to review his life by a series of strange incidents. Among other things, he escaped a fatal road accident unhurt, and he avoided being injured during a riot that resulted in the death of a young girl who had helped him flee the violence. After these experiences, the guest had asked himself, If I died today, where would I go? (*ngati ndafa lero, ndifikira kuti?*). He started to study the Qur'an but found it lacking the connection with God that he discovered in the story of Genesis. Discussions with born-again acquaintances made him realize the need to follow the real truth (*kutsatira choona chenicheni*) and the good laws (*malamulo abwino*).

This guest ended the testimony by elaborating on the importance of change among his peers. Proselytizing, he asserted, ought to target people who deny Jesus (*anthu amene amakanira Yesu*). He complained that pastors and church elders were looking for followers in other Christian churches, thereby catching fish that were already dead (*nsomba zimene zinafa kale*). "Let us not ignore another group of lost people" (*tisasiye gulu lina la anthu osokera*), he insisted, adding that many Christians are afraid of Muslims (*amawaopera asilamu*). He urged his listeners to go where Muslims are, no less than to places where the members of Gule Wamkulu gather, and preach to them, since they are still in the dark (*ali m'mdimabe*). The guest claimed particular authority over Islam by stating, "I was there, I know their teachings" (*ndinali kumeneko, maphunziro awo ndimadziwa*).

Besta Goodson, another former Muslim, likewise used a part of his testimony to highlight the special challenge—and the special urgency—to engage Muslims. His origin in Mangochi District, predominantly but by no means exclusively inhabited by Yao Muslims, was another allusion that most Malawians were able to interpret. Coupled with his account of finding Jesus a year after he had moved to Lilongwe in search of work, this background in Mangochi indicated a need to bring the good news to where he had started from. Goodson ended by expressing his desire to return to Mangochi as a pastor who would help the lost ones to receive Jesus. What both this and the testimony discussed above seem to convey is, of course, a certain missionary zeal that comes deceptively close to the rhetoric used by foreign evangelists. For many Pentecostal and evangelical preachers, particularly of North American origin, Muslims represent a target untouched by the gospel, with their demonic associations a constituency at once highly challenging and highly captivating.[35] However, the overlap in Malawians' and foreign preachers' missionary zeal must not mask very real differences. When former Muslims give testimonies on Transworld Radio, they direct their missionary gaze as much to themselves as to others. In the above examples, one guest described his origins in a Muslim family and how he knows the teachings of Islam. Goodson reinforced this guest's call for an engagement with Muslims by announcing his intent to return to his district of origin to preach the good news. These examples show how the Muslim Other is not simply virgin territory for a Christian missionary to conquer. The Other is as much within as without, not unlike those Christian relatives who disparage the need for the second birth and indulge, instead, in various ungodly practices. Ethnographic and historical specificity is, once more, of primary importance for understanding the purpose and dynamic of spiritual warfare. The desire for a radical change is palpable, but the change can only be achieved in, and made apparent through, human relationships. The former Muslim demonstrates his or her new being not by withdrawing into meaningless isolation but by seeking to transform the being of others, not least those who were constitutive of his or her previous being. Spiritual warfare, in other words, is as much about securing relationships as defeating demonic forces, as much about achieving civil peace as holding enemies at bay.

The observations in this chapter challenge the view that associates born-again Christianity in general and Pentecostalism in particular with individualization and intolerance. While the two tendencies may be associated with some instances of these religious transformations, they do not seem to further our understanding of Malawian realities. It is crucial to attend to the specific idioms and practices that inform the experience of being born again as mediated by *Ndamasulidwa*. Healing, for example, is a recurrent theme in these testimonies, the capacity to be healed and to heal others through the work of the Holy Spirit a prime proof of the new condition. Healing is a key idiom and practice in the propensity of born-again Christianity to advance peaceful public life in Malawi, a guarantee of security (*chitetezo*) in a world of affliction and satanic schemes. Praying, the practice on which healing is based, should also be seen as central to the ways in which born-again Christians in Malawi expand the scope of relatedness. The frequent references to praying in *Ndamasulidwa* are no idle gestures but describe essential means by which the born-again engages with his or her world.[36] The pragmatic deficiencies of prayer-based interventions are immediately apparent to those who do not subscribe to the born-again outlook on the world, but healing and prayer do give rise to, or are associated with, a range of public interventions that give meaning to spiritual kinship in the troubled world that most Malawians inhabit. In Chinsapo Township, the pragmatic measures that Pentecostals take for the sake of the common good include not only assistance for the sick and funerals, but also setting up business partnerships and the provision of microcredits by some church leaders. Spiritual kinship, as sustained by Pentecostal healing and prayer, also has the remarkable capacity to turn strangers, even outright adversaries such as Muslims, into members of a society in which both miracles and pragmatic support take place.

Rights and obligations, as Talal Asad and others before him have argued,[37] presuppose membership in political society. Not only does the argument cast doubt over the possibility of natural rights that would belong to humans irrespective of their recognition by any political or religious authority, it has also given rise to sharply divergent views. At one extreme, the requirement of membership is taken to a distinctly undemocratic, if not lethal, conclusion by stressing exclusion and exception.[38] Others, more keen to salvage a liberal sense of tolerance, have debated the ways in which this recognition of differences can be accommodated in liberal democracy.[39] Neither perspective offers an insight into the spiritual kinship that Pentecostalism, as mediated by *Ndamasulidwa* and as pursued in Chinsapo Township, appears to cultivate. If thinking in terms of membership is, as Richard Dagger points out, "thinking in terms of 'we' and 'they,'"[40] then these Pentecostals' determination to expand "us" to include "them" goes beyond both antidemocratic exclusion and the pluralism of primordial identities. Nor does Pentecostal membership lend itself to the nostalgic representation of migrants re-creating a community resembling a rural village in town, a representation that has informed the anthropology of urban religious movements in Africa.[41] Here is another modality of membership, one whose expansion across the various boundaries of everyday life gives the lie to both anthropological nostalgia and the communitarianism of some liberal theorists.[42]

If spiritual kinship entails a notion of the common good, the case presented in this chapter serves to release the notion from the egoistic and altruistic confines within which much liberal theory has conventionally placed it. In contrast to the choice between, as Alasdair MacIntyre has put it, goods as "mine-rather-than-others'" or "others'-rather-than-mine,"[43] genuinely common goods are "mine in so far as they are those of others." The prospect of healing, for example, evokes one such common good among the Pentecostals discussed here, conditional as it is on everyone's submission to the Holy Spirit. As mentioned, healing, through its promise of security, is inseparable from ostensibly more mundane practices, from assistance during life crises to commercial ventures, all of which inspire responsibility and obligation when the practices are pursued with brothers and sisters in Christ. The crux of the expansive momentum in this spiritual kinship lies in the accommodation of strangers, even spiritual adversaries, within the Pentecostal membership. This is why the testimonies delivered in *Ndamasulidwa* demonstrate not only the range of ways in which salvation is achieved but also the diversity of persons who experience it. The more unlikely the source of the testimony, the more convincing is the power of the Holy Spirit. By broadcasting transgressions among both Christians and Muslims, *Ndamasulidwa* also blurs the boundaries between insiders and outsiders. Although Islamophobia among Pentecostals elaborates on the association between Muslims, demonic spirits, Satanists, and witches, the testimonies by former Muslims call for an engagement with Muslims. When pursued by former Muslims among their own kin, this engagement confronts the enemy within rather than without, just as other born-again Christians must not take for granted the Christian credentials of their worldly kin. Here, Islamophobia not so much objectifies the Other for missionary interventions as demands vigilance against backsliders and false prophets in one's own midst. Far from policing some imaginary community boundaries, as nostalgic representations would have it, this vigilance is about the qualities of human relationships—particularly the conditions of trust—in contexts of abundant ethnic and religious diversity.

It bears repeating that this chapter has not been propelled by a desire to create a blueprint for democratic membership. Fundamentalist or not, Pentecostalism will strike many as "counter-cosmopolitanism," which imposes uniformity on its subjects.[44] Yet whatever may be said about the insight that Pentecostalism, as refracted in this Malawian case, affords into membership and exclusion as corollaries of democracy, the constant promise of expansion through spiritual kinship surely encourages civility that befits democracy. Broadcasters at Transworld Radio appear instrumental to cultivating this civility, motivated by a sense of public duty to proclaim that salvation is for everyone. In a country where the Christian-Muslim divide can easily be manipulated for political gain, and where poverty and inequality are rampant, the peace that spiritual warfare brings about is a veritable achievement.

Notes

1. For an analysis of the 1999 elections, see Martin Ott, Kings M. Phiri, and Nandini Patel, eds., *Malawi's Second Democratic Elections: Process, Problems, and Prospects* (Blantyre: Christian Literature Association in Malawi, 2000). Chakuamba was a Seventh-Day Adventist. The presidential and parliamentary elections in 2004 and 2009 appeared to incite much less controversy over religion, perhaps largely because, as is discussed below, Muluzi's chosen successor was a Christian.

2. That the attack was random was evident not only because the founder had avoided overtly political topics in his sermons during the election campaign. Among the township's Pentecostal pastors, he was also unusually sympathetic to the incumbent president. The founder's business had been destroyed by the Malawi Congress Party, the only

political party before the democratic transition in the early 1990s and the party fielding a Christian presidential candidate in 1999. The founder was, in private conversations, grateful for the freedoms that the new Muslim-led regime had instituted in Malawi.

3. The meanings of Islamophobia are many, depending on who uses the term. It is, for example, used by some Muslims as a tool to criticize non-Muslims. See S. Sayyid and Abdoolkarim Vakil, eds., *Thinking through Islamophobia* (London: Hurst, 2009).

4. "Religious Coexistence a Must," *Nation*, February 22, 2006.

5. Radio ownership increased from 19 percent of the population in 1987 to 50 percent in 1998, with 76 percent in urban areas having at least one radio. See Malawi, National Statistical Office, *1998 Malawi Population and Housing Census: Analytical Report* (Zomba: National Statistical Office, 2002), 136. Radio listening is often a social event, which makes radio available to those who do not own receivers. Television Malawi commenced in 1999 and reaches only a minority of residents in urban areas.

6. Three stations were associated with the Roman Catholic Church and one with the Seventh-Day Adventists. Sixteen of the twenty-one licensed stations were operational in 2006, and nine of them, including Radio Islam and Transworld Radio, had a nationwide coverage.

7. "Macra Orders Radio Islam Off the Air Temporarily," *Nation*, September 4, 2006.

8. According to David Martin, although Pentecostalism professes attachment to Christian fundamentals, it also promotes "empowerment through spiritual gifts offered to all" and represents "a fissiparous and peaceable extension of voluntarism and competitive pluralism." Martin, *Pentecostalism: The World Their Parish* (Oxford: Blackwell, 2002), 1.

9. Transworld Radio, which was founded in 1952 in the United States, was one of the first evangelical stations to reach Malawi. It began its Chichewa broadcasts from Swaziland in the 1980s and acquired an FM license from the Malawi government in 2000. See Ernst Wendland, *Sewero! Christian Drama and the Drama of Christianity in Africa* (Zomba: Kachere Series, 2005), 43. Broadcasting in African languages has always been central to Transworld Radio's operations. Its staff has long been Malawian, and they contrast their station with African Bible College Radio, which broadcasts almost exclusively in English, often programs imported from the United States.

10. Before my fieldwork commenced in Chinsapo Township, I had for several years carried out fieldwork in rural Dedza District. Township dwellers drew my attention to the testimonies delivered on Transworld Radio. The program's appeal extended well beyond those who were active Pentecostals. I conducted interviews and observed the selection of testimonies at the station's Lilongwe headquarters in 2006. My interpretations of the testimonies are based on conversations with broadcasters and township dwellers and on my appreciation of township Pentecostalism, developed over a number of years. All translations are my own and are based on a sample of twenty testimonies broadcast in 2005 and 2006.

11. Harri Englund, "The Village in the City, the City in the Village: Migrants in Lilongwe," *Journal of Southern African Studies* 28, no. 2 (2002): 137–54.

12. Harri Englund, *Prisoners of Freedom: Human Rights and the African Poor* (Berkeley: University of California Press, 2006).

13. Edward A. Alpers, "Towards a History of the Expansion of Islam in East Africa: The Matrilineal Peoples of the Southern Interior," in *The Historical Study of African Religion*, ed. T. O. Ranger and I. Kimambo (London: Heinemann, 1972); David S. Bone, "An Outline History of Islam in Malawi," in *Malawi's Muslims: Historical Perspectives*, ed. Bone (Blantyre: Christian Literature Association in Malawi, 2000).

14. Harri Englund, "Witchcraft and the Limits of Mass Mediation in Malawi," *Journal of the Royal Anthropological Institute* 13, no. 2 (2007): 305.

15. An emphasis on microcredit as a strategy of poverty alleviation was by no means uncommon in the 1990s, but Malawi's ruling elite embraced the policy preference for businesses with particular enthusiasm. As a result, trade was increasingly conducted with imported or smuggled commodities, and the size of the manufacturing sector decreased to 12 percent of the economy in 1999. See Blessings Chinsinga, "The Politics of Poverty Alleviation in Malawi: A Critical Review," in *A Democracy of Chameleons: Politics and Culture in the New Malawi*, ed. Harri Englund (Uppsala: Nordiska Afrikainstitutet; Blantyre: Christian Literature Association in Malawi, 2002), 27. Unprocessed tobacco remained the country's chief export, its prospects steadily darkened by falling world prices.

16. Englund, *Prisoners*.

17. United Nations Development Programme, *Malawi Human Development Report, 2001* (Lilongwe: UNDP, 2001), 20.

18. Even more than religion or ethnicity, regionalism came to inform Malawi's political constellations, with the three main political parties dividing the country's three administrative regions between them. See Wiseman C. Chirwa, "Democracy, Ethnicity and Regionalism: The Malawian Experience, 1992–1996," in *Democratization in Malawi: A Stocktaking*, ed. Kings M. Phiri and Kenneth R. Ross (Blantyre: Christian Literature Association in Malawi, 1998). After the 2004, and especially the 2009 presidential and parliamentary elections, this political division has appeared less clear.

19. "Muslim Body Accuses Bingu of Segregation," *Nation*, December 22, 2005.

20. "Muslim Body, Govt Fight over Maize," *Nation*, January 31, 2006.

21. "Muslims Plan Protest against Bingu," *Nation*, January 30, 2006.

22. For Ghana, see Birgit Meyer, "'Praise the Lord': Popular Cinema and Pentecostalite Style in Ghana's New Public Sphere," *American Ethnologist* 31, no. 1 (2004): 92–110; Meyer, chap. 7, this volume.

23. Similar moves among Muslims, provoked by Pentecostals, toward public preaching have been noted elsewhere in the region. On Tanzania, see Roman Loimeier, "Perceptions of Marginalization: Muslims in Contemporary Tanzania," in *Islam and Muslim Politics in Africa*, ed. Benjamin F. Soares and René Otayek (New York: Palgrave Macmillan, 2007), 145–49.

24. C. S. Lewis, *The Screwtape Letters* (London: Geoffrey Bles, 1942).

25. Harri Englund, "Pentecostalism beyond Belief: Trust and Democracy in a Malawian Township," *Africa* 77, no. 4 (2007): 477–79.

26. "Police Nab Author of 'Muslims Letter,'" *Nation*, June 5, 2007.

27. See Englund, "Witchcraft."

28. Compare the rhetoric of spiritual warfare among African immigrants in Europe, who accuse Satan of "having stayed too long within the society and [having] become an illegal immigrant that must be deported immediately." Afe Adogame, "Engaging the Rhetoric of Spiritual Warfare: The Public Face of Aladura in Diaspora," *Journal of Religion in Africa* 34, no. 4 (2004): 505. On spiritual warfare among African students, see Amy Stambach, "Spiritual Warfare 101: Preparing the Student for Christian Battle," *Journal of Religion in Africa* 39, no. 2 (2009): 137–57.

29. Transworld Radio has an audience relations department that deals with listeners who come to the station with pressing spiritual concerns. It usually seeks to identify someone in the listener's area of residence who can assist with these concerns. The person is often a pastor, not necessarily a Pentecostal, because all Protestant denominations are in principle embraced by Transworld Radio.

30. Transworld Radio does not have enough equipment and personnel to record testimonies at its listeners' homes. As a consequence, the majority of testimonies are delivered by people living in Lilongwe and Blantyre, many of whom belong to the

urban and periurban poor in areas such as Chinsapo Township. The directions to its two studios are usually given during the program. Because of its nationwide reach, the station occasionally receives guests from further afield who come to one of the cities to stay with their relatives in order to offer their testimonies to *Ndamasulidwa*.

31. I identify the testimonies in my sample by the personal names mentioned in the broadcasts.

32. Several journalists at Transworld Radio participate in recording testimonies, because guests often arrive unannounced and need to be received by whoever happens to be available. Some journalists are more interactive than others with their guests, but the most usual practice is to edit the narratives into one uninterrupted testimony.

33. The reference to self-control, in English, would seem to undermine the argument I have been making—since Harri Englund and James Leach, "Ethnography and the Meta-narratives of Modernity," *Current Anthropology* 41, no. 2 (2000): 225–48—that Pentecostalism in the African contexts where I have studied it does not necessarily entail individualization. However, it is important to pay attention to how this testimony continued—the person claimed to have self-control by "having Jesus." As I discuss below, having Jesus is a condition that requires, and is sustained by, human relationships.

34. The name of this guest was not broadcast.

35. See Mathijs Pelkmans, "'Culture' as a Tool and an Obstacle: Missionary Encounters in Post-Soviet Kyrgyzstan," *Journal of the Royal Anthropological Institute* 13, no. 4 (2007): 881–99.

36. On the importance of praying in the lives of African Pentecostals, see David Maxwell, *African Gifts of the Spirit: Pentecostalism and the Rise of a Zimbabwean Transnational Religious Movement* (Oxford: James Currey, 2006), 184–211.

37. Talal Asad, *Formations of the Secular: Christianity, Islam, Modernity* (Stanford: Stanford University Press, 2003): 129.

38. See Carl Schmitt, *Political Theology: Four Chapters on the Concept of Sovereignty*, trans. George Schwab (Chicago: University of Chicago Press, 2005); see also, for example, Chantal Mouffe, "Carl Schmitt and the Paradox of Liberal Democracy," in *Law as Politics: Carl Schmitt's Critique of Liberalism*, ed. David Dyzenhaus (Durham, NC: Duke University Press, 1998).

39. For example, Will Kymlicka, *Multicultural Citizenship: A Liberal Theory of Minority Rights* (Oxford: Oxford University Press, 1995).

40. Richard Dagger, *Civic Virtues: Rights, Citizenship, and Republican Liberalism* (Oxford: Oxford University Press, 1997), 52.

41. For a critical discussion, see Rijk A. van Dijk, "Pentecostalism, Cultural Memory and the State: Contested Representations of Time in Postcolonial Malawi," in *Memory and the Postcolony: African Anthropology and the Critique of Power*, ed. Richard Werbner (London: Zed, 1998), 159–61; van Wyk, chap. 9, this volume.

42. Liberal political theory has long been constrained by a tension between individualist and communitarian positions. Michael Sandel's argument that community is "not merely an attribute but a constituent" of identity articulated an understanding of the constitutive role played by relationships. See Sandel, *Liberalism and the Limits of Justice* (Cambridge: Cambridge University Press, 1982), 150. However, Richard Dagger, after due acknowledgments, places Sandel's argument in the communitarian mold and complains about its lack of room for freedom and autonomy. Dagger, *Civic Virtues*, 52–53. I have discussed elsewhere the nature of freedom in a perspective that takes seriously the constitutive role of relationships. See, for example, Englund, *Prisoners*, 189–90.

43. Alasdair MacIntyre, *Dependent Rational Animals: Why Human Beings Need the Virtues* (London: Duckworth, 1999), 119.

44. "Counter-cosmopolitanism" is how Kwame Anthony Appiah distinguishes universalism among so-called fundamentalist Christians and Muslims from that of proper cosmopolitans. See Appiah, *Cosmopolitanism: Ethics in a World of Strangers* (New York: Norton, 2006), 137–53. For a sense in which township Pentecostalism in Malawi may be compatible with some definitions of cosmopolitanism, see Harri Englund, "Cosmopolitanism and the Devil in Malawi," *Ethnos* 69, no. 3 (2004): 293–316.

NINE

Believing Practically and Trusting Socially in Africa
The Contrary Case of the Universal Church of the Kingdom of God in Durban, South Africa

ILANA VAN WYK

THE UNIVERSAL Church of the Kingdom of God (UCKG) in South Africa presents an ethnographic anomaly, if not in the broad school of religious studies, then at least in the study of Christianity in Africa.[1] Pastors of the UCKG actively discourage intimate, emotional relationships with God and instead encourage members to engage in one-off contracts with God through large monetary sacrifices. In the church's services, pastors brand acts of Christian charity and fellowship as useless and warn their congregations that the empathy that inspires them to help others is an instrument Satan uses in war against God. Pastors even counsel their congregations against charitable work *within* the church's ranks and especially against donations to poorer UCKG members. This is not a one-sided directive. Many church members assert that their fellows are not trustworthy and actively resist the kinds of social intimacy common in other Pentecostal-charismatic churches (PCCs). In the absence of a church community, public testimonies and mass sacrifices are striking features of the UCKG's daily services.

Despite the church's six daily services in Durban's Smith Street branch, known as the Cathedral of Faith, those who attend the UCKG have neither a shared history nor a shared identity; in fact few people even tell their families or friends that they go to the church. This is also a church that does not cater to a single social class or interest group.

Although the majority of members are black and a large number very poor, the UCKG includes many teachers, nurses, and civil servants in its ranks as well as a magistrate and a few wealthy businesspeople. Furthermore, the church membership has a high turnover rate, with most people staying for a few weeks and, at most, months. Only a handful of members have been with the church since it was "planted" in Durban, in 1993.[2] The UCKG's high turnover is not unique in the context of African Christianity.[3]

What singles the UCKG out from other local churches is that its members do not congregate for festivals or funerals,[4] nor are weddings or baptisms celebrated as community affairs. With the notable exception of the announcement of the wedding of five pastors and one assistant during my fieldwork, the announcements from the pulpit pertained only to events like the bishop's visit, the church's various campaigns against Satan, and reminders of tithing Sundays. For instance, during my fieldwork an assistant died unexpectedly in a car accident but neither her death nor her funeral was announced in the church.[5] I was later told that her funeral had been held in another branch and that her family had to organize and pay for everything. Only two people from the Smith Street branch, where she had served for almost ten years, went to her funeral. Baptisms were equally the affair of those individuals directly involved. Both mass baptisms I attended occurred after the main service. The pastors did not invite anyone to stay on, while the church's architecture precluded public participation or observation of the baptismal pool. The baptismal pool lay behind a shoulder-high wall on the stage. Sitting in the church facing the stage, one could not see anything of the baptisms, while the baptized left the stage through a back door to change into dry clothing in the bathrooms.

This lack of socializing among UCKG members is complemented by an almost mechanical relationship between the congregation and its pastors. At any time there are between six and ten pastors at the Cathedral of Faith. All are on contract for six months at most. Individual pastors never announce their departures, whereas new arrivals quietly and seamlessly take over church services from their predecessors. The pastors' unpredictable and high turnover rate undermines any lasting loyalties or bonds with a congregation, as is common in the UCKG worldwide.[6] This bond is further undermined by the minimal contact that the clergy have with the congregation outside the church's six daily services. They generally do not make home visits (I only heard of two home visits during my fieldwork) or hold informal social occasions where they could mix with their flock. The clergy live in apartments at the back of the church and return to their quarters promptly after the services. Church members can approach the officiating pastor for a window of ten minutes before and after each service. For more serious problems, they may make an appointment with a pastor through the church secretary. Few people do.

In this church, as many pastors and strong members reiterated, you can "only trust God." However, the kind of relationship that the UCKG prescribes with God is devoid of the intimacy and emotional engagement common in other Pentecostal churches. Certainly, anyone who has a typically Pentecostal experience of the Holy Spirit, namely those who experience the feelings of warmth, elation, or dizziness during the service, are summarily hauled to the front of the church to have the demons they ostensibly harbor exorcised. Dismissive of the "word informations" and emotions of other churches, the UCKG emphasizes *actions*. These actions never refer to good deeds, charity, humility, or Christian fellowship but center on an individual's ability and willingness to tithe and sacrifice money, and only money, in the church. After sacrificing, members are encouraged to *demand* their blessings from God and not to waste words on praising and worshipping. This is the UCKG pastors' answer to all health problems, poverty, loneliness, strife, and thwarted ambition.

In light of this apparently utilitarian approach to God, combined with its lack of community, the UCKG has presented a particularly problematic case for my anthropological colleagues. Many of them have exclaimed that the UCKG is not a church but an elaborate confidence trick in which a sinister corporation "uses God" to extract maximum revenue from a congregation of gullible and desperate people. The UCKG's efforts to discourage socializing within its ranks and between its members, reinforced by its emphasis on money, often strengthens anthropologists' and other academics' suspicions. With reference to eighteen months of fieldwork in Durban, I hope to destabilize these suspicions. Reaching beyond the particularity of the UCKG, I explore the implications of the UCKG's establishment of a unique brand of trust, one divorced from social intimacy and fundamentally geared to a technology that attempts to manipulate God. I argue that the UCKG's anomalous status in the ethnographic record is not due to a failure to be properly Christian,[7] or democratic, but to anthropology's failure to address the complex ways in which Christians believe practically.

Believing Practically and Trusting Socially in Anthropology

With the relatively recent upsurge in the literature on PCCs in Africa,[8] quite a number of authors have paid attention to the impact this mass movement has had on its members' conception of, and participation in, national politics and public culture. For the most part, the relationship between PCCs and public culture in Africa has been approached from three sometimes overlapping perspectives.

First, from a structural perspective, several authors have noted that Africans' intense social participation in churches has created local social worlds with strong organizational foundations in places where there has been a dearth of organized civil society.[9] Historically, churches on the continent were often instrumental in mobilizing their members to politically challenge repressive and undemocratic states,[10] frequently to their own ends and involving complex local power configurations.[11] The historical precedents of religious political resistance, combined with PCCs' financial autonomy and enormous membership, have inspired some authors to speculate about these churches' potential political transformative powers.[12] Others have been more circumspect, asserting that PCCs are politically conservative and authoritarian,[13] that local leaders are often co-opted by the state,[14] and that African states profit from PCCs' appropriation of development ideology as part of their "governmentality of the belly."[15] However, in the neoliberal era, a sizeable body of literature has optimistically noted that PCCs, in offering development, healthcare, jobs, and educational services that imploding African states cannot provide, are becoming viable alternatives to the state.[16] Nevertheless, a methodological focus on church leaders' statements and the place that PCCs occupy in a vaguely defined civil society ignores the symbolic and expressive aspects of politics as well as the everyday practices of a huge body of practitioners. This leaves us, as Ruth Marshall has noted, with "institutions, procedures, and constitutions."[17]

The second approach to PCCs focuses more closely on African practitioners, emphasizing that the heavy socializing in African churches transform converts in ways that allow for potential widespread reforms in public culture. Much of this literature centers on the ability of PCCs to transform their members into modern *individuals* better able to cope with neoliberalism's economic, political, and social agenda.[18] In this regard, authors have pointed out that PCCs modernize their members by forcing them to cut ties with economically burdensome kin and by offering consumer workshops, along with emotional, health, and financial support networks. These projects supposedly create individuals who are self-motivated, averse to rigid gender-role prescriptions, have microentrepreneurial initiative, and display flexibility to deal with the insecurity bred by neoliberalism.[19] In this body of literature, PCC church communities are often portrayed as egalitarian and organic and, as such, a counterpoint to the neoliberal state's cultural project and the general anomie of urban social contexts.

These depictions of PCCs as communities have been criticized for being nostalgic,[20] for focusing on "elite evangelists and upwardly mobile followers" whose social and religious lives are "conveniently circumscribed to warrant an exclusive focus on the form and content of their gospel,"[21] and for treating megachurches in terms of convergence and consensus. Most Africans, despite the discourse of social rupture common in born-again literature, "cannot afford to be autonomous individuals"[22] and remain fundamentally connected to and dependent on non-PCC family and neighbors.[23] Moreover, in many parts of Africa, South Africa included, people change their church affiliation often and, in Harri Englund's words, "without obvious doctrinal reasons."[24] Critics have also pointed out that the supposed villagization of African churches is an ideological and not a social process in which people try to cope with continuous economic, social, and political changes by formulating new blueprints for an ideal society.[25]

This brings me to the third approach to PCCs in Africa. Here authors focus on how the local forms of "belief" interact with Church ideologies and Church members' broader moral imagination. In this regard, recent years have seen a radical critique of our spiritual or otherworldly understandings of Christian religion.[26] Writers such as Talal Asad and Malcolm Ruel have argued that an understanding of Christianity (and conversions to it) in terms of a personal, inwardly organizing experience is a historical product of discursive processes in the West and of changes within the Western Christian tradition itself (see also Englund's introduction to this volume). Similarly, Jay Smith has showed that the word *belief* in the West historically signaled a person's commitment and trust, and it was only relatively recently that the word came to be used propositionally as a statement that could be affirmed or denied.[27] It is in this context that Englund has argued that African Christians' faith is often not propositional and that it centers on trust.[28]

Taking a major step beyond other scholars' focus on church leaders' discourses and narrowly defined church communities, Englund stresses the unity of the born-again condition in an impoverished township in Malawi's capital and the impact it has on the moral imagination.[29] Thus he argues that Chinsapo Pentecostals' inability to extract themselves from relationships with non-Pentecostals—along with their emphasis on spiritual kinship, human fallibility, and a shared existential predicament with non-Pentecostals in a world plagued by the devil—creates the conditions for an expansion of trust and civility across social boundaries. Against a body of literature that claims that forms of belief determine the boundaries of social life, Englund concludes that this generalized, if tenuous, trust lays the groundwork for the establishment of democracy in the lives of impoverished Pentecostals.[30]

The social and spiritual orientation of born-agains who attend the UCKG in Durban appears more clearly when it is contrasted with Englund's case. They trust no one in the church and confidently declare that other people, even pastors, harbor infectious demons that can destroy their lives. People in this church even denounce Christian charity as useless in their quest to become blessed. Belonging to the UCKG does not expand civility or trust in other people, quite the opposite. At the heart of this difference between the UCKG and the Pentecostal churches on Englund's field site lies a profound shift in religious discourse. In Lilongwe's Chinsapo Township, Jesus is the locus of a reborn identity and the source of people's spiritual kinship with other born-agains.[31] A trust in, or a commitment to, Jesus translates into idioms of embodiment as people claim to share in the body of Christ. By contrast, the UCKG devotes the bulk of its attention to God rather than to Jesus. As such, this religious discourse is complemented by an absence of idioms of embodiment, an emphasis on an empowered practitioner, and a very different imagination of who can be trusted. However, the effects of shifting religious focus from Jesus (in mainstream PCCs) to God (in the UCKG) is not permanent or even stable, as most people in Durban often change their church affiliation. Nor do they only move from one PCC to another but cross denominational frontiers to join the Catholic Church, the Jehovah's Witnesses, and some African-instituted churches. For the handful of people who stayed in the UCKG, trust in other people was not a straightforward issue either. Their changing fortunes influence their perception of vulnerability to, and hence their trust of, other people.

Different PCCs in Durban emphasize different aspects of Christian theology, not all of them compatible with the idealized shared body of Jesus. For instance, in some churches being a born-again gives people exclusive access to the powers of the Holy Spirit. In others, people are born again as spiritual warriors against demons that often reside in other people. And in the UCKG, born-agains are individually empowered to circumvent the mediation of Jesus altogether. However, in the above three approaches to PCCs in Africa, anthropologists have paid little attention to the very practical ways in which people "believe" in the absence of a propositional faith. Despite evidence that Africans often change their church affiliations, that PCCs tend toward pluralism, and that church communities are diverse, many authors writing on PCCs still treat churches as relatively stable institutions that produce either tangible or ideological social changes within a volatile neoliberal and urban context.

Against this body of work, Thomas Kirsch has paid attention to the constantly renewed "will to believe" among the Gwembe Tonga of Zambia.[32] He argues that the Tonga's precolonial experiences with fickle spiritual entities and spirit mediums that lost their privileged contact with particular spirits played an important role in the appropriation and continued practice of Christianity in this area. As such, Tonga religious life is governed by a pragmatic religious attitude that assumes the inconsistency of both spirits and access to those spirits. Thus people in this area regularly shift their affiliation to different churches and ancestor cults in their quest for religious efficacy.[33] In this chapter, I argue that the people who attend the UCKG in Durban have a similarly pragmatic reason for joining the church. However, in contrast to Kirsch's case, Christians in Durban maintain that their God is constant and enduring—as well as able to solve all problems. For most Christians, the problem lies in accessing this power, as they have to rely on all-too-human pastors,[34] prophets, and *izangoma* (healers). What makes the UCKG especially attractive to its new members is that its pastors teach people how to access God directly, this knowledge constituting a technology that people use to solve practical problems. Heeding Englund's criticism of attempts to identify the content of "Christian culture,"[35] let us look at the ways in which UCKG members in Durban overcome their suspicions and doubt to put their trust in a technology. This practical engagement works against the establishment of intimate social ties and generalized trust inside and outside the church.

Proving the UCKG's Technology

The UCKG pastors and bishops often emphasize that Satan sends demons to block the flow of blessings from God to "His" children on earth, preventing them from having the life of abundant health, wealth, and happiness that God promised. In order to restore God's will on earth, and thus to live a blessed life here and now, Christians have to obey the divine command to battle against Satan by praying strongly, tithing, sacrificing, occasionally fasting, and going to church. "Strong" men and women of God also have to get all demons exorcised from their physical bodies and have the empty space filled with the Holy Spirit.[36] It is an ongoing process because the evil army is continually "upgrading" and launching fresh attacks daily.

This ontological vulnerability resonates with assertions in Durban's townships that witches are constantly upgrading themselves and that they are getting more clever each day. It is widely acknowledged that witches also transcend the traditional boundaries of kinship and can now attack people beyond their own kin and neighborhood.[37] People tend to assess their lives in terms of the precarious balance they maintain between the various invisible forces that are working toward their downfall and those they try to access to get them ahead. They do not separate health issues from family problems, bad luck, unemployment, poverty, or unhappiness but treat them as troubles of the same kind. Problems are merely manifestations of a general condition of being unlucky, or bewitched. Thus all health, wealth, and happiness are tenuous and dependent on constant manipulation.

In combating the invisible forces, people in the townships of Durban turn to a variety of spiritual sources: izangoma (healers), African-instituted churches such as the Zionist and the AmaNazaretha Churches, PCCs, along with older Pentecostal, Protestant, and Catholic churches.[38] As people move from one source to another, many return to the PCCs, where they are, as one UCKG member put it, "born again and again and again." On average, my interviewees stated that they attended each church for about two years before complaining that there was too much witchcraft in the church, that they fell out with other churchgoers, or that the church "stopped working." Not one of my interviewees switched churches due to doctrinal reasons, and all ascribed their choices to some form of emic pragmatism. For many, the power of the Holy Spirit, invoked to combat evil, was not of a different order than the supernatural powers of witches. People who go to mainstream PCCs are thus very concerned with the ability of different pastors to channel the Holy Spirit effectively, especially in the wake of widespread scandals over money and sex implicating famous charismatic leaders. A large number of people left the Durban Christian Centre, a very successful local PCC, when their main pastor impregnated the church secretary. One woman said to me, "How will I get my blessings from that man if the devil got to him? The Holy Spirit doesn't work with demons."

Despite changing churches constantly, none of my interviewees ever questioned the Christian God's ability to affect change in their lives and blamed individual churches and pastors for not understanding or following God's instructions on how to go about this difficult task. Being a born-again is, however, seldom a final or once-off solution because of the ways in which a persistent, adapting enemy constantly attacks people, especially people of God. Testimonies, delivered during church services and published in its full-color newspaper and broadcast on the UCKG's daily programs on television, are essential to proving that the church's technology works against these challenges. However, in no sense do testimonies contribute to the awareness of a community, nor do they offer intimate insights into fellow members' private lives. People who listen to testimonies in the UCKG are less interested in the testifiers than in the size of and speed with which their blessings are received. In this regard, my church friends can often recall the exact amount of a financial blessing or the make and model of a car blessing, but cannot recall the testifier's name or point them out to me in the congregation. There is also a practical component to their disinterest. Since people do not generally know each other, they cannot scrutinize testimonies or compare the relative changes that the UCKG's technology has produced. As one woman remarked, "It is like those BioSlim ads with the before and after pictures; sometimes the pictures on the left don't even look like the same person [as the pictures on the right]." Even if my church friends can point out a "blessed person of God," this information is considered useless in their search for a solution to their problems. The process of "believing in"[39] or trusting the truth-value of the UCKG's claims are thus depersonalized and center on the evidence that testifiers bring to support their amazing stories: car and house keys, employment letters, bank statements, medical certificates. Such corroboration is incontrovertible. After testimonies, pastors file many of the certificates and other paper proof in ledgers to be used as "evidence" of the church's efficacy. Testifiers, for their part, are not anxious about the message they send to others, but see their testimonies as a part of a continued personal struggle with the demons.

In a fundamental sense, UCKG members' trust in the technologies of the church is dependent on this dynamic between testifiers and witnesses. It is further bolstered by the sense of spectacle in the church. The UCKG provides this in a series of exorcisms, amazing testimonies, and elaborate campaigns during which people sacrifice enormous amounts of money. The church's perceived ability to empower individuals to access God's blessings is thus created by assembling large numbers of people and fantastic things. Because most people visit the church alone, this power and the things that happen in the church are not dissected, appropriated, and individualized in a group context and thus gain added momentum by virtue of their anonymous public nature.

God's Power and Blessed Families

Few testimonies are about experiencing the Holy Spirit, the love of Jesus, or the spiritual growth often mentioned in local PCCs. In fact, the UCKG spurns other churches' focus on spiritual growth and "emotions" in favor of what is called intelligent faith. According to the church's founder, this faith is not "emotional . . . fanatic or religious" but functions "to achieve the results" that UCKG members desire.[40] For this reason, the UCKG criticizes other churches for their emphasis on "giving information about the things that God did in the past," such as reading the Bible, instead of *doing* something to alleviate their congregants' problems in the present. Praise and worship sessions, being born again, Bible study, and experiencing the Holy Spirit are thus considered "useless" in reestablishing God's intended blessed life on earth. In a similar vein, pastors brand acts of Christian charity and fellowship as "useless" and even counsel their congregations against charitable work *within* the church's ranks and especially against donations to poorer UCKG members. The money thus diverted cannot be applied to change a person's life, handing victory to the demons.

In the UCKG's emphasis on financial sacrifice as a precondition for a miraculous engagement with God, rather than, for instance, earnest pleading or prayer, the juxtaposition usually set up in anthropological literature between believing in and carrying out is effectively eliminated.[41] To believe is not only to be swayed by the evidence of blessed testifiers in the church but also to "test God" by following their example. Testing God through this sacrificial technology requires a concentrated willingness to participate over more than a month and an unwavering trust in the efficacy of the sacrifice as individuals scrape together the amounts they pledged when they entered the contract with God. Even after they have fulfilled their contracts, the pastors urge their increasingly desperate congregations to trust that God would do His part. They often admonish those who are left destitute by their sacrifices and who borrow money to buy food or pay rent for breaking their contracts with God. One pastor, for instance, asserted that such behavior amounted to "robbing God" and that those who did this would only see their lives worsen. And although there is evidence that pastors in the UCKG are pressured by those in power to maximize their sacrifice revenues,[42] it is not merely a "language-game" for those who participate.[43] For instance, one churchgoer took her participation in the church's campaigns very seriously and blamed her miserable life on her inability to collect the wildly optimistic amount that she usually pledged at the start of each campaign.

Despite frequent warnings that congregants should be distrustful of their family, friends, and neighbors, the UCKG counts "blessed families" among the six blessings that people can receive through the ministry of the church. The church defines these blessings as "prosperity, health, family, love, God's Spirit" and "salvation," or freedom from the work of demons. During the church's biannual Campaigns of Israel, many congregants take printed envelopes specifically for their "family" and "sentimental" (love) lives and offer thousands of rands to achieve a happy family life. Indeed, being single or alone is considered unnatural and against God's plans. There is "something wrong with you," if you do not desire a married and fertile life with your partner. Any deviations from this ideal are considered to be Satan's work.

In reality, church members' relationships with their families and lovers are fraught with conflict, often because of the very practices that the UCKG prescribes to obtain a blessed family. These family conflicts are especially fierce just before and after the Campaigns of Israel and tithing Sundays as families fight over the precious resources that strong members are supposed to sacrifice. Church members often refer to the conflicts that erupt in their families in the broader framework of Satan working against their covenants. They swear to "overcome" these demons, sometimes risking extreme violence, to reestablish the now fractured and brutal family lives. Thus members of the UCKG desperately wish for blessed families of God but believe that that goal can be achieved only through the church's technology.

However, since the UCKG pastors encourage their congregants to test the church's technology (and very little else), and since the efficacy of that technology is measured only in material results, the trust in the UCKG's technology is rather precarious. Most people stay in the church for only one or two campaigns before moving on to another church in the hope of finding a solution to their problems, which are often exacerbated by their attempts to "test God."

Anthropologists often relate religious belief/trust and social intimacy in churches to democracy or other political reforms. Such correlations do not take into account the plurality of PCC publics. Many African members of PCCs make pragmatic religious choices, and these choices presuppose the fundamental and necessary diversity in PCCs and the flexibility or instability of trust. These conditions make generalizations about PCCs and public culture suspect. In order to reach this conclusion, I have had to rethink the complex ways in which people believe practically.

Notes

1. In 1977, Edir Macedo founded the Igreja Universal do Reino de Deus, as the church is known in Brazil. Within a few years after its creation, the church had branches all over Brazil and the financial means to set up branches in the United States, Canada, Latin America, Europe, India, and Israel. See Paul Freston, *Evangelicals and Politics in Asia, Africa, and Latin America* (Cambridge: Cambridge University Press, 2001), 4. The first UCKG branch in Africa opened in 1991 in Angola, with a branch among a small Portuguese-speaking community in South Africa the year after. See Marcelo Pires, "A Humble Dream Comes to Global Fruition through Faith, Hard Work and Determination," *Saturday Weekend Argus* (Cape Town), February 28, 2004. However, it was not until the UCKG shifted its focus to black South Africans, in 1993, that it started to register enormous growth. The country proved to be a fertile ground, and by 1997 South Africa became the church's most successful country outside of Brazil. See Freston, "The Universal Church of the Kingdom of God: A Brazilian Church Finds Success in South Africa," *Journal of Religion in Africa* 35, no. 1 (2005): 40, 51. It continued to grow, and by the time of my fieldwork in 2004–5, the UCKG had established over two hundred branches in South Africa. Very few of the churchgoers in Durban were, however, aware of the precise origins and organizational features of the church in Brazil.

2. On the church's founding, see Marcelo Crivella, *Mutis, Sangomas and Nyangas: Tradition or Witchcraft?* (Brazil: UCKG Publications, 1999), 133; "New Church to Open," *Post*, March 31, 1993.

3. See Harri Englund, "Pentecostalism beyond Belief: Trust and Democracy in a Malawian Township," *Africa* 77, no. 4 (2007): 485–87; Thomas Kirsch, "Restaging the Will to Believe: Religious Pluralism, Anti-syncretism, and the Problem of Belief," *American Anthropologist* 106, no. 4 (2004): 699–709.

4. Other local churches often celebrated the founder's and the congregation's birthdays, the fulfillments of prophesies, and *iladi* (ladder; but the term refers to a special occasion).

5. I only learned about her death a week later, during an interview with another assistant.

6. Freston, "Universal Church," 41.

7. On the Mormons, see Fenella Cannell, "The Christianity of Anthropology," *Journal of the Royal Anthropological Institute* 11, no. 2 (2005): 335–56.

8. Birgit Meyer, "Christianity in Africa: From African Independent to Pentecostal-Charismatic Churches," *Annual Review of Anthropology* 33, no. 1 (2004): 447–74.

9. Bernice Martin, "From Pre- to Postmodernity in Latin America: The Case of Pentecostalism," in *Religion, Modernity and Postmodernity*, ed. Paul Heelas, David Martin, and Paul Morris (Oxford: Blackwell, 1998), 117–18; James Pfeiffer, "Civil Society, NGOs, and the Holy Spirit in Mozambique," *Human Organization* 63, no. 4 (2004): 359–72.

10. John W. de Gruchy and Steve de Gruchy, *The Church Struggle in South Africa*, foreword by Desmond Tutu (Johannesburg: Fortress Press, 2005); Paul Gifford, ed. *The Christian Churches and the Democratisation of Africa* (Leiden: Brill, 1995); Galia Sabar-Friedman, "Church and State in Kenya, 1986–1992: The Churches' Involvement in the 'Game of Change,'" *African Affairs* 96, no. 382, (1997): 25–52.

11. Sara Rich Dorman, "'Rocking the Boat'? Church NGOs and Democratization in Zimbabwe," *African Affairs* 101, no. 402 (2002): 75–92; Terence Ranger, "Religious Movements and Politics in Sub-Saharan Africa," *African Studies Review* 29, no. 2, 1986: 1–69.

12. B. Martin, "Pre- to Postmodernity"; David Martin, *Pentecostalism: The World Their Parish* (Oxford: Blackwell, 2002); Emilio Willems, *Followers of the New Faith: Culture Change and the Rise of Protestantism in Brazil and Chile* (Nashville: Vanderbilt University Press, 1967).

13. Christian Lalive d'Epinay, *Haven of the Masses: A Study of the Pentecostal Movement in Chile* (London: Lutterworth, 1969); Ruth Marshall, "'God Is Not a Democrat': Pentecostalism and Democratisation in Nigeria," in *The Christian Churches and the Democratisation of Africa*, ed. Paul Gifford (Leiden: Brill, 1995), 239–60. See also Gifford, *African Christianity: Its Public Role* (London: Hurst, 1998), 37; Paul Freston, "Evangelicals and Politics: A Comparison between Africa and Latin America," *Journal of Contemporary Religion* 13, no. 1 (1998): 37–49; Joel Robbins, "The Globalization of Pentecostal and Charismatic Christianity," *Annual Review of Anthropology* 33, no. 1 (2004): 134–35.

14. André Corten and Ruth Marshall-Fratani, introduction to *Between Babel and Pentecost: Transnational Pentecostalism in Africa and Latin America*, ed. Corten and Marshall-Fratani (London, Hurst, 2001); Freston, *Evangelicals*; Marshall, "'God.'"

15. Marshall, "'God,'" 240.

16. John Comaroff and Jean Comaroff, "Second Comings: Neo-Protestant Ethics and Millennial Capitalism in Africa, and Elsewhere," in *2000 Years and Beyond: Faith, Identity and the "Common Era,"* ed. Paul Gifford, David Archard, Trevor A. Hart, and Nigel Rappaport (New York: Routledge, 2003), 121; Dorman, "'Rocking the Boat'"; Ruth Marshall, "'Power in the Name of Jesus': Social Transformation and Pentecostalism in Western Nigeria 'Revisited,'" in *Legitimacy and the State in Twentieth-century Africa: Essays in Honour of A. H. M. Kirk-Greene*, ed. Terence Ranger and Olufemi Vaughan (London: Macmillan, 1993), 225.

17. Marshall, "'God,'" 240.

18. David Maxwell, "'Delivered from the Spirit of Poverty?': Pentecostalism, Prosperity and Modernity in Zimbabwe," *Journal of Religion in Africa* 28, no. 3 (1998): 350–73; Maxwell, "The Durawall of Faith: Pentecostal Spirituality in Neo-liberal Zimbabwe," *Journal of Religion in Africa* 35, no. 1 (2005): 4–32; Birgit Meyer, "'Make a Complete Break with the Past': Memory and Post-colonial Modernity in Ghanaian Pentecostalist Discourse," *Journal of Religion in Africa* 28, no. 3 (1998): 316–49; Rijk van Dijk, "The Pentecostal Gift: Ghanaian Charismatic Churches and the Moral Innocence of the Global Economy," in *Modernity on a Shoestring: Dimensions of Globalisation, Consumption and Development in Africa and Beyond*, ed. Richard Fardon, Wim van Binsbergen, and Dijk (London: Anthony Rowe, 1999). See also Rekopantswe Mate, "Wombs as

God's Laboratories: Pentecostal Discourses of Femininity in Zimbabwe," *Africa* 72, no. 4 (2002): 549–68.

19. Cf. Andrew Buckser and Stephen D. Glazier, preface to *The Anthropology of Religious Conversion*, ed. Buckser and Glazier (Lanham: Rowman and Littlefield, 2003); Glazier, "'Limin' wid Jah': Spiritual Baptists Who Become Rastafarians and Then Become Spiritual Baptists Again," in Buckser and Glazier, *Anthropology*.

20. Rijk van Dijk, "Christian Fundamentalism in Sub-Saharan Africa: The Case of Pentecostalism" (Occasional Paper, Centre of African Studies, University of Copenhagen, 2000), 10.

21. Englund, "Pentecostalism," 480.

22. Francis B. Nyamnjoh, "Reconciling the 'Rhetoric of Rights' with Competing Notions of Personhood and Agency in Botswana," in *Rights and the Politics of Recognition in Africa*, ed. Harri Englund and Nyamnjoh (London: Zed, 2004), 34–35.

23. Englund, "Pentecostalism"; Englund, chap. 8, this volume.

24. Englund, "Pentecostalism," 485–87; Kirsch, "Restaging the Will"; Ranger, "Religious Movements," 74.

25. Compare Peter Geschiere and Josef Gugler, "The Urban-Rural Connection: Changing Issues of Belonging and Identification," *Africa* 68, no. 3 (1998): 309; Wim M. J. van Binsbergen, *Religious Change in Zambia: Exploratory Essays* (New York: Routledge and Kegan Paul, 1981); Binsbergen, *Virtuality as a Key Concept in the Study of African Globalisation: Aspects of the Symbolic Transformation of Contemporary Africa* (The Hague: WOTRO, 1997).

26. Talal Asad, *Genealogies of Religion: Discipline and Reasons of Power in Christianity and Islam* (Baltimore: Johns Hopkins University Press, 1993); Cannell, "Christianity;" Malcolm Ruel, *Belief, Ritual and the Securing of Life: Reflexive Essays on a Bantu Religion* (Leiden: Brill, 1997); Marshall Sahlins, "The Sadness of Sweetness: The Native Anthropology of Western Cosmology," *Current Anthropology* 37, no. 3 (1996): 395–428.

27. Jay M. Smith, "No More Language Games: Words, Beliefs, and the Political Culture of Early Modern France," *American Historical Review* 102, no. 5 (1997): 1413–40.

28. Englund, "Pentecostalism."

29. Ibid., 486–87.

30. Ibid., 495.

31. Ibid., 486–88.

32. Kirsch, "Restaging the Will."

33. Ibid., 702–3.

34. Cf. Harri Englund, "The Quest for Missionaries: Transnationalism and Township Pentecostalism in Malawi," in *Between Babel and Pentecost: Transnational Pentecostalism in Africa and Latin America*, ed. André Corten and Ruth Marshall-Fratani (London: Hurst, 2001); Englund, "Christian Independency and Global Membership: Pentecostal Extraversions in Malawi," *Journal of Religion in Africa* 33, no. 1 (2003): 83–111.

35. Englund, "Pentecostalism." See, for example, Joel Robbins, "Continuity Thinking and the Problem of Christian Culture: Belief, Time, and the Anthropology of Christianity," *Current Anthropology* 48, no. 1 (2007): 5–38.

36. Salvation in the UCKG refers to freedom from the work of demons and evil spirits that blocks the flow of God's blessings into a person's life.

37. Cf. Harri Englund, "Witchcraft and the Limits of Mass Mediation in Malawi," *Journal of the Royal Anthropological Institute* 13, no. 2 (2007): 295–311.

38. New churches and prayer groups were constantly emerging all over the city, some in people's front rooms, others in school halls, garages, backyards, and some sharing church buildings with other congregations of different denominations.

39. Cf. Kirsch, "Restaging the Will."

40. From http://www.uckg.org.za.

41. See Kirsch, "Restaging the Will," 704–5.

42. "The Church That 'Drives Evil from the Possessed,'" *Independent*, January 13, 2001; "Kicking of Icon Outrages Brazil Catholics," *Dallas Morning News*, November 24, 1995; "See the Light: Ex-church Members Struggle to Reclaim Happiness and Financial Health," *LA Weekly*, June 29, 2001; "Demons on Broadway, Miracles, Exorcism, Catholic-Bashing: Going for Broke in the Universal Church," *LA Weekly*, July 5, 2001.

43. Cf. Kirsch, "Restaging the Will," 705.

TEN
———

The Gospel of Public Image in Ghana

MICHAEL PERRY KWEKU OKYEREFO

IS ALL that Pentecostalism has to offer a parochial religious orientation that has no effect on public culture more generally? Conflating Pentecostalism with the prosperity, or faith, gospel, Paul Gifford argued in 1991 that the sociopolitical effect of that gospel and born-again fundamentalist theology was to neglect or undermine developmental pursuits.[1] Gifford used the term *fundamentalism* to describe that aspect of Christianity that had "resolutely opposed" development through its manner of "presenting faith [that was] hardly calculated to promote self-help, self-reliance, self-esteem, self-determination, responsibility, and autonomy."[2] Four years later, Birgit Meyer pointed out that Ruth Marshall contradicted Gifford's view in the same issue of *Review of African Political Economy* by concluding that Pentecostalism in Nigeria constituted "a self-conscious movement which sees itself as changing society and making history."[3] Thirteen years on and Paul Gifford's stance remains essentially unchanged, although he concedes that some Pentecostal denominations engage in a modicum of development activity.[4] Yet Gifford's analysis of these churches is based on a view of development that is skewed in favor of a Western Enlightenment worldview. Reviewing Gifford's earlier book *African Christianity: Its Public Role*,[5] David Maxwell argues that Gifford might have gained more optimism about African creativity had he paid closer attention to local culture.[6] Patently, development cannot be conceived in economic terms only; human development goes beyond the economic to include health, education, and spiritual dimensions.

Through the provision of social amenities, two popular Ghanaian Pentecostal churches—Lighthouse Chapel International and Royalhouse Chapel International—expand their religious community to engage public culture in Ghana in ways that defy a simple compartmentalization of religion and socioeconomic development. Particularly significant are the efforts these two organizations are making in the field of health and orphan care as well as in the provision of education facilities. I conducted fieldwork in Accra between February and September 2007, conducting interviews and observing church members in addition to perusing media products and written documents. I have continued to follow the projects I describe here beyond the end of formal fieldwork.[7]

Contrary to the narrow view on development that blames developing counties for lagging behind, the World Bank and the International Monetary Fund are as much to blame as Africans themselves for the continent's failure. The structural-adjustment policies (SAPs) they imposed on African states in the 1980s and 1990s, in keeping with the philosophy of neoliberalism, were a mirage.[8] They lowered standards of living, and, after affecting the lives of millions of people, many people tried to leave Africa but some could not.[9] As a result of the SAPs, African economies have become increasingly marginalized globally, the meager incomes of the formally employed matched by state-imposed obstacles to pursue informal avenues to the production of wealth.[10] For many, survival depends on immense creativity, expressed in the Ghanaian idiom as "we are managing." Many Ghanaians have become self-made managers of their lives in the struggle to survive the harsh economic conditions generated by the SAPs.[11] Hence, rather than lift Africa out of the vicious circle into which it has been plunged, Gifford's view on development would seem to perpetuate it. If Pentecostal Christianity, as Gifford describes it, de-emphasizes hard work, then it is difficult to ascertain where its adherents get the money they contribute to their churches or to buy their Mercedes, BMWs, Pajeros, Land Cruisers, and Patrols that Gifford uses to map out their social class.[12]

Yet I share Gifford's unease about the image of Pentecostalism displayed by some of its adherents who spend endless hours in praying rather than working. Such practice supports Gifford's argument that allows little room for socioeconomic development within Pentecostalism. What I hope to show here, however, is that some (not all) Pentecostal-charismatic organizations have taken on new, unexpected roles in African public culture. The case material of this chapter points out how social services are provided by Lighthouse and Royalhouse by means of their educational and health services, and not simply by teaching morality.

These new institutional forms confound critics who doubt the rational expression of this kind of Christianity. The increasing involvement of Pentecostalism in socioeconomic development renders naive the attitude that consigns religion strictly to the private life of individuals. In everyday life, the experiences of the private and the public constantly intersect among most Ghanaians, making it difficult to draw a sharp distinction between religion as a private or public affair. What is more, the continuing importance of religion in public culture defies the prediction that religion will gradually be consigned to the private sphere in an increasingly modern-rationalist world.[13]

From Student Evangelism to Conquering the World

Lighthouse and Royalhouse belong to the most rapidly growing new churches in Ghana. Duncan Williams's Christian Action Faith Ministries International (Action Chapel, founded in 1979) and Mensa Otabil's International Central Gospel Church (founded in 1984) are older, more established, and the subjects of more previous research[14] than Lighthouse and Royalhouse, which scholars are only beginning to explore. Lighthouse and Royalhouse share the origins in student evangelistic ministries, which explains why membership is largely drawn from the professional classes. Although these churches have become transnational organizations, student evangelism on the University of Ghana campus continues to be the bedrock of their success. Lighthouse supports Campus Church as one of its branches that organizes crusades and owns buses and banners that announce its presence on campus. Lighthouse's founder holds an annual camp meeting with all the elders, shepherds, and members of this campus branch. The elders and shepherds are chosen from the student body, because the mother church believes that born-again students should be entrusted with leadership roles from a young age. Royalhouse also has a University of Ghana branch, known as Royalhouse Students and Associates. Both campus branches are engaged not only in proselytizing but also in providing a range of psychological and social support to students, thereby subscribing to a close relationship between spiritual and academic advancement. Training courses in leadership are also offered, along with significant scholarship schemes to ease students' financial hardship.

While it is interesting that many university campuses in West Africa have transformed from hotbeds of nationalist and leftist agitation to strongholds of evangelism,[15] new churches' provision of material welfare should not pass unnoticed. It is a part of a process by which churches such as Lighthouse and Royalhouse have expanded their influence and sought greater respectability for their public image in Ghana. This attempt to reach out through travel and education is evident in their founders' biographies. Lighthouse was established by Dag Heward-Mills, who was born in 1963 to a Ghanaian father and a Swiss mother. Although born in the United Kingdom, he grew up in Accra and attended the Christ the King Catholic Parish Basic School there before proceeding to Achimota School in the same city. While his family attended an Anglican church, Heward-Mills joined the Scripture Union Fellowship at Achimota School, rising to become its leader. It was on this basis that he embarked on student evangelism at the University of Ghana, where he studied medicine. He founded the Legon Calvary Road on campus in 1985, and after practicing medicine for three years, was ordained into full-time ministry in Victory Church International in London. A contemporary from the University of Ghana, Eddy Addy, studied economics and statistics and worked with the Volta River Authority, one of Ghana's leading companies, before entering full-time ministry to work with Heward-Mills. Addy's family background was in Methodism and Baptism.

The founder of Royalhouse, Sam Korankye Ankrah, was born in 1960 to a polygamous father and a Presbyterian mother. It was the mother who had him baptized as Samuel in the Presbyterian Church. Another great influence on him was the Scripture Union, which he joined at St. John's Grammar School in Accra, eventually giving his life to Christ when Joyful Way Incorporated, a nondenominational evangelistic group, visited the school.[16] He continued his education through Accra High School and entered the University of Ghana in 1984, where he founded his own evangelistic ministry, Showers of Blessings. It was this ministry that grew into Royalhouse as a result of a dramatic spiritual experience Ankrah claims to have had in Holland on June 19, 1991. He said God spoke to him that night, calling him into full-time ministry back home in Ghana. Referring to 1 Timothy 3:1, he says God offered him the office of bishop and overseer.[17] For his charitable contributions to education and health, Ankrah received in July 2008 the Order of the Volta from Ghana's president, one of the highest honors in Ghana.

There can hardly be a more decisive sign of respectability than this award, but crucial to achieving respectability have been other forms of public presence, from the architecture of the Church headquarters to transnational connections. The Qodesh, the main Lighthouse cathedral and headquarters, also known as the Mega Church, is located in North Kaneshie, a suburb of Accra.[18] It is doubtful whether any other religious building in Ghana surpasses this new cathedral and opulence. Bishop E. A. T. Sackey, one of Heward-Mills's assistants, oversees the Qodesh, leaving Heward-Mills free to exercise his duty as the general overseer of this transnational organization. Two chapels in the new cathedral complex are named after Bishops Addy and Sackey, while another is named after Heward-Mills's wife, Adelaide, a lawyer by profession and now the first lady of Lighthouse Chapel and its reverend minister. Weddings are celebrated in the Adelaide Chapel.

Worldwide, Lighthouse claims to have 687 branches in forty-one dioceses. Membership is said to be 38,756 worldwide and 27,811 in Ghana, although Eddy Addy in 2007 put the latter figure at 20,000. The Qodesh is reported to attract nearly twenty-five hundred people on a typical Sunday.[19] Although these statistics are contestable, the Sunday services I attended during fieldwork saw sizable crowds in the Qodesh's conservatively estimated seating capacity of fifteen hundred. The Church operates in thirty-four countries in Europe, the Caribbean, Australia, and North and South America, including the United States and Australia.[20] In Africa, Lighthouse has branches in Kenya, Uganda, Nigeria, Zambia, and South Africa. Membership in Ghana is spread mostly across urban areas, which is consistent with the church's strategy to become established first in the 110 district capitals before moving into rural areas. Rural ministry is in progress, with forty-six missions reported in the Ghanaian hinterland.[21] Since Lighthouse believes it has a missionary mandate according to Matthew 28:19–20,[22] the church organizes a conference to train missionaries. The ministry of the church is evangelistic, exercised through Healing Jesus Crusades, Lighthouse Media Ministries, and "over several books." Eddy Addy claims Heward-Mills has written over seventy books, of which I could find sixty-five listed on the founder's website.

Heward-Mills does not teach only through preaching and the books he has written but also by means of video- and audiocassettes. In this regard, he has acknowledged the American preacher Kenneth Hagin as one of the main influences on him. Some of Heward-Mills's books are used as training manuals in Bible schools and pastors' training programs. His own schools, the Anagkazo Bible and Ministry Training Centre and the Christ Mission Academy, are dedicated to producing practical and anointed ministers and missionaries. He has a network of pastors who receive guidance and counseling from him personally, while he publishes the magazine *A Healing Jesus* quarterly. His broadcast *The Mega Word* serves as an avenue for the proclamation of the word and miracle services.

Royalhouse Chapel takes its name from God as king. The church also uses the Akan version of Royalhouse, Ahenfie (the King's Palace), as its other official name. The headquarters is in Awudome, another suburb of Accra. The church has twenty-six local assemblies (branches) and eight international missions in New York, New Jersey, Maryland, Connecticut, North Carolina, and South, East, and North London. Royalhouse claims a total membership of twelve thousand at its headquarters and three thousand in all the other branches in Ghana. Only six of the twenty-six branches are in rural areas,[23] supporting my observation that both the locus and focus of this church are urban. The departments of the church include the media ministries, the church administration, the Christian Leadership College, and the Department of Social Services. Among the many ministries in the Department of Social Services are the Basic Trust Scholarship Project, Feed the Hungry, Rural Missions and Evangelism, Rescue to the Needy, premarital and marriage counseling, the Anglo/Francophone Ministry, and ministries for children, teens, men, women, and the elderly. This proliferation of social-service ministries demonstrates a growing organizational structure to expand the influence of the church from spiritual concerns to a wider public culture in Ghana.

Spiritual Welfare, Material Welfare

Leaders in Lighthouse and Royalhouse are consciously establishing the acceptability and respectability of their churches in Ghanaian public culture and are, by so doing, both responding to and transforming aspects of that public culture. The endeavor of Pentecostal movements to gain respectability is an interesting feature and yet often neglected in the academic literature.[24] This aspiration has to be understood in the context of considerable negative publicity about the alleged aim of these and other Pentecostal-charismatic churches to maximize economic gain. In 2006, for example, Rev. Dr. E. N. Tetteh of Worldwide Miracle Outreach in the UK, admonished ministers of God "to desist from the attitude of preaching on material things." Apostle Kwamena Ahinful, in 2007, challenged these churches to action: "What is the essence of religion if it is unable to solve human and societal problems?"[25] Pentecostal-charismatic churches and ministries subscribe, therefore, as the social services of Lighthouse and Royalhouse show, to certain procedures of the mainline churches they seek to differentiate themselves from.

The words *International* and *Continental* in many of the names of Pentecostal-charismatic churches and ministries indicate that their founders are seeking as wide an audience as possible, and thereby enhanced aspirations, which is aided by Ghanaians' international migration.[26] Going transnational and launching into social activities, both of which were traditionally associated with the mainline churches, augment the public image of these new churches. In the context of the SAPs, it is no surprise that churches and faith-based organizations have mushroomed to take over some of the functions previously performed by the state. The Registrar General's Department in Ghana indicates that 443 new religious organizations were registered in 2005.[27] The total number of companies, secular and religious, registered over the same period was 1,931. To counteract the view that Pentecostal-charismatic churches only teach morality without being developmental, I argue that they contribute to development through the social institutions they are establishing. Of particular interest are orphan care, healthcare, and education.

Lighthouse has an orphanage in Aburi, in the Eastern Region of Ghana. The home, which operates under the office of the first lady of the church, provides care and education for deprived children. Soon after its establishment, in 2006, there were nineteen orphans in the home, four boys and fifteen girls. These figures are, of course, subject to fluctuation, not least because the church intends to expand the facilities. The ages of the orphans range from babies to eleven-year-olds. The institution has an administrator who is also the resident pastor of the local branch of Lighthouse, a fact that indicates a close link between spirituality and development. Five caregivers, also referred to as mothers, cater to the daily needs of the children. These workers are all members of the church. A social worker, a nurse, and a medical doctor visit the institution occasionally. The children at the institution are trained to acquire skills such as crafts and painting. The institution also has a primary school which the children attend until they are sent to junior secondary school. The orphanage is funded through a canteen operated in its name at the Qodesh as well as through voluntary contributions from members. Lighthouse has also opened a basic school in Accra up to the junior secondary level, where some of these orphans may continue their education. In establishing the orphanage, the church sees its primary obligation of prayer bearing fruit by touching human lives. This guiding principle informs all its social projects, thereby asserting that spirituality and development are mutually inclusive.

Within the premises of the Qodesh, a huge religious empire in Accra, Lighthouse established a new hospital in 2006 with a ward that accommodates up to forty patients. During my fieldwork the hospital was staffed with four medical doctors, two of whom were church members, and nine nurses, eight of whom were church members. Five paramedic staff worked in the X-ray department, eye clinic, laboratory, and pharmacy. The hospital treated approximately twenty patients every day. The services were open to the public irrespective of their faith. Patients from the church's orphanage who could not afford medical bills, so-called agape patients, were treated free of charge. All other patients paid for treatment. The Lighthouse hospital ministry is reminiscent of the encounter between medical missionaries and converts, the link between the spiritual and the material having a long history in Africa.[28] The hospital staff used the opportunity to share the word of God with patients, an action that the staff I interviewed refused to call proselytism. Some patients I met expressed interest in joining the church, if only in appreciation of its good works in offering conventional medicine alongside spiritual healing.

Royalhouse has also started building a clinic, which is intended to provide free medical care for the underprivileged and the vulnerable, such as widows, single mothers, and orphans. As with Lighthouse, these developments affect the lives of members and nonmembers alike. In January 2007, Royalhouse launched the Royalhouse Vanguard Christian Life Assurance, an insurance policy for the future welfare of members of the church. By contributing premiums to the church's welfare or their personal life investments (or both), members are guaranteed a lump sum in the event of marriage, childbirth, hospitalization, and death of spouse or parent.[29] While the manifest objective of the scheme is to support members in difficulty, the latent objective is to ensure that members remain in the church and are committed. So the intention is not wholly religious. However, if the insurance scheme is successful for the approximately fifteen thousand Royalhouse members in Ghana, it will take some strain off meager state resources, which are unable to support the welfare of a vast majority of citizens. The church's program for feeding the hungry has to be seen in the same light. And the scholarship scheme mentioned earlier entices students to join the fellowship.

More broadly, religious broadcasts, fathers becoming authors of religious books, and the use of audio and visual recordings fulfill not only a religious goal but also a social one. Marleen de Witte notes that religious broadcasting is "the bedrock of the media industry" in Ghana.[30] The wide distribution of books written by the pastors of Pentecostal-charismatic churches is meant to "enhance their reputation,"[31] thereby augmenting their public image. Lighthouse also organizes youth camps for students and other young people during vacations. Apart from teaching them the word of God, the church gives participants workshops on leadership formation. Young people are taught skills they ultimately need to succeed, both as good Christians and as citizens of the world. The workshops are designed to promote self-help, self-reliance, self-esteem, self-determination, responsibility, and autonomy, the very qualities Gifford contends these new churches do not exhibit.[32] They contribute substantially to the transformation of the individual's welfare, for "the new spiritual power possessed by the born again individual cannot be disassociated from the 'practical' power to transform his/her social and economic world."[33]

The new gospel of public image in Ghanaian Pentecostal-charismatic circles was taken to one extreme when the International Central Gospel Church opened a university. What more public recognition does its founder and general overseer, Mensa Otabil, the self-made teacher of the nation, need beyond that of chancellor of an accredited university in a secular state?[34] He becomes a trailblazer for other Pentecostal-charismatic leaders to emulate. The inspiration he can generate in Ghanaian public culture is evident in his belief that he has the mandate to shape public discourse on individual success and wealth creation as well as on national development.

THE PROVISION of social services by Pentecostal-charismatic churches and ministries asserts their legitimate and respectable presence in Ghana. Because these services will be used by Ghanaians of any faith, they are among the means by which these new churches influence public culture. To wit, religious denominations leave their mark on the services they provide. These churches resemble, in this regard, pioneering missionary organizations by associating welfare services with proselytization. Public image in the structure of church buildings as megachurches combines with socioeconomic services to win not only souls for the church but also a conspicuous place in Ghanaian public culture. That such a connection to society and politics is sought by Royalhouse also became clear when it invited Ghana's minister of chieftaincy and culture to act as a guest speaker at the graduation ceremony of pastors in 2006. The broader trend, not addressed in this chapter, is the way in which these churches are reevaluating their attitude toward participation in institutional politics.[35]

I hope to have made it clear, therefore, that a naive belief in a miracle-working God offers no proper description of what is taking place on the ground in many African settings. The view that the political and economic reasons for so much poverty in Africa are ignored or obscured by Pentecostalism[36] does no justice to the prosperity gospel, which does not simply implore its adherents to look up to a miracle-working God or ignore poverty-creating conditions. It raises the consciousness of people to combat poverty through the skills they have acquired in these churches while all the time committing themselves to God's blessings. Preachers at Lighthouse and Royalhouse constantly hammer on this message. For example, pastors engage in founding churches, usually rising from difficult beginnings to great success.[37] The messages of achievement they preach can only drive an already ambitious youth to strive toward economic opportunity and success. This theme ran through almost all the preaching at services I attended during my fieldwork, and it runs through the advertisements for youth camps where skills can be learned to further this goal. Therefore, at least some adherents seem to understand that it is the work of their hands that will be miraculously blessed, contrary to the idle praying and moralizing some critics associate with this form of Christianity.

Scholars should, therefore, desist from misrepresenting the prosperity gospel as merely a dependency syndrome, even if it works in favor of some (notably pastors) and not all adherents. No economic system works to the advantage of an entire populace. Through giving, some are enriched, even if at the risk of impoverishing the givers. But while pastors preach against corruption, their churches increasingly provide health and educational facilities. In the context of socioeconomic difficulties and popular skepticism about the ability of the state to cater to citizens' needs, these religious leaders not only preach about the nation and national development but also go beyond the nation into a global public sphere by engaging both religious and secular transnational organizations, making a claim to discourses on democracy, human rights, and the emancipation of blacks and women.[38]

The faith clinics and schools run by these churches may not be on a large scale when compared to similar initiatives in mainline churches. Moreover, compared to some individual benefits, such as pastors being presented with Mercedes, the magnitude of the churches' social services is negligible. However, these services point to a shift in emphasis that requires more observation and analysis. Examining the media profile of Pentecostals and charismatics, J. Kwabena Asamoah-Gyadu contends, "In the last couple of years, a number of them have realized that to maintain an enduring presence in the community, values such as tolerance, religious dialogue, emphasis on hard work, and social commitment, are timeless values that need to be given a place."[39] Indeed, to found megachurches is to found powerful constituencies. Megachurches, Heward-Mills has asserted, are a challenge to governments that are constantly looking for votes; megachurches mean "more contacts and 'connections' as many people can find jobs through the church."[40] The transnational character of these churches promotes foreign earnings that are plowed into development projects such as schools and hospitals. At issue is a developmental import that a narrow view on what constitutes development fails to discern.

Notes

1. Paul Gifford, "Christian Fundamentalism and Development in Africa," *Review of African Political Economy* 19, no. 52 (1991): 9–20.
2. Ibid., 10.
3. Birgit Meyer, "'Delivered from the Powers of Darkness': Confessions of Satanic Riches in Christian Ghana," *Africa* 65, no. 2 (1995): 252; Ruth Marshall, "'Power in the Name of Jesus,'" *Review of African Political Economy* 19, no. 52 (1991): 37.
4. Paul Gifford, *Ghana's New Christianity: Pentecostalism in a Globalising African Economy* (London: Hurst, 2004), 161.
5. Paul Gifford, *African Christianity: Its Public Role* (London: Hurst, 1998).
6. David Maxwell, "In Defence of African Creativity," *Journal of Religion in Africa* 30, no. 4 (2000): 476.
7. To the extent that my analysis may be seen to present a positive account of some forms of Pentecostalism in Ghana, I ought to make it clear that I am not a Pentecostal myself. My religious background is in Roman Catholicism.
8. James Ferguson, *Global Shadows: Africa in the Neoliberal World Order* (Durham: Duke University Press, 2006), 11.
9. Paul Stoller, *Money Has No Smell: The Africanization of New York City* (Chicago: University of Chicago Press, 2002), 17.

10. Ragnhild Overå, "When Men Do Women's Work: Structural Adjustment, Unemployment and Changing Gender Relations in the Informal Economy of Accra, Ghana," *Journal of Modern African Studies* 45, no. 4 (2007): 541.

11. In Ghana, as elsewhere in Africa, many functions that were traditionally the prerogatives of the state have been taken up by foreign donors and religious and nongovernmental organizations. See Nicolas van de Walle, *African Economies and the Politics of Permanent Crisis, 1979–1999* (Cambridge: Cambridge University Press, 2001), 276. The consequences of the belt-tightening liberalization policies in Ghana since the mid-1980s included a drastic reduction in public spending on health and education. The SAPs came to be replaced with Poverty Reduction Strategy Papers, whose drafting was expected to involve more collaboration between African governments, civil society, and international aid and lending institutions. On closer inspection, the process has continued to impose donor-driven constraints on democratic governance in countries such as Ghana. See Lindsay Whitfield, "Trustees of Development from Conditionality to Governance: Poverty Reduction Strategy Papers in Ghana," *Journal of Modern African Studies* 43, no. 4 (2005): 641–64.

12. Gifford, *Ghana's New Christianity*, 26.

13. The narrow view on development I criticize here finds a parallel in the Habermasian notion of the public sphere that represents, in Marleen de Witte's words, "a modernist discourse that emphasizes rationality and leaves no room for the passions, desires, emotions, and 'magic' that that are also part of modernity." De Witte, "Altar Media's Living Word: Televised Charismatic Christianity in Ghana," *Journal of Religion in Africa* 33, no. 2 (2003): 173. Distinctions are drawn too sharply in this notion of the public sphere, because the British, French, and German polities that Jürgen Habermas wrote about were not devoid of emotional expression any more than Pentecostal-charismatic Christianity is entirely deficient in rational, critical debate. Cf. Craig Calhoun, "Habermas and the Public Sphere," introduction to *Habermas and the Public Sphere*, ed. Calhoun (Cambridge, MA: MIT, 1992), 3.

14. Paul Gifford, "Ghana's Charismatic Churches," *Journal of Religion in Africa* 24, no. 3 (1994): 241–65; Gifford, *Ghana's New Christianity*; Akosua K. Darkwah, "Aid or Hindrance? Faith Gospel Theology and Ghana's Incorporation into the Global Economy," *Ghana Studies* 4 (2001): 7–29; De Witte, "Altar," 172–202.

15. Ebenezer Obadare, "White-Collar Fundamentalism: Interrogating Youth Religiosity on Nigerian University Campuses," *Journal of Modern African Studies* 45, no. 4 (2007): 517–37.

16. D. Amanor, "Royalhouse Chapel International: Its Vision, History and Impact," (Bachelor of Divinity diss., Trinity Theological Seminary, Legon, Ghana, 2006), 12.

17. Ibid. 1 Timothy 3:1 reads: "This [is] a true saying, If a man desire the office of a bishop, he desireth a good work."

18. In Hebrew *qodesh* means holy, hallowed, or sanctified.

19. Data office, Lighthouse Chapel International, Accra.

20. Lighthouse Chapel International, http://www.daghewardmills.org.

21. Data office, Lighthouse Chapel International, Accra.

22. Matthew 28:19–20 reads: "Go ye therefore, and teach all nations, baptizing them in the name of the Father, and of the Son, and of the Holy Ghost: Teaching them to observe all things whatsoever I have commanded you: and, lo, I am with you always, [even] unto the end of the world. Amen."

23. Pastor Hannah Yawson, administrator of Royalhouse.

24. However, see David Maxwell, *African Gifts of the Spirit: Pentecostalism and the Rise of a Zimbabwean Transnational Religious Movement* (Oxford: James Currey, 2006).

25. E. N. Tetteh, *Ghanaian Times,* September 21, 2006; Kwamena Ahinful, *Daily Guide,* July 21, 2007.

26. See Margaret Peil, "The Development and Practice of Religion in an Accra Suburb," with K. A. Opoku, *Journal of Religion in Africa* 24, no. 3 (1994): 201.

27. Ghana, Registrar General's Department, *Companies Registered: Report From January 1, 2005, to December 31, 2005.* Accra: Registrar General's Department.

28. Adrian Hastings, *The Church in Africa, 1450–1950* (Oxford: Clarendon Press, 1994), 275–78.

29. Royalhouse Chapel International, http://www.royalhousechapel.org.

30. De Witte, "Altar," 172.

31. Gifford, "Ghana's Charismatic Churches," 256.

32. Gifford, "Christian Fundamentalism," 10, 18.

33. Marshall, "Power," 36.

34. Otabil has been chancellor of the Central University since its founding in 1988.

35. Marshall, "Power," 35; Maxwell, *African Gifts.*

36. Gifford, "Christian Fundamentalism," 13–14.

37. Dag Heward-Mills, *The Mega Church* (Accra: Parchment House, 1999).

38. De Witte, "Altar"; Harri Englund, "The Quest for Missionaries: Transnationalism and Township Pentecostalism in Malawi," in *Between Babel and Pentecost: Transnational Pentecostalism in Africa and Latin America,* ed. André Corten and Ruth Marshall-Fratani (London: Hurst, 2001); Englund, "Christian Independency and Global Membership: Pentecostal Extraversions in Malawi," *Journal of Religion in Africa* 33, no. 1 (2003): 83–111.

39. J. Kwabena Asamoah-Gyadu, "Reshaping Sub-Saharan African Christianity," *Media Development: Journal of the World Association for Christian Communication* 52, no. 2 (2005): 21.

40. Heward-Mills, *Mega Church,* 16–17.

Bibliography

Abe, Toshiharu. "The Concepts of Chira and Dhoch among the Luo of Kenya: Transition, Deviation and Misfortune." In *Themes in Socio-Cultural Ideas and Behaviour among the Six Ethnic Groups of Kenya,* edited by Nobuhiro Nagashima. Tokyo: Hitotsubashi University, 1981.

Abu-Lughod, Lila. "The Romance of Resistance: Tracing Transformations of Power through Bedouin Women." *American Ethnologist* 17, no. 1 (1990): 41–55.

Achebe, Chinua. *Morning Yet on Creation Day.* London: Heinemann, 1975.

Adeokun, L. A., and R. M. Nalwadda. "Serial Marriages and AIDS in Masaka District." *Health Transition Review* 7 (suppl.) (1997): 49–66.

Adogame, Afe. "Engaging the Rhetoric of Spiritual Warfare: The Public Face of Aladura in Diaspora." *Journal of Religion in Africa* 34, no. 4 (2004): 493–522.

Akin, David. "Concealment, Confession, and Innovation in Kwaio Women's Taboos." *American Ethnologist* 30, no. 3 (2003): 381–400.

Alpers, Edward A. "Towards a History of the Expansion of Islam in East Africa: The Matrilineal Peoples of the Southern Interior." In *The Historical Study of African Religion,* edited by T. O. Ranger and I. Kimambo. London: Heinemann, 1972.

Amanor, D. "Royalhouse Chapel International: Its Vision, History and Impact." Bachelor of Divinity diss., Trinity Theological Seminary, Legon, Ghana, 2006.

Anderson, Allan. *An Introduction to Pentecostalism: Global Charismatic Christianity.* Cambridge: Cambridge University Press, 2004.

Anderson, Benedict. *Imagined Communities: Reflections on the Origin and Spread of Nationalism.* London: Verso, 1991.

Appadurai, Arjun. *Fear of Small Numbers: An Essay in the Geography of Anger.* Durham, NC: Duke University Press, 2006.

Appiah, Kwame Anthony. *Cosmopolitanism: Ethics in a World of Strangers.* New York: Norton, 2006.

Asad, Talal. *Formations of the Secular: Christianity, Islam, Modernity.* Stanford: Stanford University Press, 2003.

———. *Genealogies of Religion: Discipline and Reasons of Power in Christianity and Islam.* Baltimore: Johns Hopkins University Press, 1993.

Asamoah-Gyadu, J. Kwabena. *African Charismatics: Current Developments within Independent Indigenous Pentecostalism in Ghana.* Leiden: Brill, 2005.

———. "Reshaping Sub-Saharan African Christianity." *Media Development: Journal of the World Association for Christian Communication* 52, no. 2 (2005): 21.

Ashforth, Adam. *Witchcraft, Violence, and Democracy in South Africa.* Chicago: University of Chicago Press, 2005.

Ayany, Samuel. *Kar chakruok mar Luo.* 1951. Reprint, Kisumu: Equatorial Publishers, 1989.

Balogun, Odun F. *Ngũgĩ and African Postcolonial Narrative: The Novel as Oral Narrative in Multigenre Performance.* Quebec: World Heritage Press, 1997.

Barber, Karin, ed. *Africa's Hidden Histories: Everyday Literacy and Making the Self.* Bloomington: Indiana University Press, 2006.

———. *The Anthropology of Texts, Persons, and Publics: Oral and Written Culture in Africa and Beyond.* Cambridge: Cambridge University Press, 2007.

———. Introduction to *Readings in African Popular Culture,* edited by Barber. Bloomington: Indiana University Press, 1997.
Bateye, B. O. "Female Leaders of New Generation Churches as Change Agents in Yorubaland." PhD diss., Obafemi Awolowo University, Ile-Ife, 2001.
Beidelman, T. O. *Colonial Evangelism: A Socio-historical Study of an East African Mission at the Grassroots.* Bloomington: Indiana University Press, 1982.
Berger, Peter, ed. *The Desecularization of the World: Resurgent Religion and World Politics.* Grand Rapids: Eerdmans, 1999.
Binsbergen, Wim M. J. van. *Religious Change in Zambia: Exploratory Studies.* London: Routledge and Kegan Paul, 1981.
———. *Virtuality as a Key Concept in the Study of African Globalisation: Aspects of the Symbolic Transformation of Contemporary Africa.* The Hague: WOTRO, 1997.
Birmingham, David, and Phyllis M. Martin, eds. *History of Central Africa.* 2 vols. London: Addison Wesley Longman, 1983.
Bompani, Barbara. "African Independent Churches in Post-apartheid South Africa: New Political Interpretations." *Journal of Southern African Studies* 34, no. 3 (2008): 665–77.
Bone, David S. "An Outline History of Islam in Malawi." In *Malawi's Muslims: Historical Perspectives,* edited by Bone. Blantyre: Christian Literature Association in Malawi, 2000.
Bornstein, Erica. *The Spirit of Development: Protestant NGOs, Morality, and Economics in Zimbabwe.* New York: Routledge, 2003.
Bruce, Steve. *God Is Dead: Secularization in the West.* Oxford: Wiley-Blackwell, 2002.
———. *Religion in the Modern World: From Cathedrals to Cults.* Oxford: Oxford University Press, 1996.
Buckser, Andrew, and Stephen D. Glazier, eds. *The Anthropology of Religious Conversion.* Lanham, MD: Rowman and Littlefield, 2003.
Cabrita, Joel. "Isaiah Shembe's Theological Nationalism, 1920s–1935." *Journal of Southern African Studies* 35, no. 3 (2009): 609–25.
Calhoun, Craig, ed. *Habermas and the Public Sphere.* Cambridge, MA: MIT Press, 1992.
Campbell, James T. *Songs of Zion: The African Methodist Episcopal Church in the United States and South Africa.* Chapel Hill: University of North Carolina Press, 1998.
Cannell, Fenella. "The Christianity of Anthropology." *Journal of the Royal Anthropological Institute* 11, no. 2 (2005): 335–56.
Carmody, Brendan. "Religious Education and Pluralism in Zambia." In *Religion and Education in Zambia,* edited by Carmody. Ndola: Mission Press, 2004.
Carotenuto, Matthew. "Riwuok e teko: Cultivating Identity in Colonial and Postcolonial Kenya." *Africa Today* 53, no. 2 (2006): 53–73.
Casanova, José. *Public Religions in the Modern World.* Chicago: University of Chicago Press, 1994.
Castells, Manuel. *The Rise of the Network Society.* Oxford: Blackwell, 1996.
Chabal, Patrick. *Africa: The Politics of Suffering and Smiling.* London: Zed, 2009.
Chanock, Martin. *Law, Custom and Social Order: The Colonial Experience in Malawi and Zambia.* Cambridge: Cambridge University Press, 1985.
Chidester, David. *Savage Systems: Colonialism and Comparative Religion in Southern Africa.* Charlottesville: University Press of Virginia, 1996.
Chinsinga, Blessings. "The Politics of Poverty Alleviation in Malawi: A Critical Review." In *A Democracy of Chameleons: Politics and Culture in the New Malawi,* edited by Harri Englund. Uppsala: Nordiska Afrikainstitutet; Blantyre: Christian Literature Association in Malawi, 2002.

Chirwa, Wiseman C. "Democracy, Ethnicity and Regionalism: The Malawian Experience, 1992–1996." In *Democratization in Malawi: A Stocktaking*, edited by Kings M. Phiri and Kenneth R. Ross. Blantyre: Christian Literature Association in Malawi, 1998.

Chong, H. Kelly. "Negotiating Patriarchy: South Korean Evangelical Women and the Politics of Gender." *Gender and Society* 20, no. 6 (2005): 697–724.

Cohen, David W., and E. S. Atieno Odhiambo. "Ayany, Malo, and Ogot—Historians in Search of a Luo Nation." *Cahiers d'études africaines* 27, nos. 105–6 (1987): 269–86.

———. *Burying SM: The Politics of Knowledge and the Sociology of Power in Africa*. London: James Currey, 1992.

———. *Siaya: The Historical Anthropology of an African Landscape*. London: James Currey, 1989.

Coldham, Simon. "The Effect of Registration of Title upon Customary Land Rights in Kenya." *Journal of African Law* 22, no. 2 (1978): 91–111.

Comaroff, Jean. *Body of Power, Spirit of Resistance: The Culture and History of a South African People*. Chicago: University of Chicago Press, 1985.

———. "The Diseased Heart of Africa: Medicine, Colonialism, and the Black Body." In *Knowledge, Power, and Practice: The Anthropology of Medicine and Everyday Life*, edited by Shirley Lindenbaum and Margaret Lock. Berkeley: University of California Press, 1993.

Comaroff, Jean, and John L. Comaroff. *Christianity, Colonialism, and Consciousness in South Africa*. Vol. 1 of *Of Revelation and Revolution*. Chicago: University of Chicago Press, 1991.

———. *The Dialectics of Modernity on a South African Frontier*. Vol. 2 of *Of Revelation and Revolution*. Chicago: University of Chicago Press, 1997.

———. Introduction to *Modernity and Its Malcontents: Ritual and Power in Postcolonial Africa*, edited by Jean Comaroff and John Comaroff. Chicago: University of Chicago Press, 1993.

———. "Occult Economies and the Violence of Abstraction: Notes from the South African Postcolony." *American Ethnologist* 26, no. 2 (1999): 279–303.

Comaroff, John L., and Jean Comaroff. "Second Comings: Neo-Protestant Ethics and Millennial Capitalism in Africa, and Elsewhere." In *2000 Years and Beyond: Faith, Identity and the "Common Era,"* edited by Paul Gifford, David Archard, Trevor A. Hart, and Nigel Rapport. New York: Routledge, 2003.

Cook, David, and Michael Okenimkpe. Introduction to *Ngũgĩ wa Thiong'o: An Exploration of His Writings*, edited by Cook and Okenimkpe. London: Heinemann, 1997.

Cooper, Barbara M. "Anatomy of a Riot: The Social Imaginary, Single Women, and Religious Violence in Niger." *Canadian Journal of African Studies* 37, nos. 2–3 (2003): 467–512.

———. *Evangelical Christians in the Muslim Sahel*. Bloomington: Indiana University Press, 2006.

———. "Population and Piety: Demographic Imperatives and Sudan Interior Mission Interventions in the Sahel, 1930–1960." Paper presented at fiftieth anniversary meeting, African Studies Association, New York, October 18, 2007.

———. "La rhétorique de la 'mauvaise mère.'" In *Niger 2005: Une catastrophe si naturelle*, edited by Xavier Crombé and Jean-Hervé Jézéquel. Paris: Karthala, 2007.

Corten, André, and Ruth Marshall-Fratani, eds. *Between Babel and Pentecost: Transnational Pentecostalism in Africa and Latin America*. London: Hurst, 2001.

Cotran, Eugene. "Marriage, Divorce and Succession Laws in Kenya: Is Integration or Unification Possible?" *Journal of African Law* 40, no. 2 (1996): 194–204.

Bibliography

Crivella, Marcelo. *Mutis, Sangomas and Nyangas: Tradition or Witchcraft?* Brazil: UCKG Publications, 1999.
Crossley, Nick, and John Michael Roberts, eds. *After Habermas: New Perspectives on the Public Sphere.* Oxford: Blackwell, 2004.
Crumbley, Deidre Helen. "Impurity and Power: Women in Aladura Churches." *Africa* 62, no. 4 (1992): 505–22.
Dagger, Richard. *Civic Virtues: Rights, Citizenship, and Republican Liberalism.* Oxford: Oxford University Press, 1997.
Darkwah, Akosua K. "Aid or Hindrance? Faith Gospel Theology and Ghana's Incorporation into the Global Economy." *Ghana Studies* 4 (2001): 7–29.
Dawkins, Richard. *The God Delusion.* London: Bantam Press, 2006.
Deeb, Lara. *An Enchanted Modern: Gender and Public Piety in Shi'i Lebanon.* Princeton: Princeton University Press, 2006.
de Gruchy, John W., and Steve de Gruchy. *The Church Struggle in South Africa.* Foreword by Desmond Tutu. Johannesburg: Fortress Press, 2005.
de Witte, Marleen. "Altar Media's *Living Word:* Televised Charismatic Christianity in Ghana." *Journal of Religion in Africa* 33, no. 2 (2003): 172–202.
———. "The Spectacular and the Spirits: Charismatics and Neo-traditionalists on Ghanaian Television." *Material Religion* 1, no. 3 (2005): 314–35.
———. "Spirit Media: Charismatics, Traditionalists, and Mediation Practices in Ghana." PhD diss., University of Amsterdam, 2008.
Devy, Ganesh. "Translation and Literary History: An Indian View." In *Post-colonial Translation: Theory and Practice,* edited by Susan Bassnett and Harish Trivedi. New York: Routledge, 1999.
Dijk, Rijk van. "Christian Fundamentalism in Sub-Saharan Africa: The Case of Pentecostalism." Occasional Paper, Centre of African Studies, University of Copenhagen, 2000.
———. "Contesting Silence: The Ban on Drumming and the Musical Politics of Pentecostalism in Ghana." *Ghana Studies* 4 (2001): 31–64.
———. "From Camp to Encompassment: Discourses of Transsubjectivity in the Ghanaian Pentecostal Diaspora." *Journal of Religion in Africa* 27, no. 2 (1997): 135–59.
———. "Negotiating Marriage: Questions of Morality and Testimony in the Ghanaian Pentecostal Diaspora." *Journal of Religion in Africa* 34, no. 4 (2004): 438–67.
———. "The Pentecostal Gift: Ghanaian Charismatic Churches and the Moral Innocence of the Global Economy." In *Modernity on a Shoestring: Dimensions of Globalisation, Consumption and Development in Africa and Beyond,* edited by Richard Fardon, Wim van Binsbergen, and Dijk. London: Anthony Rowe, 1999.
———. "Pentecostalism, Cultural Memory and the State: Contested Representations of Time in Postcolonial Malawi." In *Memory and the Postcolony: African Anthropology and the Critique of Power,* edited by Richard Werbner. London: Zed, 1998.
Dilger, Hansjörg. "Healing the Wounds of Modernity: Salvation, Community, and Care in a Neo-Pentecostal Church in Dar es Salaam, Tanzania." *Journal of Religion in Africa* 37, no. 1 (2007): 59–83.
Dinwiddy, Hugh. "Biblical Usage and Abusage in Kenyan Writing." *Journal of Religion in Africa* 19, no. 1 (1989): 27–47.
Dirks, Nicholas B., ed. *Colonialism and Culture.* Ann Arbor: University of Michigan Press, 1992.
Dorman, Sara Rich. "'Rocking the Boat'? Church NGOs and Democratization in Zimbabwe." *African Affairs* 101, no. 402 (2002): 75–92.
Eagleton, Terry. *Reason, Faith, and Revolution: Reflections on the God Debate.* New Haven: Yale University Press, 2009.

Bibliography

Eickelman, Dale F., and Jon W. Anderson, eds. *New Media in the Muslim World: The Emerging Public Sphere*. Bloomington: Indiana University Press, 1999.

Eliot, T. S. *Essays, Ancient and Modern*. London: Faber and Faber, 1936.

Ellis, Stephen, and Gerrie ter Haar. "Religion and Politics: Taking African Epistemologies Seriously." *Journal of Modern African Studies* 45, no. 3 (2007): 385–401.

———. *Worlds of Power: Religious Thought and Political Practice in Africa*. London: Hurst, 2004.

Elster, Jon, ed. *Deliberative Democracy*. Cambridge: Cambridge University Press, 1998.

Engelke, Matthew. *A Problem of Presence: Beyond Scripture in an African Church*. Berkeley: University of California Press, 2007.

Englund, Harri. "Christian Independency and Global Membership: Pentecostal Extraversions in Malawi." *Journal of Religion in Africa* 33, no. 1 (2003): 83–111.

———. "Cosmopolitanism and the Devil in Malawi." *Ethnos* 69, no. 3 (2004): 293–316.

———. "The Dead Hand of Human Rights: Contrasting Christianities in Post-transition Malawi." *Journal of Modern African Studies* 38, no. 4 (2000): 579–603.

———. "Pentecostalism beyond Belief: Trust and Democracy in a Malawian Township." *Africa* 77, no. 4 (2007): 477–99.

———. *Prisoners of Freedom: Human Rights and the African Poor*. Berkeley: University of California Press, 2006.

———. "The Quest for Missionaries: Transnationalism and Township Pentecostalism in Malawi." In Corten and Marshall-Fratani, *Between Babel and Pentecost*.

———. "The Village in the City, the City in the Village: Migrants in Lilongwe." *Journal of Southern African Studies* 28, no. 2 (2002): 137–54.

———. "Witchcraft and the Limits of Mass Mediation in Malawi." *Journal of the Royal Anthropological Institute* 13, no. 2 (2007): 295–311.

Englund, Harri, and James Leach. "Ethnography and the Meta-narratives of Modernity." *Current Anthropology* 41, no. 2 (2000): 225–48.

Epstein, A. L. *Politics in an Urban African Community*. Manchester: Manchester University Press, 1958.

Evans-Pritchard, E. E. "Luo Tribes and Clans." *Rhodes-Livingstone Journal* 7 (1949): 24–40.

———. "Marriage Customs of the Luo of Kenya." In *The Position of Women in Primitive Societies and Other Essays in Social Anthropology*, edited by Evans-Pritchard. London: Faber and Faber, 1965.

———. *The Nuer: A Description of the Modes of Livelihood and Political Institutions of a Nilotic People*. Oxford: Oxford University Press, 1940.

Fabian, Johannes. *Jamaa: A Charismatic Movement in Katanga*. Evanston, IL: Northwestern University Press, 1971.

Fanon, Frantz. *The Wretched of the Earth*. Harmondsworth: Penguin, 1967.

Ferguson, James. *Expectations of Modernity: Myths and Meanings of Urban Life on the Zambian Copperbelt*. Berkeley: University of California Press, 1999.

———. *Global Shadows: Africa in the Neoliberal World Order*. Durham, NC: Duke University Press, 2006.

Fernandez, James W. *Bwiti: An Ethnography of the Religious Imagination in Africa*. Princeton: Princeton University Press, 1982.

Fields, Karen. "Charismatic Religion as Popular Protest: The Ordinary and the Extraordinary in Social Movements." *Theory and Society* 11, no. 3 (1982): 321–61.

———. *Revival and Rebellion in Colonial Central Africa*. Princeton: Princeton University Press, 1985.

Fisher, W. Singleton, and Julyan Hoyte. *Africa Looks Ahead: The Life Stories of Walter and Anna Fisher of Central Africa*. London: Pickering and Inglis, 1948.

Bibliography

Flora, Cornelia Butler. "Pentecostal Women in Colombia: Religious Change and the Status of Working-Class Women." *Journal of Interamerican Studies and World Affairs* 17, no. 4 (1975): 411–25.

Francis, Elizabeth. "Migration and Changing Divisions of Labour: Gender Relations and Economic Change in Koguta, Western Kenya." *Africa* 65, no. 2 (1995): 197–215.

Freston, Paul. "Evangelicals and Politics: A Comparison between Africa and Latin America." *Journal of Contemporary Religion* 13, no. 1 (1998): 37–49.

———. *Evangelicals and Politics in Asia, Africa, and Latin America*. Cambridge: Cambridge University Press, 2001.

———. "The Universal Church of the Kingdom of God: A Brazilian Church Finds Success in South Africa." *Journal of Religion in Africa* 35, no. 1 (2005): 33–65.

Geissler, Wenzel, and Ruth Prince. *The Land Is Dying: Contingency, Creativity and Conflict in Western Kenya*. New York: Berghahn, 2009.

———. "Life Seen: Touch and Vision in the Making of Sex in Western Kenya." *Journal of Eastern African Studies* 1, no. 19 (2007): 123–49.

Geschiere, Peter. *The Perils of Belonging: Autochthony, Citizenship, and Exclusion in Africa and Europe*. Chicago: University of Chicago Press, 2009.

Geschiere, Peter, and Josef Gugler. "The Urban-Rural Connection: Changing Issues of Belonging and Identification." *Africa* 68, no. 3 (1998): 309–19.

Gewald, Jan-Bart, Marja Hinfelaar, and Giacomo Macola, eds. *One Zambia, Many Histories: Towards a History of Post-colonial Zambia*. Leiden: Brill, 2008.

Gifford, Paul. *African Christianities and Public Life: A View from Kenya*. London: Hurst, 2009.

———. *African Christianity: Its Public Role*. London: Hurst, 1998.

———, ed. *The Christian Churches and the Democratisation of Africa*. Leiden: Brill, 1995.

———. "Christian Fundamentalism and Development in Africa." *Review of African Political Economy* 19, no. 52, no. 1991): 9–20.

———. "Ghana's Charismatic Churches." *Journal of Religion in Africa* 24, no. 3 (1994): 241–65.

———. *Ghana's New Christianity: Pentecostalism in a Globalising African Economy*. London: Hurst, 2004.

———. *The New Crusaders: Christianity and the New Right in Southern Africa*. London: Pluto Press, 1991.

Gikandi, Simon. *Ngũgĩ wa Thiong'o*. Cambridge: Cambridge University Press, 2000.

———. "On Culture and the State: The Writings of Ngũgĩ wa Thiong'o." *Third World Quaterly* 11, no. 1 (1989): 149–56.

Glazier, Stephen D. "'Limin' wid Jah': Spiritual Baptists Who Become Rastafarians and Then Become Spiritual Baptists Again." In Buckser and Glazier, *The Anthropology of Religious Conversion*.

Goode, Luke. *Jürgen Habermas: Democracy and the Public Sphere*. London: Pluto Press, 2005.

Gould, Jeremy. "Subsidiary Sovereignty and the Constitution of Political Space in Zambia." In Gewald, Hinfelaar, and Macola, *One Zambia*, 275–93.

Gray, Richard. *Black Christians and White Missionaries*. New Haven: Yale University Press, 1990.

Green, Maia. "Confronting Categorical Assumptions about the Power of Religion in Africa." *Review of African Political Economy* 33, no. 110 (2006): 635–50.

———. *Priests, Witches and Power: Popular Christianity after Mission in Southern Tanzania*. Cambridge: Cambridge University Press, 2003.

Griffith, R. Marie. *God's Daughters: Evangelical Women and the Power of Submission*. Berkeley: University of California Press, 1997.

Bibliography

Gunner, Liz. *The Man of Heaven and the Beautiful Ones of God: Writings from Ibandla lama Nazaretha, a South African Church*. Leiden: Brill, 2002.
Haar, Gerrie ter. *Spirit of Africa: The Healing Ministry of Archbishop Milingo of Zambia*. London: Hurst, 1992.
Habermas, Jürgen. "On the Relation between the Secular Liberal State and Religion." In *The Frankfurt School on Religion: Key Writings by the Major Thinkers*, edited by Eduardo Mendieta. New York: Routledge, 2005.
———. *The Structural Transformation of the Public Sphere: An Inquiry into a Category of Bourgeois Society*. Cambridge, MA: MIT Press, 1989.
Hackett, Rosalind I. J. "Charismatic/Pentecostal Appropriations of Media Technologies in Nigeria and Ghana." *Journal of Religion in Africa* 28, no. 3 (1998): 258–77.
Hall, Stuart, and Tony Jefferson, eds. *Resistance through Rituals: Youth Subcultures in Post-war Britain*. London: Hutchinson, 1976.
Hansen, Karen Tranberg. *Salaula: The World of Secondhand Clothing and Zambia*. Chicago: University of Chicago Press, 2000.
Hastings, Adrian. *The Church in Africa, 1450–1950*. Oxford: Clarendon Press, 1994.
Haugerud, Angelique. *The Culture of Politics in Modern Kenya*. Cambridge: Cambridge University Press, 1993.
Hay, Margaret. "Women as Owners, Occupants, and Managers of Property in Colonial Western Kenya." In *African Women and the Law: Historical Perspectives*, edited by Hay and Marcia Wright. Boston: African Studies Center, Boston University, 1982.
Heward-Mills, Dag. *The Mega Church*. Accra: Parchment House, 1999.
Hinfelaar, Hugo. *History of the Catholic Church in Zambia, 1895–1995*. Lusaka: Bookworld, 2004.
Hinfelaar, Marja. "Legitimizing Powers: The Political Role of the Roman Catholic Church, 1972–1991." In Gewald, Hinfelaar, and Macola, *One Zambia*, 129–43.
———. *Respectable and Responsible Women: Methodist and Roman Catholic Women's Organizations in Harare, Zimbabwe (1919–1985)*. Zoetermeer, Netherlands: Boekencentrum, 2001.
Hirschkind, Charles. *The Ethical Soundscape: Cassette Sermons and Islamic Counterpublics*. New York: Columbia University Press, 2006.
Hitchens, Christopher. *God Is Not Great: How Religion Poisons Everything*. New York: Atlantic Press, 2008.
Hodgson, Dorothy. *The Church of Women: Gendered Encounters between Maasai and Missionaries*. Bloomington: Indiana University Press, 2005.
Hoehler-Fatton, Cynthia. *Women of Fire and Spirit: History, Faith, and Gender in Roho Religion in Western Kenya*. Oxford: Oxford University Press, 1996.
Hofmeyr, Isabel. *The Portable Bunyan: A Transnational History of* The Pilgrim's Progress. Princeton: Princeton University Press, 2004.
Hokkanen, Markku. *Medicine and Scottish Missionaries in the Northern Malawi Region, 1875–1930: Quests for Health in a Colonial Society*. Lewiston, NY: Edwin Mellen Press, 2008.
Horton, Robin. "African Conversion." *Africa* 41, no. 2 (1971): 85–108.
Hunt, Nancy Rose. "'Le bébé en brousse': European Women, African Birth Spacing, and Colonial Intervention in Breast Feeding in the Belgian Congo." In *Tensions of Empire: Colonial Cultures in a Bourgeois World*, edited by Frederick Cooper and Ann Laura Stoler. Berkeley: University of California Press, 1997.
———. *A Colonial Lexicon of Birth Ritual, Medicalization, and Mobility in the Congo*. Durham, NC: Duke University Press, 2003.

Bibliography

Johnson-Hanks, Jennifer. "On the Politics and Practice of Muslim Fertility: Comparative Evidence from West Africa." *Medical Anthropology Quarterly* 20, no. 1 (2006): 12–30.

Johnston, Sandy. *Under the Radar: Pentecostalism in South Africa and Its Potential Social and Economic Role*. Johannesburg: Centre for Development and Enterprise, 2008.

Jules-Rosette, Bennetta. *African Apostles: Ritual and Conversion in the Church of John Maranke*. Ithaca: Cornell University Press, 1975.

Kaggia, Bildad. *Roots of Freedom, 1921–1963: The Autobiography of Bildad Kaggia*. Nairobi: East African Publishing House, 1975.

Kalusa, Walima. "Disease and the Remaking of Missionary Medicine in Colonial Northwestern Zambia: A Case Study of Mwinilunga District, 1902–1964." PhD diss., Johns Hopkins University, 2003.

Karega, John B. "Theology and Literature: Religions in the Works of Ngũgĩ wa Thiong'o." PhD diss., Catholic University of Leuven, 1988.

Kasoma, Francis P. *The Press in Zambia: The Development, Role, and Control of National Newspapers in Zambia, 1906–1983*. Lusaka: Multimedia Publications, 1986.

Keane, Webb. "Materialism, Missionaries, and Modern Subjects in Colonial Indonesia." In *Conversion to Modernities: The Globalization of Christianity*, edited by Peter van der Veer. New York: Routledge, 1996.

Kibwana, Kibwana, and Lawrence Mute, eds. *Law and the Quest for Gender Equality in Kenya*. Nairobi: Claripress, 2000.

Kimani, V. N. "Human Sexuality: Meaning and Purpose in Selected Communities in Contemporary Kenya." *Ecumenical Review (WCC)* 56, no. 4 (2004): 404–21

Kirsch, Thomas G. "Restaging the Will to Believe: Religious Pluralism, Anti-syncretism, and the Problem of Belief." *American Anthropologist* 106, no. 4 (2004): 699–709.

———. *Spirits and Letters: Reading, Writing and Charisma in African Christianity*. New York: Berghahn, 2008.

Klaits, Frederick. *Death in a Church of Life: Moral Passion during Botswana's Time of AIDS*. Berkeley: University of California Press, 2010.

Kolawole, Mary Ebun Modupe. "Kofi Awoonor as a Prophet of Conscience." *African Languages and Cultures* 5, no. 2 (1992): 125–32.

Komakoma, Joseph. *The Social Teaching of the Catholic Bishops and Other Christian Leaders in Zambia: Major Pastoral Letters and Statements, 1953–2001*. Ndola: Mission Press, 2003.

Kymlicka, Will. *Multicultural Citizenship: A Liberal Theory of Minority Rights*. Oxford: Oxford University Press, 1995.

Lalive d'Epinay, Christian. *Haven of the Masses: A Study of the Pentecostal Movement in Chile*. London: Lutterworth, 1969.

Landau, Paul. *The Realm of the Word: Language, Gender, and Christianity in a Southern African Kingdom*. London: James Currey, 1995.

Latour, Bruno. *We Have Never Been Modern*. New York: Harvester Wheatsheaf, 1993.

Lazarus, Neil. *Resistance in Postcolonial African Fiction*. New Haven: Yale University Press, 1990.

Lewis, C. S. *The Screwtape Letters*. London: Geoffrey Bles, 1942.

Lindquist, Galina, and Simon Coleman. "Against Belief?" *Social Analysis* 52, no. 1 (2008): 1–18.

Loimeier, Roman. "Perceptions of Marginalization: Muslims in Contemporary Tanzania." In *Islam and Muslim Politics in Africa*, edited by Benjamin F. Soares and René Otayek. New York: Palgrave Macmillan, 2007.

Lonsdale, John. "Moral Ethnicity and Political Tribalism." In *Inventions and Boundaries: Historical and Anthropological Approaches to the Study of Ethnicity and Nationalism*, edited by Preben Kaarsholm and J. Hultin. Roskilde, Denmark: International Development Studies, Roskilde University, 1994.

———. "The Prayers of Waiyaki: The Political Uses of the Kikuyu Past." In *Revealing Prophets: Prophecy in East African History*, edited by David Anderson and Douglas H. Johnson. London: James Currey, 1995.

Luginaah, Isaac, David Elkins, Eleanor Maticka-Tyndale, Tamara Landry, and Mercy Mathui. "Challenges of a Pandemic: HIV/AIDS-Related Problems Affecting Kenyan Widows." *Social Science and Medicine* 60, no. 6 (2005): 1219–28.

MacIntyre, Alasdair. *Dependent Rational Animals: Why Human Beings Need the Virtues*. London: Duckworth, 1999.

Maffesoli, Michel. *The Contemplation of the World: Figures of Community Style*. Minneapolis: University of Minnesota Press, 1996.

Mahmood, Saba. *Politics of Piety: The Islamic Revival and the Feminist Subject*. Princeton: Princeton University Press, 2005.

Maina, W. "Kenya: The State, Donors and the Politics of Democratization." In *Civil Society and the Aid Industry*, edited by Alison Van Rooy. London: Earthscan, 1998.

Malawi. National Statistical Office. *1998 Malawi Population and Housing Census: Analytical Report*. Zomba: National Statistical Office, 2002.

Malungo, J. R. S. "Sexual Cleansing (Kusalazya) and Levirate Marriage (Kunjilila mung'anda) in the Era of AIDS: Changes in Perceptions and Practices in Zambia." *Social Science and Medicine* 53, no. 3 (2001): 371–82.

Marsden, Magnus. *Living Islam: Muslim Religious Experience in Pakistan's North-West Frontier*. Cambridge: Cambridge University Press, 2005.

———. "Talking the Talk: Debating Debate in Northern Afghanistan." *Anthropology Today* 25, no. 2 (2009): 20–24.

Marshall, Ruth. "'God Is Not a Democrat': Pentecostalism and Democratisation in Nigeria." In Gifford, *Christian Churches*.

———. *Political Spiritualities: The Pentecostal Revolution in Nigeria*. Chicago: University of Chicago Press, 2009.

———. "Power in the Name of Jesus." *Review of African Political Economy* 19, no. 52 (1991): 21–37.

———. "'Power in the Name of Jesus': Social Transformation and Pentecostalism in Western Nigeria 'Revisited.'" In *Legitimacy and the State in Twentieth-century Africa: Essays in Honour of A. H. M. Kirk-Greene*, edited by Terence Ranger and Olufemi Vaughan. London: Macmillan, 1993.

Marshall, Will, ed. *With All Our Might: A Progressive Strategy for Defeating Jihadism and Defending Liberty*. Lanham, MD: Rowman and Littlefield, 2006.

Martin, Bernice. "From Pre- to Postmodernity in Latin America: The Case of Pentecostalism." In *Religion, Modernity, and Postmodernity*, edited by Paul Heelas, David Martin, and Paul Morris. Oxford: Blackwell, 1998.

Martin, David. *Pentecostalism: The World Their Parish*. Oxford: Blackwell, 2002.

Mate, Rekopantswe. "Wombs as God's Laboratories: Pentecostal Discourses of Femininity in Zimbabwe." *Africa* 72, no. 4 (2002): 549–68.

Mathuray, Mark. "Resuming a Broken Dialogue: Prophecy, Nationalist Strategies, and Religious Discourses in Ngũgĩ's Early Work." *Research in African Literatures* 40, no. 2 (2009): 40–62.

Maughan-Brown, David. "Matigari and the Rehabilitation of Religion." *Research in African Literatures* 22, no. 4 (1991): 173–80.

Maxwell, David. *African Gifts of the Spirit: Pentecostalism and the Rise of a Zimbabwean Transnational Religious Movement*. Oxford: James Currey, 2006.

Bibliography

———, ed. *Christianity and the African Imagination: Essays in Honour of Adrian Hastings.* With Ingrid Lawrie. Leiden: Brill, 2002.

———. *Christians and Chiefs in Zimbabwe: A Social History of the Hwesa People, c. 1870s–1990s.* Edinburgh: Edinburgh University Press, 1999.

———. "'Delivered from the Spirit of Poverty?': Pentecostalism, Prosperity and Modernity in Zimbabwe." *Journal of Religion in Africa* 28, no. 3 (1998): 350–73.

———. "The Durawall of Faith: Pentecostal Spirituality in Neo-liberal Zimbabwe." *Journal of Religion in Africa* 35, no. 1 (2005): 4–32.

———. "In Defence of African Creativity." *Journal of Religion in Africa* 30, no. 4 (2000): 468–81.

———. "Post-colonial Christianity in Africa." In McLeod, *World Christianities*, 401–21.

Mboya, Paul. *Luo kitigi gi timbegi* (A Handbook of Luo Customs). Kisumu: Anyange Press, 1938.

McCracken, John. "Church and State in Malawi: The Role of the Scottish Presbyterian Missions, 1875–1965." In *Christian Missionaries and the State in the Third World*, edited by Holger B. Hansen and Michael Twaddle. Oxford: James Currey, 2002.

McGee, Gary B. "Pentecostal Missiology: Moving beyond Triumphalism to Face the Issues." *Pneuma* 16, no. 2 (1994): 276–77.

McKenna, Joseph C. *Finding a Social Voice: The Church and Marxism in Africa.* New York: Fordham University Press, 1997.

McLeod, Hugh, ed. *World Christianities c. 1914–c. 2000.* Vol. 9 of *The Cambridge History of Christianity.* Cambridge: Cambridge University Press, 2006.

Meebelo, H. S. *African Proletarians and Colonial Capitalism: The Origins, Growth and Struggles of the Zambian Labour Movement to 1964.* Lusaka: Kenneth Kaunda Foundation, 1986.

Meyer, Birgit. "Christianity in Africa: From African Independent to Pentecostal-Charismatic Churches." *Annual Review of Anthropology* 33, no. 1 (2004): 447–74.

———. "Commodities and the Power of Prayer: Pentecostalist Attitudes towards Consumption in Contemporary Ghana." *Development and Change* 29, no. 4 (1998): 751–77.

———. "'Delivered from the Powers of Darkness': Confessions of Satanic Riches in Christian Ghana." *Africa* 65, no. 2 (1995): 236–55.

———. "From Imagined Communities to Aesthetic Formations: Religious Mediations, Sensational Forms, and Styles of Binding." In *Aesthetic Formations: Media, Religion, and the Senses,* edited by Meyer. New York: Palgrave Macmillan, 2009.

———. "Impossible Representations: Pentecostalism, Vision, and Video Technology in Ghana." In Meyer and Moors, *Religion, Media,* 290–312.

———. "'Make a Complete Break with the Past': Memory and Post-colonial Modernity in Ghanaian Pentecostalist Discourse." *Journal of Religion in Africa* 28, no. 3 (1998): 316–49.

———. "Money, Power and Morality: Popular Ghanaian Cinema in the Fourth Republic." *Ghana Studies* 4 (2001): 65–84.

———. "Pentecostal and Neo-liberal Capitalism: Faith, Prosperity and Vision in African Pentecostal-Charismatic Churches." *Journal for the Study of Religion* 20, no. 2 (2007): 5–28.

———. "'Praise the Lord': Popular Cinema and Pentecostalite Style in Ghana's New Public Sphere." *American Ethnologist* 31, no. 1 (2004): 92–110.

———. "Religious Revelation, Secrecy, and the Limits of Visual Representation." *Anthropological Theory* 6, no. 4 (2006): 431–53.

———. "Religious Sensations: Why Media, Aesthetics, and Power Matter in the Study of Contemporary Religion." In Vries, *Religion,* 704–23.

Bibliography

———. *Translating the Devil: Religion and Modernity among the Ewe in Ghana.* Edinburgh: Edinburgh University Press, 1999.
Meyer, Birgit, and Annelies Moors, eds. *Religion, Media, and the Public Sphere.* Bloomington: Indiana University Press, 2006.
Miller, Donald E., and Tetsunao Yamamori. *Global Pentecostalism: The New Face of Christian Social Engagement.* Berkeley: University of California Press, 2007.
Miller, Joseph C. *Way of Death: Merchant Capitalism and the Angolan Slave Trade, 1730–1830.* Madison: University of Wisconsin Press, 1988.
Mitchell, J. Clyde, ed. *Social Networks in Urban Situations: Analyses of Personal Relationships in Central African Towns.* Manchester: Manchester University Press, 1969.
Mouffe, Chantal. "Carl Schmitt and the Paradox of Liberal Democracy." In *Law as Politics: Carl Schmitt's Critique of Liberalism*, edited by David Dyzenhaus. Durham, NC: Duke University Press, 1998.
Mũgo, Micere. *Visions of Africa: The Fiction of Chinua Achebe, Margaret Laurence, Elspeth Huxley and Ngũgĩ wa Thiong'o.* Nairobi: Kenya Literature Bureau, 1978.
Mukonyora, Isabel. *Wandering a Gendered Wilderness: Suffering and Healing in an African Initiated Church.* New York: Peter Lang, 2007.
Mukuka, Catherine. *A Christian Nation versus a Secular State: The Making of a Constitution.* Lusaka: Abiyah Publishing House, 2006.
Mwaura, Philomena N. "'A Burning Stick Plucked Out of the Fire': The Story of Rev. Margaret Wanjiru of JIAM." In *Her-Stories: Hidden Histories of Women of Faith in Africa*, edited by Isabel A. Phiri, D. B. Govinden, and Sarojini Nadar. Pietermaritzburg: Cluster Publications, 2002.
———. "Gender and Power in African Christianity: African Instituted Churches and Pentecostal Churches." In *African Christianity: An African Story*, edited by Ogbu Kalu. Pretoria: University of Pretoria, 2005.
Mwikisa, Wamulungwe P. "The Limits of Difference: Ngũgĩ wa Thiong'o's Redeployment of Biblical Signifiers in *A Grain of Wheat* and *I Will Marry When I Want*." In West and Dube, *Bible in Africa*, 163–83.
Ngũgĩ, James. "James Ngũgĩ Interviewed by Fellow Students at Leeds University." Interview by Alan Marcuson, Mike González, and Dave Williams. In *Ngũgĩ wa Thiong'o Speaks: Interviews with the Kenyan Writer*, edited by Reinhard Sander and Bernth Lindfors. Trenton, NJ: Africa World Press, 2006.
Ngũgĩ wa Thiong'o. *A Grain of Wheat.* Nairobi: East African Educational Publishers, 1967.
———. *Homecoming.* London: Heinemann, 1972.
———. "I Try Witchcraft." *Alliance High School Magazine*, September 1957, 21–22.
———. *The River Between.* Nairobi: East African Educational Publishers, 1965.
———. *Weep Not, Child.* Nairobi: East African Educational Publishers, 1984.
Ntozi, James. "Widowhood, Remarriage and Migration during the HIV/AIDS Epidemic in Uganda." *Health Transition Review* 7 (suppl.) (1997): 125–44.
Nyamnjoh, Francis B. "Reconciling the 'Rhetoric of Rights' with Competing Notions of Personhood and Agency in Botswana." In *Rights and the Politics of Recognition in Africa*, edited by Harri Englund and Nyamnjoh. London: Zed, 2004.
Obadare, Ebenezer. "White-Collar Fundamentalism: Interrogating Youth Religiosity on Nigerian University Campuses." *Journal of Modern African Studies* 45, no. 4 (2007): 517–37.
Ocholla-Ayayo, A. B. C. *The Luo Culture.* Wiesbaden: Steiner, 1980.
———. *Traditional Ideology and Ethics among the Southern Luo.* Uppsala: Scandinavian Institute of African Studies, 1976.

Bibliography

Oduyoye, Mercy Amba. *Daughters of Anowa: African Women and Patriarchy.* Maryknoll, NY: Orbis, 1995.
Ogot, Bethwell A. *Migration and Settlement, 1500–1900.* Vol. 1 of *History of the Southern Luo.* Nairobi: East African Publishing House, 1967.
——. *Politics and the AIDS Epidemic in Kenya, 1983–2003.* Kisumu: Anyange Press, 2004.
Ogutu, G. E. M. *Ker Jaramogi Is Dead, Who Shall Lead My People? Reflections on Past, Present, and Future Luo Thought and Practice.* Kisumu: Palwa Search Publications, 1995.
Okeyo, T. M., and A. K. Allen. "Influence of Widow Inheritance on the Epidemiology of AIDS in Africa." *African Journal of Medical Practice* 1, no. 1 (1994): 20–25.
Olajubu, Oyeronke. *Women in the Yoruba Religious Sphere.* Albany: State University of New York Press, 2003.
Ortner, Sherry. "Resistance and the Problem of Ethnographic Refusal." *Comparative Studies in Society and History* 37, no. 1 (1995): 173–93.
Ott, Martin, Kings M. Phiri, and Nandini Patel, eds. *Malawi's Second Democratic Elections: Process, Problems, and Prospects.* Blantyre: Christian Literature Association in Malawi, 2000.
Overå, Ragnhild. "When Men Do Women's Work: Structural Adjustment, Unemployment and Changing Gender Relations in the Informal Economy of Accra, Ghana." *Journal of Modern African Studies* 45, no. 4 (2007): 539–63.
Pala, Achola O. "Changes in Economy and Ideology: A Study of the Joluo of Kenya (with Special Reference to Women)." PhD diss., Harvard University, 1977.
——. "Daughters of the Lakes and Rivers: Colonization and the Land Rights of Luo Women." In *Women and Colonization: Anthropological Perspectives,* edited by Mona Etienne and Eleanor Leacock. New York: Praeger, 1980.
Parkin, David. *The Cultural Definition of Political Response: Lineal Destiny among the Luo.* London: Academic Press, 1978.
Parpart, Jane L. *Labor and Capital on the African Copperbelt.* Philadelphia: Temple University Press, 1983.
Peel, J. D. Y. *Aladura: A Religious Movement among the Yoruba.* Oxford: Oxford University Press, 1968.
——. "Christianity and the Logic of Nationalist Assertion in Wole Soyinka's *Ìsarà.*" In Maxwell, *Christianity,* 127–56.
——. "'For Who Hath Despised the Day of Small Things?': Missionary Narratives and Historical Anthropology." *Comparative Studies in Society and History* 37, no. 3 (1995): 581–607.
——. *Religious Encounter and the Making of the Yoruba.* Bloomington: Indiana University Press, 2000.
Peil, Margaret. "The Development and Practice of Religion in an Accra Suburb." With K. A. Opoku. *Journal of Religion in Africa* 24, no. 3 (1994): 198–227.
Pelkmans, Mathijs. "'Culture' as a Tool and an Obstacle: Missionary Encounters in Post-Soviet Kyrgyzstan." *Journal of the Royal Anthropological Institute* 13, no. 4 (2007): 881–99.
Pels, Peter. *A Politics of Presence: Contacts between Missionaries and Waluguru in Late Colonial Tanganyika.* Amsterdam: Harwood Academic, 1999.
Peterson, Derek R. *Creative Writing: Translation, Bookkeeping, and the Work of Imagination in Colonial Kenya.* Portsmouth, NH: Heinemann, 2004.
——. "Writing in Revolution: Independent Schooling and Mau Mau in Nyeri." In *Mau Mau and Nationhood: Arms, Authority and Narration,* edited by E. S. Atieno Odhiambo and John Lonsdale. Oxford: James Currey, 2003.
Pfeiffer, James. "Civil Society, NGOs, and the Holy Spirit in Mozambique." *Human Organization* 63, no. 4 (2004): 359–72.

Bibliography

———. "Condom Social Marketing, Pentecostalism, and Structural Adjustment in Mozambique: A Clash of AIDS Prevention Messages." *Medical Anthropology Quarterly* 18, no. 1 (2004): 77–103.

Phiri, Isabel A. "President Frederick J. T. Chiluba of Zambia: The Christian Nation and Democracy." *Journal of Religion in Africa* 33, no. 4 (2003): 401–28.

———. "Why African Churches Preach Politics: The Case of Zambia." *Journal of Church and State* 41, no. 2 (1999): 323–47.

———. *Women, Presbyterianism and Patriarchy: Religious Experience of Chewa Women in Central Malawi*. Blantyre: Christian Literature Association in Malawi, 1997.

Pierre, Jemima. "Anthropology and the Race of/for Africa." In *Disciplinary and Interdisciplinary Encounters*, vol. 1 of *The Study of Africa*, edited by Paul Tiyambe Zeleza. Dakar: CODESRIA, 2006.

Port, Mattijs van de. "Priests and Stars: Candomblé, Celebrity Postscripts, Discourses, and the Authentication of Religious Authority in Bahia's Public Sphere." *Postscripts: The Journal of Sacred Texts and Contemporary Worlds* 1, no. 2–3 (2005): 301–24.

Potash, Betty. "Wives of the Graves: Widows in a Rural Luo Community." In *Widows in African Societies: Choices and Constraints*, edited by Potash. Stanford: Stanford University Press, 1986.

Potts, Deborah. "Counter-urbanization on the Zambian Copperbelt? Interpretations and Implications." *Urban Studies* 42, no. 4 (2005): 583–609.

Prince, Ruth. "Salvation and Tradition: Configurations of Faith in a Time of Death." *Journal of Religion in Africa* 37, no. 1 (2007): 84–115.

Pritchett, James A. *Friends for Life, Friends for Death: Cohorts and Consciousness among the Lunda-Ndembu*. Charlottesville: University of Virginia Press, 2007.

———. *The Lunda-Ndembu: Style, Change, and Social Transformation in South Central Africa*. Madison: University of Wisconsin Press, 2001.

Pugliese, Christiana. *The Life and Writings of Gakaara wa Wanjau*. Bayreuth: Eckhard Breitinger, 1995.

Ranger, Terence. "Religious Movements and Politics in Sub-Saharan Africa." *African Studies Review* 29, no. 2 (1986): 1–69.

Raringo. *Chike Jjaduong e Ddalane* (The Rules of the Old Man in His Home). Nairobi: Three Printers and Stationers, 2001.

Richards, Audrey. *Land, Labour and Diet in Northern Rhodesia: An Economic Study of the Bemba Tribe*. London: Oxford University Press, 1939.

Robbins, Joel. "Continuity Thinking and the Problem of Christian Culture: Belief, Time, and the Anthropology of Christianity." *Current Anthropology* 48, no. 1 (2007): 5–38.

———. "The Globalization of Pentecostal and Charismatic Christianity." *Annual Review of Anthropology* 33, no. 1 (2004): 134–35.

Ruel, Malcolm. *Belief, Ritual and the Securing of Life: Reflexive Essays on a Bantu Religion*. Leiden: Brill, 1997.

Sabar-Friedman, Galia. "Church and State in Kenya, 1986–1992: The Churches' Involvement in the 'Game of Change.'" *African Affairs* 96, no. 382 (1997): 25–52.

Sackey, Brigid M. *New Directions in Gender and Religion: The Changing Status of Women in African Independent Churches*. Lanham, MD: Rowman and Littlefield, 2006.

Sahlins, Marshall. *Islands of History*. Chicago: University of Chicago Press, 1985.

———. "The Sadness of Sweetness: The Native Anthropology of Western Cosmology." *Current Anthropology* 37, no. 3 (1996): 395–428.

Sandel, Michael J. *Liberalism and the Limits of Justice*. Cambridge: Cambridge University Press, 1982.

Bibliography

Sayyid, S., and Abdoolkarim Vakil, eds. *Thinking through Islamophobia*. London: Hurst, 2009.

Schmitt, Carl. *Political Theology: Four Chapters on the Concept of Sovereignty*. Translated by George Schwab. Chicago: University of Chicago Press, 2005.

Schoffeleers, Matthew. "Ritual Healing and Political Acquiescence: The Case of the Zionist Churches in Southern Africa." *Africa* 61, no. 1 (1991): 1–25.

Schulz, Dorothea A. "'Charisma and Brotherhood' Revisited: Mass-Mediated Forms of Spirituality in Urban Mali." *Journal of Religion in Africa* 33, no. 2 (2003): 146–71.

———. "Morality, Community, Publicness: Shifting Terms of Public Debate in Mali." In Meyer and Moors, *Religion, Media*, 132–51.

Scott, James C. *Domination and the Arts of Resistance: Hidden Transcripts*. New Haven: Yale University Press, 1990.

———. *Weapons of the Weak: Everyday Forms of Peasant Resistance*. New Haven: Yale University Press, 1985.

Shepperson, George A., and Thomas Price. *Independent African: John Chilembwe and the Origins, Setting and Significance of the Nyasaland Native Rising of 1915*. Edinburgh: Edinburgh University Press, 1958.

Shipton, Parker. "Debts and Trespasses: Land, Mortgages, and the Ancestors in Western Kenya," *Africa* 62, no. 3 (1992): 357–88.

———. "The Kenyan Land Tenure Reform: Misunderstandings in the Public Creation of Private Property." In *Land and Society in Contemporary Africa*, edited by R. E. Downs and S. P. Reyna. Hanover, NH: University Press of New England, 1988.

———. "Land and Culture in Tropical Africa: Soil, Symbols, and the Metaphysics of the Mundane." *Annual Review of Anthropology* 23, no 1 (1994): 347–77.

Sicherman, Carol. "The Leeds-Makerere Connection and Ngũgĩ's Intellectual Development," *Ufahamu: Journal of the African Activist Association* 23, no. 1 (1995): 5–6.

Silberschmidt, Margarethe. *"Women Forget That Men Are the Masters": Gender Antagonism and Socio-economic Change in Kisii District, Kenya*. Uppsala: Nordiska Afrikainstitutet, 1999.

Simatei, Tirop. "Colonial Violence, Postcolonial Violations: Violence, Landscape, and Memory in Kenyan Fiction." *Research in African Literatures* 36, no. 2 (2005): 85–94.

Simpson, Anthony. *"Half-London" in Zambia: Contested Identities in a Catholic Mission School*. Edinburgh: Edinburgh University Press, 2003.

Smith, Jay M. "No More Language Games: Words, Beliefs, and the Political Culture of Early Modern France." *American Historical Review* 102, no. 5 (1997): 1413–40.

Smith, Wilfred Cantwell. *Belief and History*. Charlottesville: University Press of Virginia, 1977.

———. *Faith and Belief*. Princeton: Princeton University Press, 1979.

Spinks, Charlotte. "Panacea or Painkiller? The Impact of Pentecostal Christianity on Women in Africa." *Annual Journal of Women for Women International* 1, no. 1 (2003): 21–24.

Stambach, Amy. "Spiritual Warfare 101: Preparing the Student for Christian Battle." *Journal of Religion in Africa* 39, no. 2 (2009): 137–57.

Stoller, Paul. *Money Has No Smell: The Africanization of New York City*. Chicago: University of Chicago Press, 2002.

Stolow, Jeremy. "Religion and/as Media." *Theory, Culture and Society* 22, no. 4 (2005): 119–45.

Stotesbury, John A. *The Logic of Ngũgĩ's Use of Biblical and Christian Reference in* A Grain of Wheat. Joensuu, Finland: University of Joensuu, 1985.

Strathern, Marilyn. "Cutting the Network." *Journal of the Royal Anthropological Institute* 2, no. 3 (1996): 517–35.

Strayer, Robert W. *The Making of Mission Communities in East Africa: Anglicans and Africans in Colonial Kenya, 1875–1935.* London: Heinemann, 1978.
Sundkler, Bengt. *Bantu Prophets in South Africa.* Oxford: Oxford University Press, 1948.
Swynnerton, R. J. M. *A Plan to Intensify the Development of African Agriculture in Kenya.* Nairobi: HM Stationery Office, 1954.
Tarnopolsky, Christina. "Platonic Reflections on the Aesthetic Dimensions of Deliberative Democracy." *Political Theory* 35, no. 3 (2007): 288–312.
Taylor, Charles. *A Secular Age.* Cambridge, MA: Harvard University Press, 2007.
Thomas, Lynn. *Politics of the Womb: Women, Reproduction, and the State in Kenya.* Berkeley: University of California Press, 2003.
Trapnell, Colin, and J. N. Clothier. *The Soils, Vegetation and Agricultural System of North Western Rhodesia: A Report of the Ecological Survey.* Lusaka: Government Printer, 1937.
Turner, Victor W. *The Forest of Symbols: Aspects of Ndembu Ritual.* Ithaca: Cornell University Press, 1967.
Ukpong, Justin S. "Developments in Biblical Interpretation in Africa: Historical and Hermeneutical Directions." In West and Dube, *Bible in Africa*, 11–28.
United Nations Development Programme. *Malawi Human Development Report, 2001.* Lilongwe: UNDP, 2001.
van de Walle, Nicolas. *African Economies and the Politics of Permanent Crisis, 1979–1999.* Cambridge: Cambridge University Press, 2001.
Vansina, Jan. *Kingdoms of the Savanna: A History of Central African States until European Occupation.* Madison: University of Wisconsin Press, 1966.
Vaughan, Megan. *Curing Their Ills: Colonial Power and African Illness.* Cambridge: Polity Press, 1991.
———. "Exploitation and Neglect: Rural Producers and the State in Malawi and Zambia." In *History of Central Africa: The Contemporary Years since 1960*, edited by David Birmingham and Phyllis M. Martin. London: Longman, 1998.
Vries, Hent de. "In Media Res: Global Religion, Public Spheres, and the Task of Contemporary Comparative Religious Studies." In Vries and Weber, *Religion and Media*, 3–42.
———, ed. *Religion: Beyond a Concept.* New York: Fordham University Press, 2008.
Vries, Hent de, and Samuel Weber, eds. *Religion and Media.* Stanford: Stanford University Press, 2001.
Walsh, Michael. "The Religious Ferment of the Sixties." In McLeod, *World Christianities*, 304–22.
Warner, Michael. *Publics and Counterpublics.* New York: Zone, 2002.
Weber, Max. *The Protestant Ethic and the Spirit of Capitalism.* New York: Charles Scribner's Sons, 1920.
Wendland, Ernst. *Sewero! Christian Drama and the Drama of Christianity in Africa.* Zomba: Kachere Series, 2005.
Werbner, Richard. "The Political Economy of Bricolage." *Journal of Southern African Studies* 13, no. 1 (1986): 151–56.
West, Gerald O., and Musa W. Dube, eds. *The Bible in Africa: Transactions, Trajectories, and Trends.* Leiden: Brill, 2000.
White, Landeg. *Magomero: Portrait of an African Village.* Cambridge: Cambridge University Press, 1987.
White, Louise. *Comforts of Home: Prostitution in Colonial Nairobi.* Chicago: University of Chicago Press, 1990.
Whitfield, Lindsay. "Trustees of Development from Conditionality to Governance: Poverty Reduction Strategy Papers in Ghana." *Journal of Modern African Studies* 43, no. 4 (2005): 641–64.

Bibliography

Willems, Emilio. *Followers of the New Faith: Culture Change and the Rise of Protestantism in Brazil and Chile.* Nashville: Vanderbilt University Press, 1967.

Willis, Justin. "The Nature of a Mission Community: The Universities' Mission to Central Africa in Bonde." *Past and Present* 140, no. 1 (1993): 127–54.

Wilson, Gordon M. *Luo Customary Law and Marriage Laws Customs.* Nairobi: Government Printers, 1968.

Woodhead, Linda, ed. *Religions in the Modern World: Traditions and Transformations.* New York: Routledge, 2002.

Wright, Marcia. *Strategies of Slaves and Women: Life-Stories from East/Central Africa.* New York: Lilian Barber, 1993.

Zeleza, Paul Tiyambe. *Rethinking Africa's Globalization.* Vol. 1, *The Intellectual Challenges.* Trenton, NJ: Africa World Press, 2003.

Contributors

BARBARA M. COOPER is a professor of history at Rutgers University. Her research explores the intersections between culture and political economy, with a focus on gender, religion, and family life. She is author of *Marriage in Maradi: Gender and Culture in a Hausa Society in Niger, 1900–1989* and *Evangelical Christians in the Muslim Sahel*, which won the Melville J. Herskovits Award of the African Studies Association.

HARRI ENGLUND is a reader in the Department of Social Anthropology at the University of Cambridge. His research interests include human rights and the moral imagination, and African-language debates on socioeconomic inequality. He has written and edited several books on the social and cultural dimensions of liberalization in Africa, including *Prisoners of Freedom: Human Rights and the African Poor*, which won the Amaury Talbot Prize of the Royal Anthropological Institute.

MARJA HINFELAAR is an affiliate of the National Archives of Zambia. Her current research interests are church-state relations and the political history of Zambia. She is author of *Respectable and Responsible Women: Methodist and Roman Catholic Women's Organizations in Harare, Zimbabwe (1919–1985)* and coeditor (with Jan-Bart Gewald and Giacomo Macola) of *One Zambia, Many Histories: Towards a History of Post-colonial Zambia*.

NICHOLAS KAMAU-GORO lectures in the Department of Literary and Communication Studies, Laikipia University College, Egerton University, Kenya. His recently completed PhD dissertation examines the poetics of language and the quest for a socially relevant aesthetic ideology in the work of Ngũgĩ wa Thiong'o.

BIRGIT MEYER is professor of cultural anthropology at Amsterdam's Vrije Universiteit. She is author of *Translating the Devil: Religion and Modernity among the Ewe in Ghana*; editor of *Aesthetic Formations: Religion, Media, and the Senses*; and coeditor (with Peter Geschiere) of *Globalization and Identity: Dialectics of Flow and Closure*, (with Peter

Pels) of *Magic and Modernity: Interfaces of Revelation and Concealment*, and (with Annelies Moors) of *Religion, Media, and the Public Sphere*.

MICHAEL PERRY KWEKU OKYEREFO lectures in sociology at the University of Ghana. His research interests span the fields of religion and public culture, the sociology of literature, and the sociology of education. He is author of *The Cultural Crisis of Sub-Saharan Africa as Depicted in the African Writers' Series: A Sociological Perspective*.

DAMARIS PARSITAU lectures in African Christianities at Egerton University, Kenya. She is finalizing her doctoral dissertation on Pentecostalism and civic engagement in Kenya. Her areas of interest include global Pentecostalism, religion and gender, feminist theologies, religion and health, and religion and popular culture.

RUTH PRINCE is Smuts Fellow at the Centre of African Studies, University of Cambridge. Her research focuses on East Africa and explores Christianity, kinship and gender, healing, medicine, and historical anthropology. She is coauthor (with Paul Wenzel Geissler) of *The Land Is Dying: Contingency, Creativity, and Conflict in Western Kenya* and coeditor (with Philippe Denis and Rijk van Dijk) of a special issue of *Africa Today* on Christianity and AIDS in Africa.

JAMES A. PRITCHETT is a professor of anthropology and director of the African Studies Center at Michigan State University. He is author of *The Lunda-Ndembu: Style, Change, and Social Transformation in South Central Africa* and *Friends for Life, Friends for Death: Cohorts and Consciousness among the Lunda-Ndembu*. He also has an interest in the African diaspora and has studied communities of African-descended people in the Caribbean and in South and Central America.

ILANA VAN WYK holds a research fellowship at the London School of Economics and Political Science. Her doctoral research was on the Universal Church of the Kingdom of God in Durban, South Africa. Her current research focuses on gambling, the national lottery, and the perceptions of luck in a Cape Town settlement.

Index

Achebe, Chinua, 67
Addy, Eddy, 207, 208
agriculture, 11, 33–35
Ahinful, Kwamena, 210
Akinola, Peter, 90, 93
Anamela, Njekwa, 56
Anderson, Allan, 16
Anderson, Benedict, 159
Anglican Church, 14, 114, 116, 180, 207
Angola, 58
Ankrah, Sam Korankye, 207
Appadurai, Arjun, 90, 106
Appiah, Kwame Anthony, 188n44
Armah, Ayi Kwei, 67
Asad, Talal, 22n35, 51, 151, 182, 193
Asamoah-Gyadu, J. Kwabena, 214
Australia, 139, 208
Awonoor, Kofi, 67

Barber, Karin, 8, 36
belief, 9, 18, 193–94
Bible, 4, 14, 30, 54, 68, 71, 73, 74, 76, 77, 78, 79–81, 83, 94, 97, 123, 135, 142, 161, 173, 198
Bonsam, Kwaku, 166n39
Botswana, 139
Brazil, 200n1
British South Africa Company, 29
Bruce, Steve, 19n2

Casanova, José, 20n2, 53, 151
Castells, Manuel, 162
Catholic Church, 12, 14, 16, 29, 33, 37, 40, 42, 52–63, 116, 180, 194, 196; Second Vatican Council, 12, 53–54, 59
Chabal, Patrick, 15
Chakuamba, Gwanda, 167, 184n1
Chichewa, 18, 168, 169, 170, 178
chiefs, 27, 35, 42
Chilembwe, John, 21n23
Chiluba, Frederick, 50, 57, 58–60
Chilumpha, Cassim, 172
Chona, Mainza, 57
Christian independence, 5, 16, 133, 194, 196
Christian Missions in Many Lands, 29–30, 37, 40, 41
Christmas, 100
Church of Scotland, 68
civic virtues, 155, 156, 184, 194
clothing, 36–38, 160–61
Cohen, David, 118
colonialism, 6, 28, 31, 37, 45, 69, 71–73, 75, 77, 111, 153–54
Comaroff, Jean, 6, 7, 22n26

Comaroff, John, 6, 7
Conrad, Joseph, 79
conversion, 44–45, 92, 94, 158, 170
Cooper, Barbara, 13, 157

Dagger, Richard, 183, 187n42
Dawkins, Richard, 20n3
development, 19, 120, 123, 149, 156, 204–6, 210–14
De Witte, Marleen, 161, 212, 215n13
Dholuo, 110, 111, 118, 123, 126n1
Dinwiddy, Hugh, 83

Egypt, 2, 4
Eliot, T. S., 68
Ellis, Stephen, 3
English, 31, 44, 69, 73, 77, 78, 83
Englund, Harri, 17, 18, 193–94, 195
Ethiopia, 58, 67
Ethiopianism, 21n23
Europe, 10, 15, 28, 37, 51, 151, 208

faith-based organizations, 16, 156, 210
Faith Evangelistic Ministries, 131, 137–38
Faith for Healing Life Church, 167–68
Fanon, Frantz, 69, 77, 80
Ferguson, James, 51
fertility, 13, 89–92, 107, 199
Fields, Karen, 6–7, 51
Fisher, Walter, 29–30, 37
fostering, 95, 100
Freemasons, 174
funerals, 110, 111–12, 118, 125, 182, 190

Gadhafi, Mu'ammar, 171
gender relations, 13–15, 91, 92–94, 106, 113, 115, 117, 124, 126, 132–34. *See also* patriarchy
Ghana, 15, 17, 19, 132–33, 149–50, 205, 210, 213; cultural policy in, 149, 157, 161–62; student evangelism in, 206–7; 2008 elections in, 150, 155
Gifford, Paul, 15, 204–5, 212
Gikandi, Simon, 77
Gĩkũyũ, 77, 78
Gitonga, Arthur, 134
God, 9, 18, 30, 44, 50, 57, 71, 75, 94, 101, 104, 123, 135, 137, 138, 139, 140, 141, 143, 158, 159, 160, 175, 177, 178, 180, 189, 191, 194, 195–200, 207, 209
Green, Maia, 45, 51
Griffiths, Marie, 133
Griswold, Eliza, 90
Gule Wamkulu, 175, 180, 181

Index

Habermas, Jürgen, 10, 151, 155, 156, 215n13
Hagin, Kenneth, 208
Hansen, Karen Tranberg, 38
Hastings, Adrian, 4–5
Hausa, 100
healing, 6, 7, 30, 32, 132, 138, 142, 182, 183
Heward-Mills, Adelaide, 208
Heward-Mills, Dag, 207, 208–9, 214
Hinfelaar, Marja, 12
Hirschkind, Charles, 2, 157
Hitchens, Christopher, 20n3
HIV/AIDS, 14, 109–10, 113, 114, 115–17, 120, 122, 123
Holland, 207
Holy Spirit, 17–18, 142, 156, 159, 161, 175, 176, 182, 183–84, 195, 196–97, 198
Horton, Robin, 32
human rights, 14, 53, 59, 110, 115–16, 122, 125, 154, 168, 214

Indonesia, 118
International Central Gospel Group, 161
International Monetary Fund, 150, 205
Internet, 91, 110, 119, 144–45n18
Islam, 1, 7, 8, 15, 19n1, 92, 93, 94, 96, 98, 99, 135, 137, 138, 143, 151, 154, 157, 161, 168, 170, 172, 177, 180–81. *See also* Muslims

Jehovah's Witnesses, 56, 194. *See also* Watchtower
Jesus, 44, 50, 74, 80, 81–82, 93, 98, 138, 140, 178, 179, 180, 181, 194, 198, 207
Jesus Is Alive Ministries, 131, 134–37
Johnson-Hanks, Jennifer, 89–90, 106
Joshua, T. B., 150

Kalusa, Walima, 30
Kamanda, Maina, 136
Kamanga, Reuben, 57
Kamau-Goro, Nicholas, 12–13, 14
Kamenju, Grant, 69
Karega, John, 82
Kaunda, Kenneth, 50, 55, 57, 65n47
Keane, Webb, 118
Kenya, 14, 67, 70, 78, 79, 80, 81, 83, 208; constitution in, 135–36, 138; economy in, 113, 116; "Luo tradition" in, 109–10, 117–25; widow inheritance in, 109–26
Kenya Broadcasting Commission, 123
Kibaki, Mwai, 136
kinship, 110, 118, 119, 123, 126, 192–93, 196, 199; spiritual, 176, 182–84, 194
Kirsch, Thomas, 195
Kiwala, Lucia, 141
Kwach, Justice, 122–23

Laden, Osama bin, 173
language, 4, 6, 12, 77, 78
leadership, 14–15, 60, 62, 77, 106, 131–45, 163, 206

Lewis, C. S., 173
Lighthouse Chapel International, 205–14
literacy, 42
Livingstone, David, 37
Lunda, 30–31, 40

Macedo, Edir, 200n1
MacIntyre, Alasdair, 183
Maffesoli, Michel, 160
Mahmood, Saba, 20n12
Malawi, 6, 17, 67, 139; Muslim-Christian relations in, 168–76, 184; poverty in, 170–71, 172, 186n15; 1999 elections in, 167, 171; 2004 elections in, 171–72, 184n1, 185n18
Malewezi, Justin, 168
Mambo, John, 65n47
marriage, 94–95, 96, 103–4, 111–15, 136, 140, 143, 180, 199
Marshall, Ruth, 8, 192, 204
Martin, David, 185n8
Marxism, 7, 12, 54, 56, 58, 69
mass media, 10, 17, 41, 90, 91–92, 104–7, 109–10, 115, 119, 121, 124, 136–37, 150, 154–55, 157, 159, 161–62, 169, 172, 173, 212
Mathuray, Mark, 75
Matjeke, Samuel, 136
Maxwell, David, 16, 50, 133, 204
McCracken, John, 58
medicine, 11, 13, 19, 29–32, 95, 175, 211
Meebelo, Henry, 56
membership, 17–18, 43, 45, 46, 106, 158, 169–70, 182–84, 190, 195
Methodism, 16, 207
Meyer, Birgit, 10, 17, 18, 102, 204
Middle East, 2, 3, 171
Milingo, Emmanuel, 57
Mills, John Atta, 150
missions, 5–6, 11, 13, 16, 27–49, 54, 72, 82, 92–100, 114, 153, 181, 211
modernity, 30, 45, 71, 73, 74, 117, 118
Moi, Daniel Arap, 118–19, 124
money, 19, 36, 161, 189, 191, 196, 198
Moors, Annelies, 10
Mozambique, 58
Msiska, Tom, 60
Mukuka, Catherine, 61
Muluzi, Bakili, 167, 168, 170, 184n1
music, 40, 102, 103, 178
Muslims, 13, 17, 89–90, 91, 93, 94, 96, 98, 100–104, 107, 135, 168, 170–76, 180–84. *See also* Islam
Mutharika, Bingu wa, 171–72
Mwaura, Philomena, 132, 133
Mwikisa, Wamulungwe, 76, 77, 78

naming, 96–98, 101–4
nationalism, 12–13, 68–69, 70, 71, 77, 82
Nazareth, Peter, 69
Ndhlovu, Peter, 61
neoliberalism, 17, 60, 155–56, 192–93, 205

Index

Ngũgĩ wa Thiong'o, 13, 67; aesthetic of, 76–77; biblical tropes of, 70–76; and change of names, 76; education of, 68–69, 78; and Mau Mau, 78–79, 82, 83
Niger, 13, 90, 91–92; and the French administration, 100; growth of the Christian community in, 94–96; Muslim-Christian relations in, 93–107
Nigeria, 90, 150, 158, 204, 208

Odhiambo, E. S. Atieno, 118
Odinga, Raila, 122–23, 144–45n18
Ogutu, G. E. M., 120–23
Okyerefo, Michael, 18
orphans, 210–11
Otabil, Mensa, 161, 206, 212
Otieno, S. M., 118, 120, 122, 124

Parsitau, Damaris, 14, 158
patriarchy, 13–14, 93, 99, 110, 117, 118–19, 124, 131–32, 133, 136–37, 142, 143. *See also* gender relations
Pentecostalism, 14–19, 52, 54, 59–60, 62–63, 102, 105, 114, 120, 142–43, 149–51, 168, 172–76, 194, 196–97, 200, 210; and prosperity gospel, 16–19, 133, 150, 155, 160–61, 204–6, 213–14; and women, 132–34
Peterson, Derek, 28
Phiri, Isabel, 50
politics and religion, 2–3, 7–8, 15, 50, 150, 167–68, 171, 192
polygamy, 92–93
Pope Benedict XIV, 61
Pope Paul VI, 52
popular culture, 4, 28, 36
Potts, Deborah, 63n4
Prince, Ruth, 14
Pritchett, James, 11–12, 19, 158
Protestantism, 16, 41, 45, 60, 75, 98, 156, 196
public culture, 3–4, 8–9, 10–11, 12–13, 14, 28, 41, 46–47, 83, 105, 111, 125, 137, 143, 172, 192, 200, 205, 209, 212–13
publics, 8–9, 18, 19, 41, 45, 78, 111, 150–51, 153, 157, 159
public sphere, 10–11, 17, 149–53, 155, 156, 159, 161–62

Qur'an, 96, 173, 180

radio, 13, 17, 41, 42, 52, 58–59, 91, 104, 105, 106, 119, 123, 149, 150, 158, 168–88
Radio Islam, 168–69
Ranganathan, M. A., 65n47
Ranger, Terence, 5
Rawlings, J. J., 149
Reformation, 9
resistance, 6–7, 14, 73
Richards, Audrey, 48n21
ritual, 13, 30, 32, 46, 96–104, 111–12

Royalhouse Chapel International, 205–14
Ruel, Malcolm, 9, 193

Sackey, E. A. T., 208
Sackey, Brigid, 132
Sandel, Michael, 187n42
Satanism, 61, 168, 170, 172, 173–74, 175, 179
Saudi Arabia, 171
secularization, 1–2, 19, 51–52, 61–62, 63, 105, 151–52
sex, 112–13, 116, 120, 123–24, 125, 137, 158, 179, 196
Schoffeleers, Matthew, 7
Seychelles, 139
Single Ladies Interdenominational Fellowship, 131, 139–42
Smith, Jay, 193
Smith, Wilfred Cantwell, 9
South Africa, 7, 18, 144–45n18, 172, 189, 193, 208
Soyinka, Wole, 67
Spinks, Charlotte, 133
spiritual warfare, 150, 168, 169, 174, 176–84, 186n28
Stotesbury, John, 82
style, 17, 36, 37, 43, 153, 157, 160–61
Sudan, 67
Sudan Interior Mission, 92–93, 98

Tani, Grace, 133
Tanzania, 67, 139
Taylor, Charles, 151
television, 52, 59, 106, 134, 150, 197
ter Haar, Gerrie, 3
testimonies, 18, 176–84, 189, 197–98
Tetteh, E. N., 209
Todd, Brenda, 135
Transworld Radio, 169, 176–78, 184, 185n9, 186nn29–30, 187n32
trust, 9, 18, 169, 184, 191, 193–94, 195, 197–200
Turner, Victor, 32

Uganda, 67, 75, 139, 208
United Democratic Front, 170–72
United Kingdom, 207
United States, 1, 15, 33, 37, 98, 116, 138, 208
Universal Church of the Kingdom of God, 18, 195–200; pastors in, 189, 190–91

van Binsbergen, Wim M. J., 32
van Wyk, Ilana, 18, 163
Vaughan, Megan, 55
violence, 90
Virgin Mary, 140

Wahome, Elizabeth, 131, 139–42
Wairimu, Teresia, 131, 137–39
Wangare, Margaret, 132
Wanjiru, Margaret, 131, 134–37, 138, 139
Warner, Michael, 9, 111
Watchtower, 6. *See also* Jehovah's Witnesses

Index

Weber, Max, 156
Werbner, Richard, 7
Williams, Duncan, 206
witchcraft, 7, 134–35, 144–45n18, 158, 168, 175, 178, 180, 196
Woodhead, Linda, 142
World Bank, 150, 205

youth, 38–39, 40, 44, 56, 121, 172, 212

Zambia, 6, 11–12, 28–29, 36, 67, 208; as a Christian nation, 58–63; and evolutionary assumptions, 51, 62–63; and media, 55, 58–59; and religious education, 54; and scientific socialism, 56–58; and trade unions, 57
Zimbabwe, 139
Zionism, 6–7
Zirimu, Elvania, 69
Zirimu, Pio, 69

www.ingramcontent.com/pod-product-compliance
Lightning Source LLC
Chambersburg PA
CBHW031241290426
44109CB00012B/388